MR. SMITH GOES TO SCHOOL AND STAYS AND STAYS AND STAYS

HOW TO BECOME AN EDUCATOR IN ONLY 84 YEARS

DONALD E. SMITH, PH.D.

authorHOUSE®

AuthorHouse™ LLC
1663 Liberty Drive
Bloomington, IN 47403
www.authorhouse.com
Phone: 1-800-839-8640

I have tried to make the following narrative as accurate and factual as possible. But, time and
age get in the way of accuracy. I have only my memory on which to rely in relating most of
what I've written about my own education and my work in the field of education. Because it
covers almost eighty-four years, some details might be innacurate or misplaced in time sequence.
So, if you read of something that you did or observed and you have a different memory of it,
combine it with my version. Between the two of us, we might just arrive at the truth. Or, not.

Published by AuthorHouse   09/10/2014

ISBN: 978-1-4969-3824-4 (sc)
ISBN: 978-1-4969-3823-7 (e)

Library of Congress Control Number: 2014915924

CONTENTS

How did I decide to become a teacher? Was it by default? Was it a classic example of that old saw, "Those who can, do. Those who can't, teach?" In my case, the decision was helped along by the words and actions of several individuals and one world-class corporation.

My paternal grandmother, Jenny, had been a teacher. She had finished the eighth grade and went to a so-called normal school to get her teaching certificate. She taught me to read before I began my schooling. It was, probably, a mistake. She saw something in me that prompted her to say to me, "You should be a teacher. You're always explaining things."

My dad, while trying to show me how to assemble some plumbing, said in disgust, "You can't do a damn thing but read! You might as well be one of those sissy teachers."

My high school coach, Joe, said one day in health class, "You'd make a good teacher. How about grading my test papers for me after class?" It became a regular routine. It was wrong, but it gave me a sense of pride and power. I received new respect from my peers.

My high school English and journalism teacher, Mrs. "Wee," said: "You write well. You have a gift. Have you thought of teaching?"

A graduate assistant at Akron University who helped teach a creative writing class said, "Your explanation of the meaning of that assigned short story was very creative, but entirely wrong. But, you showed that you could take an idea and make it your own. Have you considered getting a degree in education?"

My wife, Joy, never questioned my choice of becoming a teacher. She was supportive fully even though we both knew that we'd never have much money. Being wealthy was never our goal.

All through my undergraduate degree courses I worked nights at Goodyear Tire and Rubber Company. I reported nightly and the supervisor sent me to departments where help was needed. I suffered through heat, lampblack, soapstone, sulfur and the endless kidding and teasing of the grizzled veterans who delighted in making a college kid's life miserable. But, Goodyear let me work the shifts that fit my schedule and provided me with enough money to pay for my college tuition and to buy groceries and pay the rent. I learned that I wasn't cut out to work in a factory. That period of five years firmed my resolve to earn a teaching degree.

And, then, there was me. I knew my limitations. Dad was correct. I was terrible at doing things with my hands. I loved the idea of working with ideas. I became involved fully with becoming the best teacher that I could be. Channeling Kurt Vonnegut, "And, so it goes."

"It is the mark of an educated mind to be able to entertain a thought without accepting it."

Aristotle

A Chance Meeting

I had gone to the mall for some last-minute Christmas shopping. "Didn't you used to be my teacher?" I looked up. An elderly man with white hair and beard was looking at me. I didn't recognize him. He looked much too old to have been my student. But, he persisted by saying, "I think that you were my English teacher back in the early 50's."

I stopped walking and asked him for his name. "Bob," he answered. "Bob Nichols." The name evoked a string of memories. Memories that had lain dormant for over sixty years. "How old are you, Bob?" "I'm seventy-five," he replied. The numbers worked. I'm eighty-three now. Back then, I was twenty-two and he was, probably, thirteen or fourteen.

"Well, Bob," I said. "You have a great memory." Bob just looked at me and smiled. "I always remember people who made a difference in my life. Back then, I was a big problem, always in trouble. You helped to change me. Sometimes, it was with a hug. Sometimes, with a swat with your paddle. I graduated and went to college. Recently, I retired from my successful law practice. Oh, yes, I remember you."

I felt the lump growing in my throat. I averted my eyes that had begun to water. Maybe, just maybe, being a teacher had been worth it. Maybe, it had been a good choice after all. Grandma and the others had seen something in me that has taken me a life-time to understand.

"Education is the transmission of civilization."

Will Durant

PROLOGUE

I stopped cleaning out my desk and slumped back in my chair. I had hoped to get through this without the emotion that had begun to well up.

I shouldn't have been surprised. After all, I'd spent thirty-three years working in various jobs in the field of education. The work had been my life. So much so, that I'd almost neglected everything else. Now, what would lie beyond? Had I chosen to retire too soon? Would I be able to live on my retirement? Should I find another job in another field? Should I reconsider?

I looked around my office. It had been my second home. I had tried to make it a place where students, colleagues and parents would feel comfortable. I'd made it a place that I'd hoped was non-threatening. The desk lamp glowed warmly with its subdued light. I had always disliked the harshness of bright overhead lighting. Tasteful paintings and photographs hung on the walls.

All except my desk was in semi-shadow. I didn't want it to look like a principal's office. Bad things happened often in those offices. The large windows that formed one wall were covered with heavy draperies. I had tried to isolate my office from the outside world. I had created my own insular world.

Memorabilia from my foreign travels were displayed on my desk and on tables and shelves. Most of the trappings of my business duties were hidden from sight. I had made myself into a ninja principal. My created personna was that of a quiet, kindly administrator who disliked many of the required duties of a typical high school principal.

I knew that evening in June, 1984 that I had no more to offer. I was tired and had nothing left. It was time. I had always known that I'd realize when I'd had enough. And, God knows, I'd had enough.

Time, that quick-silver thing. We only have the present. The past slithers in and out of memory. The future is a tenuous dream-scape only dimly imagined through a smoky mirror.

The memories flooded back. How had I reached this point? What had motivated me to pursue a career that promised little in the way of monetary rewards? Dad had called male teachers "Sissies." The College of Education was given second-class status among the university's more prestigious programs. Yet, here I was, thirty-three years later, ready to retire.

That night in 1984 I made a plan. The plan has taken thirty years to reach fulfillment. Only now, do I feel ready to implement it. I will try to bring back to life my memories as a student, teacher, guidance counselor, principal, university instructor and overseas' volunteer in order to give them substance and order.

I will try to reconstruct those experiences which formed my career as an educator. I will write of those things that remain embedded forever in my psche - those things that shaped and molded me into what society calls an "Educator." I will flesh in and color those events and those people who contributed to my success and my failures.

Sitting in this room that housed eighteen of those thirty-three years, I promised myself that I would not only write of real events, people and happenings, but, also, write of how I think that education could serve better the young people who depend on education to prepare them for their futures. In order to do that, I would blur purposely the lines between reality and the realm of ideas. The reader could decide what really happened. It wouldn't matter.

To be a little trite, education supplies the life-blood to both individuals and society as a whole. It's how we hand down the teachings, ideas and accomplishments of those who've gone before. It's how we equip young people to face future changes and challenges.

Teachers are the agents through which these past events and new ideas reach the minds of today's students. I have been proud to have been part of this process. I'm proud to be called an educator and proud to be called a teacher. Are the two terms inter-changeable? I've always thought that I'd rather be known as a teacher. Somehow, it seems more personal and warm.

The life of a teacher is not easy. That life is evolving always. It is changing endlessly. Each day offers a new set of challenges. It's not for those who thrive on routine. Making daily lesson plans is, often, a fool's job. Things and days never turn out as planned.

As in most things in life, there were many things done incorrectly and many things left undone. Even worse, there were many things that shouldn't have been done.

I can't change any of that. What I can do is write of what did happen. My plan in this book is to write of what took place as I slouched off to my private Bethlehem and to write of what should have happened given the gifts of hindsight and experience.

As is customary to say, "To protect the innocent, I've not always used real full names. If names seem familiar to those who walked the walk with me, it's, probably, true."

This book is for those who've given their lives to this noble profession. It's for those who've spent more time with their students and colleagues than they have with their own   families. It's for those who've lived with the frustrations that come from seeing their idealism crushed by realities.

It's, also, for the students who managed to jump the hurdles that we set up for them. We bask in the glow of their accomplishments. It's, also, for those students who fell along the way. We share the blame with them.

I hope that this book brings back memories to both students and teachers. For students, I hope that it helps them to re-live a time when the future was bright and their eyes glowed in anticipation. It was a time when they didn't know what they couldn't do. A time when their bodies responded quickly and easily to every command. A time that should have been the best of times.

As teachers, we should have made it so. Anything less, meant that we failed.

Did you love being a teacher? Did you love those whom you taught? Did that love equal the love that was received from those whom you taught? If your answer to those questions is an unqualified "Yes," then you deserve the title of teacher. Your legacy will follow you down through time. You will be remembered. And, if you did your job with skill and humanity, those memories that you evoked will be good.

What follows is the story of the influences in my life that caused me to become an educator and the experiences that I had during my career. It's not an unusual story. Many thousands of educators followed similar paths. It's the story of struggles. Struggles that are both very personal and very universal. If struggles make one strong, then, certainly, educators are among the strongest of people.

"I have come to believe that a great teacher is a great artist and that there are as few as there are of any other great artists. Teaching might even be the greatest of the arts since the medium is the human mind and spirit."

John Steinbeck

Part One

GRADES ONE AND TWO - CARROLLTON, OHIO

"Showing up at school already able to read is like showing up at the undertakers already embalmed: people start worrying about losing their jobs."

Florence King

I hid my toy car behind my reading book. I kicked the foot of the girl who sat ahead of me. I stuck out my tongue at Harry who had made a face at me. I had finished the silly little reading assignment well before anyone else in the class. I had asked to read one of the bigger more interesting books that was on the book shelf. But, no, the teacher made me read about Jack and Jill with the rest of the class. I had been reading books from the library even before I began the first grade. That was Grandma Smith's fault. She had taught me to read when I was four years old.

Carrollton had no kindergarten. Back then, they weren't common. Being born in February, I had to wait until the next September to begin the first grade. I was seven years old and bored to death. I was a victim of the depression, my birth date and silly school policies. I didn't know those things then, but I suffered from them all during my school days.

I don't remember a lot of those days, but what I do remember remains firmly embedded in my mind and psyche.

I couldn't wait to start school. Summer passed slowly. I asked Mom almost daily as to when school would begin. I practiced walking the four blocks to the elementary school. I counted the number of steps

Donald E. Smith, Ph.D.

from my front door to the front door of the school. I walked around the school building and looked in all of the windows. I pretended that I was sitting in one of those empty chairs in the first grade room. At night, in my bed, I rehearsed what I'd say when the teacher asked for my name and for something about me. "My name is Donald E. Smith and I live at 21 South High Street in Carrollton, Ohio. My Mom's name is Leta Smith and my Dad is Earl Smith. Mom is sick most of the time. He is a night watchman at the Carrollton Pottery Company. I have a sister named Phyllis. I like to read and listen to the radio. My Dad gets mad when I read in bed. He makes me turn off the light and go to sleep."

Finally, the big day came. I awoke very early. Dad was still in bed and Mom was bustling around the kitchen preparing breakfast. My stomach felt funny. The odor of eggs and bacon made me queasy. I sat down at the table and picked at my food. Mom said, "Eat up, you have a big day ahead." After drinking my milk, I made a quick bathroom stop. I hoped that I wouldn't be sick.

I picked up my metal lunch box that Mom had filled with a peanut butter and jelly sandwich, an apple and a home-made cupcake. The thermos contained chocolate milk.

It was raining outside, so Mom made me wear that dumb yellow raincoat with a hood. Worst of all, she made me wear those new high boots with the metal buckles. I had seen boys walking to school without wearing rain clothes. I wanted to look like them. I wanted to look tough and fearless. I wanted to look like a big boy. I knew that I'd be teased. I'd worn this stuff before and the older boys told me to go home to mommy.

Mom insisted on giving me a hug and a kiss as I opened the door to leave. She hardly ever does that. I hoped that no one saw it. I took a deep breath and started down the sidewalk. At Oak Street, I turned left. At Pine Street, I turned right. The school lay just ahead. I merged with several other children and hoped nobody said anything about my ridiculous outfit. Luckily, the rain pelted down hard and every one kept his head down while trudging ahead.

I started up the front steps of the school. I didn't know it then, but this was one of my life's defining moments. I had started my educational journey. I had begun a trip that was to last a life time. Eighty-three years later, it is still in progress.

I mingled with the crowd of childen who joked with one another while searching for their assigned classrooms. I didn't see any one whom I knew. I only knew a few other kids. My family didn't mix much with other people. I looked at the room assignments that were posted on the wall of the main corridor. My name was listed under: "Mrs. Gladys Mitchel - Grade One - room 113." I looked for familiar names on that list. I saw the name of one boy whom I knew. Bobby Hefton belonged to the Methodist Church where my mom and I attended sporadically. He was my age, but much bigger. He liked to act tough and was a bully. Just my luck! Dad had told me to hit him in the face if he continued to pick on me. I had never hit any one in the face or any place else. Just one more reason to be nervous.

I found room 113 and peeked inside. Several students were already inside and seated. I saw a seating chart on the wall with names on it. Because I could already read, I walked over and saw my name on the second seat from the front in the row next to the windows. I went over and sat down without looking around. I felt a tap on my back. I turned around and Bobby's freckled face was two inches from mine. He said: "How did you get this seat? I told him I'd looked on the seating chart. He insisted, "How did you know?" I replied: "I can read. that's how." "No, you can't," he said. Just then, Mrs. Mitchel returned to the room and gave both of us a stern look. "There will be no arguing in my classroom!"

By nine o'clock, the last of the students took their seats. A bell rang and Mrs. Mitchel stood in front of the class holding a yardstick. She gave us a lecture about how she expected good behavior from every one. She appointed two girls to pass out two little reading books that featured Jack and Jill and a bunch of goofy-looking animals.

She pointed out the long banners across the top of the chalkboards that displayed the letters of the alphabet both in capital letters and in

3

cursive writing. Another banner displayed the numbers from one to one hundred. She told us that before we left her room we would understand all of this. She expected all of us to pass on to the second grade.

Then, the dreaded moment came when she asked us to introduce ourselves. She made each of us stand, speak loudly and keep our heads up. We went in alphabetical order of our last names. So, I had a chance to listen to many students before it was my turn. Some children were so traumatized that they couldn't utter a word. Mrs. Mitchel told them that they would get another chance tomorrow, but they'd better do it then or else.

Some, especially, the girls, did a good job. They spoke clearly, looked around, smiled and, obviously, enjoyed the limelight. I envied them. Even Bobby was able to do a reasonable job while mugging for the girls. My turn was approaching quickly.

Sam Slaughter was next. He mumbled, sweated and, finally, was able to blurt out the required information. "Donald Smith," Mrs. Mitchel announced in stentorian tones.

It was not my finest moment. As I arose to speak, Bobby whispered, "Ok, wise guy, tell 'em how smart you are." I started to talk and nothing came out. Mrs. Mitchel glared at me. "Donald, just tell us your name, where you live and about your family."

I tried again and had the same result. It was as if that nasty proverbial cat had picked my tongue for his morning snack. I heard Bobby snicker, "Gotcha!"

Mrs. Mitchel said finally: "Well, Donald, it looks like you will be doing this again tomorrow. You'd better practice tonight at home." I had no plans to tell mom and dad. I would do it tomorrow. I would.

The remainder of the day went by slowly. We practiced sounding out the letters and the numbers. It was kid-stuff for me. The next day's speech weighed heavily on my mind. I avoided Bobby at lunch time and struck up a conversation with a boy named David and a red-headed girl named Joan. They were both quiet and offered sympathy about my aborted speech.

The three o'clock bell rang loudly. We got up to leave and Mrs. Mitchel said sternly, "I dismiss you, not the bell. Take your seats!" When she, finally, dismissed us, we had to line up in single file and walk down the corridor to the front door.

As I walked slowly towards home, I decided that school was not a happy place after all. I had to do things that made me uncomfortable and obey rules that seemed silly. It would not be the last time that my illusions about school and schooling would be shattered. Tomorrow had to be better.

I remember not sleeping well that night. I kept my problem to myself. That's been a life-long habit. The next morning dawned bright and sunny. I didn't have to wear the dreaded raincoat and high boots. I marched off to school with resolve. I would make that silly little speech. I would.

I took my seat. Bobby leaned over my shoulder and whispered: "I can't wait to hear your speech." Was now the time to do what dad had told me to do? I didn't have time to do anything. Mrs. Mitchel walked down the aisle towards us and admonished: "You boys have been told to not talk once you are seated." I didn't know what being seated had to do with not talking, but we both complied.

The first business of the day was to finish the little introductory speeches. Seven of us had that to do. I was next to last, so, once again, I had time to structure my thoughts. Joey Bowden was up first. He seemed to be a little strange. He kept his head down and seldom spoke. He had eaten by himself yesterday and I thought that I had seen him crying when we were in the restroom before class resumed after lunch.

He got up to speak and started to shake all over. Several students laughed at him. Bobby almost wet himself by laughing so hard. Mrs. Mitchel told every one to be quiet and Let Joey speak. But, Joey didn't speak. He bolted from the room and ran down the hall with Mrs. Mitchel in hot pursuit. We all sat in stunned silence.

When Mrs. Mitchel returned, she told us that Joey was ill and would be sent home for the day. I felt very bad about Joey. I felt very bad for me. What if I had a similar problem? The next speakers managed to get out their information without much drama.

Once again, I heard my name called. I stood up and said almost too loudly: "My name is Donald Smith." I looked around and realized that no one really was paying much attention. I had flattered myself by thinking that I would be the center of attention. It was a valuable lesson to learn that other people don't care much about what you say or how you say it. So, I continued on with the remainder of my spiel. I looked around for reactions or comments. None came except for Mrs. Mitchel saying, "Next is Mary Thomas."

Even Bobby was subdued. He said nothing to me. I turned around and looked at him. He didn't look so big today. It was almost as if he sensed that his words hadn't really bothered me. So, the fun was gone from saying them. That day, I sensed that I could stand on my own and face down obstacles that had seemed unsurmountable before.

I did worry about Joey. Would he return tomorrow? Even then, my seven year old mind had processed that Joey might need my help. I resolved to do something to make him feel better.

The remainder of the day went by without any incidents that brought back memories. I know that we continued to practice saying the names of the letters and numbers. We were asked to identify the letters in the two little books that had been handed out. I felt my first, but not my last, taste of boredom in a school setting. I wanted to get on with the excitement of reading real books and discussing what happened in them. That's how Grandma Smith had taught me. That's how I wanted first grade to be. Instead, we labored on with the stuff that I'd already mastered. If only Mrs. Mitchel had known about dividing the class into ability groups and providing suitable material for each group. I can't really blame her for not knowing, but she, surely, must have sensed that I and a few others were capable of doing much more.

Slowly, as the days wore on, I made friends with a few students who shared my interest in reading. David and Joan, in particular, were able to read nearly as well as I could. We ate together and walked home together after school. We talked about asking Mrs. Mitchel if we could get some books from the library to use instead of the insipid ones handed out in the classoom. Yes, I know, we didn't act like your typical first graders. I guess that we weren't.

We decided to ask her. I think that it was about the fourth or fifth day of school. We approached her timidly. I blurted out the request. At first, she acted surprised. Then, she acted irritated. She said, "I am supposed to use the books that I've given to you. Those are the only ones that we're allowed to use. You will read what I tell you to read. Don't fill your minds with some of that junk that is being handed out in public libraries. That's it! Don't ask me again." I remember her words and her tone of voice. It made an impression. School was not what I expected. I had hoped that it would be a place where dreams would come alive. My dream was that I could read all of the books in the world. I dreampt that teachers and students would be happy and no one would be cross or cranky. But, Mrs. Mitchel was almost always cross and cranky. The school books were stupid. Some kids were mean and nasty. Some kids were sad and lonely. Welcome to the world of education. Welcome to the real world.

Looking back, I can't believe how rigid and unbending the teachers and rules were in my first two years of school in Carrollton, Ohio. At the time, I just accepted that this was how school was supposed to be. I went along because I didn't know how things should be. I just knew that I was bored and so were most of the other kids. My parents weren't knowledgeable enough to know that parents could have some influence in changing things. I complained at home about being forced to do the same things as all of the other students even though I was far ahead of them in my reading skills. Mom and Dad just told me to do what I was told and quit complaining.

During this time, I believe that I developed a life-long aversion to mathematics. I did it, but I never really understood it. That has been true all through my time in algebra, geometry, calculus and statistic courses.

I never learned cursory writing. I used printed letters, mostly capitals. I do to this day. I thank the Gods that be for the use of typewriters and, now, the computer.

later in the first grade, I began to receive recognition for my reading and writing skills. I won an award for the most books read and for writing simple little stories. I won our class' spelling bee. Mrs. Mitchel began to warm up to the idea of allowing library books to be used for reading assignments.

Bobby and I reached a sort of truce after I hit him hard in the stomach after he threw one of my books into the trash can. It felt good to feel him gasp for air and double over.

Poor Joey continued to fall behind in our class work. He became more withdrawn and began to miss a lot of school. I offered to help him with his work, especially the reading assignments. I think that he appreciated my attempts, but he was too shy to establish a friendship. Before the year was over, he and his family moved from Carrollton.

Profiting from hindsight, I realize that many of these problems could have been averted by the usage of some of the modern-day procedures and policies. Bobby would be classified as a bully and treated as such. Joey would have received help from personnel trained to handle special students. Students would be identified as being gifted or as being in need of specialized, individualized attention.

Teachers would have been given training in identifying students who needed more challenges in order to reach their potentials.

But, it was in the 1930's and schools weren't in the business of coddling special students. Staying in lock-step was the mode of operation. It was up to the student to fit in. Schools weren't designed to meet students' needs.

My time in second grade in Carrollton was a reprise of the first grade. Nothing changed except the degree of difficulty in reading and arithmetic. We had a smattering of science and what we now call Social Studies. There were no art or music classes. Playing on the play ground was our physical education.

On the home front, Dad's job as a night watchman at the defunct pottery company was terminated. The buildings were due for destruction. Dad became irritable and short-tempered. I stayed away from him when at all possible. We ate a lot of jello and macaroni. I needed some new shoes, pants and shirts. Mom was sick a lot of the time. Something had to change.

> *"Don't limit a child to your own learning,*
> *for he was born in another time."*
>
> Rabindranath Tagore

Part Two

GRADES THREE, FOUR AND FIVE - RANDOLPH, OHIO

The "Something" came in the form of an invitation from my Mom's parents to move to Randolph, Ohio to help them run the general store which they owned. We could live in a small attachment on the back of the store. Change was in the air.

During the summer following my year in second grade we made the big move. I remember having mixed feelings about leaving the little house on High Street where the railroad tracks bordered our back yard. I had made a few friends and I didn't like the idea of trying to make new ones. But, we had no money and dad had no future in Carrollton. He had left the army after World War I with no appreciable skills except a strong back and a stubborn mind. We had no choice.

Dad rented a big truck and he and a few male friends loaded our meager possessions into it and we set off north up state route thirty. Randolph, Ohio was a small rural community about twelve miles east of Akron. My grandparents owned the only general store in the vicinity. It catered to townspeople and to the farmers from the surrounding area. It sold groceries, feed, grain, tools, hardware, clothing and various sundries.

They lived in a large three-story victorian home that featured fire places in almost every room. We were to live in a small attached building in the back of the store. We had no indoor plumbing. We got water from an outside pump. The outhouse was in the barn, some thirty yards behind the house. I was informed that my job was to empty the slop-jars daily. They resided under the beds in the three very small bedrooms.

My sister, Phyllis, who was twelve years older than me, made the move with us. She planned to attend Hammel-Actual Business College in Akron.

So, off we went, Dad driving the truck and a friend of his driving my mom, me and my sister in his car. We didn't own a car. We looked like the Okies leaving the dust bowl for greener grounds. I remember feeling a wave of apprehension that was tempered with a layer of excitement.

We settled into our new home. It was small and cramped. From a door on the second floor I could enter the second floor of the store. The second floor of the store was for storage. In the middle of the floor was an opening from which one could look down into the center of store below. I spent a lot of time lying on my stomach peering down at the customers, my grandfather and my dad. Sometimes, I used my water pistol to spray the unsuspecting targets. Once, I used my pea shooter. It was the last time. As I lay gloating about my marksmanship, dad came up behind me and gave me hard slap on the side of my head. He was angry with me, but I thought that I detected just the hint of a smile.

We had moved during the summer so that I had time to adjust to our new surroundings before I would start third grade in my new school. It was about a quarter of a mile up route 44 from our house. Daily, I received warnings about walking along that road to get to school. The traffic was heavy and fast. I had several practice walks before school began in early September.

Randolph wasn't much a town. The houses were few and far between. The only child near my age was a girl who lived across the street from the store. Most of the children came from outlying farms. One day, the girl and her parents came into the store. I was outside hitting stones against the barn wall with my baseball bat. My dad, the girl and her parents came outside. They said that I would be welcome to come to their home to play with the girl. The parents and my dad had decided that we both needed a playmate. Well, she was a pretty girl with red hair. I didn't object although I was intimidated by her forthright mannerisms and bold smile. I learned quickly that girls play differently than boys. They can, also, be very bossy. When I went to play with her, she had already decided what to play and how to play it. We, usually, played with a set of toy farm animals and buildings. The thing that I really liked about her was that she loved to read as much as I did. We exchanged books and discussed each one of them.

My summer was composed mainly of store duties. I swept the wooden floors and stocked the shelves with things brought from the second floor. One day, I took a candy bar from the glass case and put it in my pocket. My granddad saw me do this and told me that I was a thief and would never amount to any good. I wasn't paid for doing this daily work and I felt justified in taking a piece of candy once in a while. My maternal grandparents were stern and almost emotionless. They were far different from my other grandparents who still lived in Carrollton. Grandma Jenny had encouraged my reading and dreaming. Grandpa Joe was a sweet-spirited alcoholic who beguiled me with far-fetched stories of his imaginary accomplishments. I knew that he'd never held a regular job. I missed both of them very much.

I dreaded the nights. Dad and my sister, Phyllis, had begun to quarrel almost nightly about her late hours and her beer-drinking at the local dance hall. I lay in bed listening to his cursing and her defiant responses. It ended usually with dad stomping off and her crying behind her closed bedroom door. Just before school was to begin, she moved to Akron to share an apartment with her girl friend. She enrolled for business classes at Hammel-Actual Business College and worked as a retail clerk to support herself. Soon, she began to win honors as a typist and stenographer.

The first day of school arrived. I woke up in the morning at five o'clock. I used the slopjar by first placing a sheet of toilet paper across the water to mask the sounds. I splashed cold water on my face and rubbed water through my hair to slick it down. I left my pajama bottoms on so that my scratchy woolen pants wouldn't itch my legs. They were longer than my pants, so I had to roll them up at the bottom. I put on my only dress shirt and a cotton sweater. My newly polished shoes glowed in the early morning light. My parents were still asleep and I tip-toed down to the kitchen. I knew how to cook oatmeal, so I began the process. It was a long process that required my putting coal in the coal stove and lighting it. I took out the big cooking pot and put in the oatmeal, salt and water. I was a big boy now and I wanted to do things myself. The oatmeal began to bubble. I heard my parents walking around on the upstairs floor. Soon, they both came down and acted surprised at my being up so early.

Mom came to help me and dad sat at the table and demanded his coffee. The lecture began. Walk against the traffic . Look both ways when you cross the road. Don't get in a car with strangers if they offer you a ride. Don't get your clothes dirty. Be respectful to your new teacher. Try to make friends. Take care of your new books. Eat all of the lunch that I packed. Come straight home after school. Don't dawdle. I never learned what dawdle meant. If you have homework, do it immediately when you get home. Ad nauseum!

Later, as I left the house to begin my new journey, Mom said: "Be a good boy. Mind your teacher." Dad muttered: "Don't get in any trouble. I don't want to have to hear bad things from your teacher."

Armed with those words of wisdom, I marched off north up route 44 to begin a new chapter of my educational experiences.

Along the way I passed a car dealership and a church with a small graveyard beside it. I was early, so I opened the gate to the graveyard and entered. I had visited this place before. I found peace and quiet there especially after a night of listening to Dad and Phyllis arguing loudly. Now, I just wanted a few minutes alone to think about how I would handle a new school. I only knew a few other children in the area and those only from seeing them in the store. Oh, yes, and Sally from across the street with whom I exchanged books. I picked out a granite stone and sat on it for a while. I heard children from the road laughing and joking with one another. I would really try to make some friends today. I needed some.

I hoped that my teacher would be kind and smile a lot. My last two teachers seldom smiled. I hoped that I wouldn't meet another Bobby. I didn't like to hit people. I got up and walked slowly out of the grave yard.

The school sat back a long way from the road. The long cement walk teemed with excited students. I was carried along with the crowd up to the front door. Inside, the class lists were posted. I looked for grade three classes. I found my name on the list for Mrs. Waters in room 211. Donald E. Smith looked boring compared to the other names. There were a lot of foreign sounding last names. At least, they looked foreign to me. Every one seemed to know every one else. I guess that they had all been going to Randolph schools all of their lives. I would be an outsider. I longed to be an insider.

I climbed the stairs to the second floor and found room 211. Many students were already inside and seated. They seemed anxious for school to begin. Me, not so much. I looked through the door's glass window to check for possible trouble spots. I spotted a large curly-haired boy who was shoulder-punching a small blonde boy. The smaller boy flinched with each hit. I vowed to keep away from that curly-haired guy. There was no teacher in sight.

As I stood peering through the glass, I heard a voice behind me say: "If this is your assigned room, please go inside. The tardy bell is going to ring." Mrs. Waters was a short woman of substantial girth. She had an authoratative voice that sounded strangely masculine, a lot like my dad. I did as I was told.

I found a seating chart posted on the chalkboard. My name was on the last seat in the row by the chalkboard. At least, no one sat behind. In front of me was a boy named Glenn. I took my seat behind Glenn. He turned around and said: "Hi, my name is Glenn, what's your name?" I liked Glenn immediately.

The bell rang loudly. Mrs. Waters took her place in front of the class and looked over her new brood. She took a long time to speak. "When I stand in front of the class, you are to get quiet and listen. I will not tolerate any of you talking while I am standing in front of you. Is that clear?" Well, I guess that it was. No one made a sound. I wondered where all of the nice teachers were that I'd read about in some of my library books. They were warm, caring and motherly. I guessed that teachers were all taught to be like the three that I'd had so far. They were not warm, caring and motherly.

The day went by in a predictable way. Books were passed out. Mrs. Waters expounded on her room rules. There were more rules than the number of possible offenses that I could list. Looking back, the tone of the entire day was negative. The things you shouldn't do were far more numerous than than the things that you should do. I was almost afraid to move in fear of violating one of those things. Fear must have been what she most wanted to instill in us. I wonder how many children were turned off to learning and education back in those days.

At lunch time, I sat with Glenn whom I found lived on a farm about a mile from the school. He was easy to talk to and even invited me to visit him at the farm on the weekend. We could play in the barn and jump on the big haystacks from the top barn window. I hoped that dad would take me. But, he was always busy at the store and didn't like to be bothered with family things.

The afternoon session was, mostly, listening to Mrs. Waters extol the virtues of being prompt, courteous and industrious, not necessarily in that order. I do remember that she assigned homework that very first night.

The days flowed by predictably. I still disliked mathematics and I still liked anything to do with words. I got along with almost everyone in the class. I avoided the large curly-headed boy, but I suspected that he had had his eyes on me and was planning something.

I, finally, coaxed dad into taking me out to the farm where Glenn lived. He arranged with Glenn's dad for me to stay and play for several hours. Glenn's dad was to drive me home. I enjoyed climbing around on the bales of hay inside the barn and jumping out of the top floor onto the huge haystack. I felt very brave and adventurous. Inside the barn the barn cats chased the mice and the pigeons flew around with abandonment. It was a whole new world for me. I got to watch the cows being milked and the the pigs being fed slop from the troughs. Glenn was lucky. He had this fascinating world to live in plus the house had an inside bathroom with a flush toilet.

Mrs. Waters seemed to grow grouchier by the day. Every little thing annoyed her. Criticism flowed from her like the little drops of persperation that dropped from her forehead even on the cold days of late fall. She told us that we were the worst class that she'd ever had. And, she'd had plenty of classes in her over thirty years of teaching. The grouchier that she got, the worst the class acted. I almost felt sorry for her. Almost.

I remember clearly the day that Henry broke into tears. Henry came from a very poor family that lived in a ramshackle old house just past the cemetery. I'd heard dad say to one of the store's customers that Henry's dad was a drunk and his mom slept with other men. I didn't know what was so bad about sleeping with someone. But, it did seem like a strange thing to do. Dad complained about the family running up a big bill at the store and never making payments. I heard a lot of stuff lying up there on the second floor of the store.

The day in question Henry had not turned in his homework and had shown up at school looking dirty and disheveled. Mrs. Waters laid into him about those things and a lot of other stuff she dredged up. Poor Henry just stood looking helpless. The kids all knew that Henry was slow. "Slow" covered a lot of problems. I'm sure that today Henry would have been placed in a special needs' class and given a lot of individual help with his learning diabilities.

Henry started to cry. Then, he started to wail. Wailing is a lost art. In all of my years in education, I've never heard another student wail. I felt really bad for him. I think that the other kids did, too. I have my doubts about the large curly-haired boy. I think that I saw him smirk and nudge the boy sitting next to him.

The more that Henry wailed, the angrier that Mrs. Waters became. She said, "Henry, stop that right now or I'll take you down to the principal and he'll give you something real to cry about."

Henry stopped abruptly. He got up from his seat, ran out of the door and down the hall. Mrs. Water's mouth dropped open as she looked down the hallway at the fleeing Henry. She came back into the room and announced that Henry was in big trouble now and to let this be a lesson to all you who don't do their homework and show up without wearing clean clothes and smelling of body odor.

Henry never returned to our school. Soon after this incident, the family moved. The grocery bill was never paid. Dad talked about the thieving family for years afterwards.

My math problems continued. I did the homework and passed the tests, but I never really understood what I was doing or why I was doing it. I wish that back in my early school years that someone recognized my dilemna and did some type of intervention. But, teachers were not trained to do those things back then and counselors were non-existant. But, I am to blame, also. I was too timid to tell anyone about my problem. My report cards reflected the problem, but nobody at school or at home paid attention to it. I always recieved top grades in everything but math. My math grades were, usually, C's and D's. Certainly, those were warning flags.

It's difficult dredging up specifics from so long ago. But, the things that I remember must have been important to me. I remember the day that the large curly-headed boy came up behind me and knocked the books from my arms. I was more surprised than angry and I just bent down to pick them up. He towered over me and said with a smirk: "You think you're so smart getting those good grades and always being asked to read. My dad says that store your family owns overcharges everybody."

That did it. Now, I was mad. I turned around and hit him hard in the stomach. He doubled over in pain. I felt a quick rush of excitement and pleasure. It was a repeat of what happened to the bully in Carrollton. Before Curly could recover and retaliate, Mrs. Waters arrived on the scene and told both us to report to the principal's office. It was my first official visit to that inner sanctum that I'd heard other kids speak of in awe.

Donald E. Smith, Ph.D.

On the way to the office, Curly muttered under his breath that he'd get me later. I just looked at him and gave my first smirk. It wouldn't be my last.

Principal Barlow loomed over the two of us as we sat on uncomfortable seats facing him. He was a tall man with a big belly that extended over his large metal belt buckle. He questioned us about what had happened. Curly said that I hit him in the stomach. I said that Curly had knocked my books on the floor and ran his mouth about me and the family store. Mr. Barlow just looked at us without expression. Finally, he said: "You are both wrong. I can't let this go without punishing each of you. You will both stay after school this evening and write an essay about what you did wrong and how you plan to correct your behavior. I expect better from both of you. You are good boys who made a mistake. I know that you will learn from this. That's all. I'll see both of you in my office at 3:30." Years later I would remember Mr. Barlow and his practical humanity. I modeled some of my actions as a principal on how he treated situations and people.

I gave a silent sigh of relief. I had expected to be paddled. I looked over at Curly. He was sweating and his eyes had been watering. I believed that I had won a victory. I could write that essay blindfolded. Curly would have trouble doing it. Also, I'd felt his fat belly beneath my fist and had heard his yelp of pain. I don't think that I was or am sadistic or cruel, but vengeance had been mine and it had felt good.

We walked back to our classroom in a subdued manner carefully avoiding to touch each other or make eye contact. Mrs. Waters opened the door and said, "I hope that you both have learned a lesson. I hope that Mr. Barlow paddled both of you. I will not tolerate that kind of behavior in my classroom." Curly and l exchanged a quick glance.

I wish that I could say that my three years in Randolph Elementary School were years of learning, fun and excitement. They weren't. I have trouble today remembering any highlights or periods of elation or depression. It was a period of flatness. Nothing stands out. I continued to excel in verbal skills. I continued to just get by in mathematical skills.

My teachers in grades four and five were cut from the same cloth as Mrs. Waters had been. We were given homework. The next day, we discussed the homework. We were given busy work to do in class while the teachers hovered over us. Visual aids and field trips were not used as tools of the trade. We had no guest speakers. The monotony numbed our brains. We had no creative outlets for our youthful energies. Rote learning was the rule of the day. I was asked frequently to read aloud from our textbooks. I was a good reader and enjoyed my role. But, other kids began to resent my role as the perceived teachers' pet. I played defense and started to "Ham it up" as I read by injecting my own material into the reading assignment. The other students laughed at this. The resentment stopped. The teachers frowned openly, but I think they enjoyed the few interludes of fun into what were, usually, long boring days.

During the fifth grade, my parents became tired of my humming and singing as I played alone at home. My mom asked if I'd like to learn to play an instrument. I said that I would, but we had no money to buy a piano or horn of some kind. I wrote it off as just an idle comment.

About a week later, a man walked into the store carrying an instrument case. He told dad that this was a real bargain. His son had quit playing and it was just taking up space at home. He told dad that he could have it for five dollars. I watched dad hand over five bills. I wondered what the case contained.

What it contained was an hawaiian guitar. Of all of the world's musical instruments, this would have been my last choice. Who plays this instrument outside of Hawaii? None of the popular music of the day used this thing. I had heard it played on the radio and it sounded like old people music. I'd be laughed out of Randolph. Were my parents serious? It turned out that they were. They arranged for me to take lessons from a young lady who was majoring in music at near-bye Kent State University. She would come to our house every Wednesday evening at seven o'clock to give me lessons.

At first, I rebelled as best as an eleven year old could rebel. I pouted and sulked, but the lessons began. After about three lesssons, I had learned to play a few basic chords, hold the guitar on my lap and use the metal bar to vibrate the strings. Not much music sounds good while being played by this instrument. Only Hawaiian songs sound reasonably good. And, they are suspect. During the next summer, I took part in a recital at Kent State that featured my teacher's ten students. We played together and each of us played a small solo. I was embarrassed and frightened. I endured many sleepless nights before the concert date. I hoped that no kids from school were there or even knew about my lessons. I had kept it a secret at school. Soon after the recital, I persuaded my parents that this was leadng nowhere. I quit taking lessons before the end of the summer. I resumed my singing and humming career.

I kept the guitar for several more years. My dad later sold it for ten dollars. In that, his investment paid off. This had been my first exposure to "Culture." I had learned some things about music theory and practice. My school wasn't providing these experiences. It was only later that music and art became integral parts of a school's curricula.

The summer before I was to enter grade six in Randolph, rumors of impending war in Europe began to surface. I heard about Hitler and his rush to power on the radio and read it in the newspaper. Our economy had not bounced back from our country's worst recession and the general store began to feel the results. I heard dad and granddad discussing the fact that the store was having trouble supporting two families. Dad looked worried and Mom cried sometimes at night after I'd gone to bed. I worried, too. I don't think that I knew then why I was worried, but worry has a way of infiltrating those who are around the worriers.

Dad had been taking correspondence courses that would enable him to be licensed as a stationary engineer. I wasn't sure what that was, but I knew it had to do with steam boilers and other similar things. In July of 1941, he recieved his license by registered mail. Mom and Dad began discussing what they should do. What was decided was that Dad would go to Akron and look for a job in some of the city's industries.

By late August, it looked like war was imminent and that the United States might be involved. A branch of Goodyear Tire and Rubber

Company, later to be called Goodyear Aircraft, was hiring in anticipation of producing war armament. Dad was hired to supervise the boilers at plant one at Goodyear Aircraft during the four o'clock to midnight shift.

It was during this time that Phyllis, growing tired of the lack of adventure in her life, decided to move to California to stay with the family of a childhood friend. She was able to secure a job as secretary to a major at the March Field, the air force base in Riverside. It was a big move for a rather shy girl from Carrollton, Ohio. She had been on a few trips with our great aunt to Chicago and Baltimore, but never on her own. She took Greyhound buses to the west coast. She wrote occasionally saying that she enjoyed the climate and her work.

Dad's new job would require our moving to Akron before school began in September. Granddad owned a home in the Ellet area of East Akron. It had been vacated recently by the former tenants. We made the move the week before school was to begin. In more ways than one, it proved to be a momentous move.

"Education's purpose is to replace an empty mind with an open one."

Malcolm Forbes

Part Three

GRADES SIX - TWELVE - AKRON, OHIO

The two-story house on Sieber Avenue seemed huge in comparison with our little place in Randolph. My bedroom was big. It extended across the whole front of the second floor. Its three windows faced the street. I could see across the street and up and down the street in both directions. I used my prized ten-power telescope to keep track of the neighborhood's events.

My room had a huge walk-in closet. It not only housed my meager supply of clothes, but had room for my desk and an old filing cabinet that I'd been allowed to bring from the store. In effect, I had a two-room apartment. Two other big bedrooms with big closets were for my parents and my sister who had moved back with us in order to save money. A large bathroom, complete with a bathtub, commode and big closet completed the second floor. The bathtub had a hose connected to the faucet so that we could take a shower. This was luxury beyond my best fantasies.

Downstairs, there was a big living room with a fireplace, a large dining room, a library with built-in bookshelves and a kitchen almost as big as our last home. Behind the kitchen was a breakfast nook where we ate most of our meals. The full basement housed a coal furnace. It had a conveyer attached to an opening in the foundation where coal trucks could unload the weekly ton of coal during winter season. It was my job to feed the conveyer from the coal stored in the coal bin. While doing this job, I wore striped bib overalls and a train engineer's hat.

Best of all, the Ellet school was just across my back yard on the next street. It was, at most, a two-minute trip. I did have to navigate through the back yard of a grumpy old couple to get there, but they were usually asleep or cat-napping. When they did see me, they just yelled. By that time, I was already far up the school driveway.

Grades six through eight were housed in portable buildings behind the main building which housed grades nine through twelve. Each portable was heated by a coal stove. Students were given the job of shoveling in the coal. I was experienced in that and quickly won a starting position.

There were two sixth grade portables. There were two seventh grade and two eighth grade portables. The seventh and eighth graders moved from building to building to take English, social studies and arithmetic. But, I'm getting ahead of myself. The summer was not over yet.

The day that we moved in was dark and rainy so I stayed inside and helped mom and dad with the unpacking. The next day was perfect. It was a good omen. I got up early and started to check out my surroundings. On our left, was a house about the same size and shape as ours. I saw a man open the front door. He had his shirt off. He was the hairiest man I'd ever seen and ever would see. He was covered, back and front, with dense, black curly hair. He looked like a black bear. But, he smiled at me and said: "Hi, there, you can call me Bud." Somehow, Bud didn't fit this bear of a man. I hesitated in answering and he told me that he was Mr. Hughes and I could call him that instead if it made me more comfortable. He said that he and his wife and daughter lived there and he hoped that we could be friends. Later, I would meet the friendly Mrs. Hughes and their daughter whom everyone called "Piggy." So, next door we had Piggy and the Bear.

On our right side there was a small one-story bungalow. As I glanced over, I saw a black haired girl coming out of the front door followed by a little boy, maybe, two years old. I continued looking and the girl looked away shyly. The little boy stuck out his tongue at me.

I liked the idea of a pretty girl living next door. She might have been older than me, but it was difficult to tell. I said: "Hi" and she responded with another "Hi." Then, she took the little boy and went back inside.

Little did I know, that the black-haired girl would become my wife of, now, 64 years. Serendipity occurs to all who believe in it.

It was a great place to live. At night, the many kids in the neighborhood played kick-the-can and hide and seek. We made up a game called "Chase" that required pulling a flag from the pants of the one whom you were chasing. It got a little too rough and injuries mounted up and the girls dropped out. When darkness fell, you could hear mothers calling us to come home all up and down the street.

I continued to watch the black-haired girl that everyone called Joy. I liked that name. It fit her well. I was impressed with how she took care of the little boy who lived in the same house. She was patient and considerate with him even through his frequent tantrums. What really impressed me was her relationship with her good friend Naomi who lived across the street. Naomi was born with severe curvature of the spine. She had what is commonly called a "Hump back." Joy was very kind and understanding with her. She always made certain that Naomi was treated just like everyone else in spite of her physical limitations.

In time, I learned that Joy's dad had been killed by a drunken hit-skip driver when she was eight years old. Her mother went off to Florida and Joy came to Seiber Avenue to live with her brother, his wife and their two year old boy. Joy became the built-in baby sitter and unpaid housekeeper. She handled all of this with quiet dignity. She was someone whom I liked instinctively. That liking would, eventualy, turn into love.

Labor Day came and with it came the opening of the school year. I had, already, become acquainted with quite a few students. I had become close with Bill and Bob who lived across the street and a few others who came to play our nightly games.

I had looked in the portable room that would house my sixth grade class. It was American primitive. The pot-bellied stove occupied one corner at the front of the room. The teacher's desk occupied the other front corner. Clothes hooks were mounted all along one side wall. Chalkboards were on the front and other side wall. Old fashioned ink well desks were bolted to the floor in five rows of six desks each. It looked like a room straight out of a McGuffey Reader.

I awoke on the first day of school at six o'clock. Mom had made me take a bath the night before, so I just washed my face and patted down my hair. I heard mom bustling about in the kitchen. The smell of eggs and bacon wafted all the way upstairs to my bedroom. I put on black dress pants and a short-sleeved gray shirt. My brown shoes looked out of place, but my black ones had worn out. I tiptoed past my parent's bedroom where my dad was still sleeping. He worked from four to midnight and he, often, didn't go to bed until three o'clock in the morning. It wasn't prudent to awaken him.

I ate a hurried breakfast although I didn't need to be in school until eight fifteen. I wanted to be early so that I could avoid a dramatic late entrance when all eyes would be on me. At seven thirty, I put on the jacket that mom had insisted that I wear. She always admonished me about "Catching my death of cold." She leaned over for a hug. I was surprised. Neither parent was a frequent hugger. She felt warm and soft. I wish that she had hugged me more often.

I darted across our back yard, squeezed through between two garages, ran fast across the back yard of the Grumpies and appeared on the driveway leading to the school. I was one of many. They laughed, squealed and yelled insults at each other. I knew no one. An older boy bumped against me and said harshly, "Watch where you're going you little squirt." I was about to respond with a clever riposte, but thought better of it. I'd rather live to respond another day. Someone behind me said: "Hi, Don, I hope you have a good day." It was Joy. I told her to have a good day, too. I watched her enter the main high school building. That meant that she must be at least in the ninth grade. I had not asked her previously. Well, I was sure that she wouldn't want to pal around with an immature kid. We could still be friends.

I stopped outside of the portable and took a deep breath. I was starting school in my third new school. I wondered if it would be much different. I hoped that it would. Already, at age 12, I knew what a good teacher and a good school should be. It should be a place where I feel happy and a place where exciting things are happening. It should be a place where I actually learn some new things. It should be a place where I'm made to feel part of what is happening. I want to wake up each school day morning in anticipation of what was to come.

I want my teachers to be people whom I respect and look up to. I want them to find out about me as a real person, not just as a name on a seating chart. I want them to smile more than frown. I want them to praise me for doing well and tell me how to correct things that I am doing poorly. I want their rules to be fair and to be enforced fairly. I want to be treated exactly as all the others are treated.

So, I entered Portable Number 6A and started my time as a student in the Akron Public Schools. That time would last seven years.

Mrs. Landon greeted me with a cheery "Good morning, look for your name on the seatng chart and please take your seat. I hope you have a good day." Already, I knew that I would.

After we were seated, Mrs. Landon told us that we could change seats if we could do it without confusion and without arguments. But, we would have to keep our new seats for at least six weeks. I looked around. Several students were moving to new seats. I didn't know any of the kids in class. So, I stayed where I was. But, I appreciated Mrs. Landon giving us the opportunity to change. She seemed like a swell lady. I had never in my five previous years in school really liked my teachers. They all seemed stuffy, stern and unapproachable. I looked again at Mrs. Landon. She was watching the class move around with a little smile on her face and a knowing look in her eyes. I felt excited about the year. I would work hard and make her proud of me. Making her proud was to be a major goal for me during that year. What a gift she had. I knew her all of fifteen minutes and she had won my heart.

My sixth grade year went by quickly. Mrs. Landon did a great job in motivating us to do our best. I continued to do well in all things related to English and history. I liked the science experiments that she had us do. Later, I used some of the hands-on things that she had us do in our science time. Even the slowest among us enjoyed seeing things freeze up, blow up and steam up. Mathematics remained a mystery to me. I memorized the way she told us to solve problems, but the how and why of it remained a black hole of imponderables.

She showed great patience with all of us when we didn't understand something. She offered to help us after class if we wanted the help. I have to admit that I, sometimes, feigned having a problem just to sit next to her and listen to her advice.

There were very few discipline problems in her class during that year. We didn't act up or out because we knew that she liked us and wanted us to do well. In my experience as a student and an educator that is an unusual situation. I felt that I wanted to protect her. And, I wasn't alone. If anyone became rude or unruly, most of us joined in a chorus to tell that miscreant to sit down, shut up and shape up.

My misgivings as to being a new kid on the block vanished quickly. Mrs. Landon insisted that all of her students be treated with respect. The students who were having trouble keeping up with their work were offered additional help. She organized a small group of the better students to help those students who had difficulties. It was my first taste of peer tutoring. In time, I became one of the tutors, just not in arithmetic.

My grades and my attitude towards school flourished. I was very sad when the school year came to a close. Mrs. Landon brought each one of up to her desk individually. She told us how much she had enjoyed our being in her class and that she would miss all of us. She, even, gave us her home phone number so that we could call her anytme we needed help or advice. I knew then that if I were a teacher, I'd like to be just like her.

It was one of my best school years. I liked my teacher. I received good grades. I got along well with my classmates. I enjoyed our new house, especially my big bedroom and closet. I spent a lot of time up there reading and daydreaming. My Dad and Mom seemed to be happier, too. Dad had a good job and more money to spend. We ate better and I even had some new clothes for my growing body. Evenings were spent playing in the street with a large group of neighborhood children. I began to notice girls more. I realized that they were good for more than teasing or copying homework from. I began to notice more the dark-haired girl who lived next door. She and her brother and sister-in-law sat on their front porch almost every evening when the weather was good. I heard them singing as they sat in the swing and the rockers. I liked to sing and I wished that I could join them. One evening, her brother called out to me to come over and sing with them. It was another one of those life-changing moments. My boyish tenor voice blended well with his bass, his wife's alto and Joy's soprano. I became a regular. We sang mosly the oldies, but we managed a few modern up-beat songs, too. Joy and I began to exchange furtive glances. But, it would be almost three years later before those glances turned into something more substantial.

The next summer flew by quickly. Life had fallen into a predictable routine. I was anxious for fall and my entry into the seventh grade. Grade seven marked the beginning of adolescence. I would be changing classes for each subject and have several different teachers. I had watched with envy when those seventh and eighth graders moved from one building to another. Of course, in cold or bad weather, it didn't seem very appealing.

Finally, September came. I had a couple of new shirts, some new pants and a pair of saddle oxfords to wear. I ran through the back yards filled with anticipation. I reported to Mrs. Smith's room for homeroom and my first class. She was my science teacher. She had the reputation of being tough, but fair. I knew almost everyone in grade seven by now. There was Sam, the tough guy. I'd keep an eye on him. Bobby, the scrawny red-haired boy who lived on my street was thought to be a sissy and got picked on a lot. Virginia always had the best grades in everything. Burt was the adventurous one. He was always in a lot of trouble. Last year, he had tried to get me to break into an empty house near where he lived. He got angry when I refused.

Gwen was a flirt. Her boyfriend was in high school already. She was supposed to "Put out." I didn't really understand what that meant. But, when she winked at me one day I felt very nervous and started to perspire. Burt said he'd explain it to me some day. There were many more distinctive characters whom I could describe. Some more will appear later.

Mrs. Smith told us to take our assigned seats. She explained briefly what she would be teaching and what she expected from us. She was a kind of no-nonsense person whom I sensed would not tolerate bad behavior. I didn't plan to test her. She wrote the next day's assignment on the chalkboard. She said that she wanted each of us to have a notebook to write the assignment in each day. Homework would count for one third of our grade. Class participation and tests would each count one third. I liked it that we knew exactly what to expect. It would be a business-like class. And, that wouldn't be a bad thing. I liked to know exactly what was expected of me. What was expected was that we would learn to love science and mathematics. She told us that she would make it interesting and fun. She did. I even learned that math could be fun. Sometimes.

The bell rang and we were to move to our social studies class. I loved history and geography. I hoped that the teacher did, too. Mr. Wallace was cut from different cloth. He wore a black suit, white shirt and skinny black tie. He greeted us with a lifeless "Come in. Look for your name on the seating chart and sit down. No talking will be allowed unless I call upon you to speak. Is that understood?" Well, that was easy to understand. We weren't dummies.

If ever a teacher could ruin one's love of history and geography, Mr. Wallace could. His lectures were dry. He assigned the questions at the end of each chapter for homework and we spent most of the class taking turns reading aloud from our textbooks. He had mean eyes and no one dared to disobey his strict orders. Even Burt was cowed by this man's possible ability to exact revenge if we got out of line. He kept a wooden paddle by his desk. It had holes drilled in it to increase the velocity of his swing. Once in a while, he picked up the paddle and carressed it lovingly. I heard him use it only one time. The yelps of pain coming from the little alcove that housed the coat hooks was terrifying. Burt had had the temerity to challenge the rules in spite of his fear of Mr. Wallace. Burt told me in private that he would get even.

I managed to sustain my love of the social studies in spite of Mr. Wallace. I expanded my knowledge of the lessons by using books from the school's library and the Ellet Branch Library of the Akron system. I vowed if, by same miracle, I would ever be a teacher, I would be the exact opposite of Mr. Wallace.

We moved to the next portable. It housed our language arts' class. Language arts was really just grammar, spelling, literature and writing. Miss Lightner was our teacher. The first thing that I noticed was that she was young, Very young. Gwen looked older and more worldly than she did. She was too thin. She wore glasses and her hair was pulled back in a severe bun. She used make-up only sparingly. As we entered, she looked frightened. I would learn later that this was her first teaching job.

She was to teach my favorite subject. I hoped that she would be a good teacher. The kids came in with the knowledge from friends whom they'd met at lunch that Miss Lightner was easy pickings. Some of them planned to give her a hard time. Her looks and mannerisms made me feel sorry for her even before the class began. She looked around the room and said, "Please take your seats after checking to see where you are to sit." Hardly anyone obeyed her tentative request. Burt was the ring leader of those who remained standing, laughing and joking. Some of us sat down and waited for Miss Lightner to take charge. We waited in vain. Finally, Virginia, who was our academic leader by virtue of her good grades last year. said, "Come on, you guys, give her a chance to talk to us." With some peer pressure from some of us, the rowdies sat down.

Miss Lightner stood before the class and seemed at a loss for words. Finally, she spoke in a quiet voice. "I love the English language and I hope that you do, too. I chose to be a teacher because I want to teach you to love it, also. I want you to love to read and to be able to write well enough to express your thoughts." I liked this. It was exactly what I wanted, also.

Unfortunately, she was would be unable to complete her stated goal. It was sad to see. The boneheads in the class made her life miserable. They laughed at her attempts to settle us down. Paper wads and paper clips flew through the air. When she went to the chalkboard and began to write, all hell would break loose. She seemed at a loss as to what to do. A few of my friends and I tried to get the miscreants to give her a chance to teach. She, obviously, knew her material from the little that we could hear. I told Sam and Burt that they were being jerks. I made the age-old appeal about their mothers. "Would you like your mother treated that way." They both said: "Yeah, that would be a hoot." Nothing worked. The principal, Mr. Hyre, made a surprise visit to the class after he'd heard of the commotion that went on daily. He gave a stern speech about how he expected good behavior from now on. Ten minutes after he left, the trouble begin again.

I was at a loss as to what to do. Some of got together and stayed after school to express our apologies to Miss Lightner. She said that she didn't blame us. It was just a few students whom she felt were bad. She added that they weren't really bad. They were just being kids and she liked all of us. She felt that she was failing all of us. She should be doing a better job. But, I could tell that the job was getting her down. She came to class looking tired and deeply sad. I could tell that she wasn't getting much sleep. We left feeling sad, also. That was in October. In November, she started missing school frequently. We had a lot of substitute teachers. Our learning ground to almost a complete halt.

On a bright, bitterly cold day in December we heard the news. Mr. Hyre came to our class and asked the substitute to give him a few minutes to talk to us. He said simply: "Miss lightner was found dead last night in her apartment." We were shocked. Even Burt and Sam looked pale. About a week later, the news circulated through the school that she had committed suicide by taking an overdose of sleeping pills. She had been under a doctor's care for depression for several weeks.

I wanted to kill some of the worst behaved students. Burt and Sam were on my hit list. I didn't know how or when, but I'd make them pay. Miss Lightner had been a kind, sweet person. She hadn't deserved to be treated like she'd been treated. I think that all us, including the most guilty, learned something from this terrible incident. I know that I became much more aware of how cruelty towards others can have devastating effects. I learned, also, that the inaction of some us to correct the problem made us accessories. To this day, I feel guilty about not doing more to prevent her death. I vowed never to let that happen again. I hope that, somehow, somewhere, she understands and forgives us.

That vivid memory overshadows anything else that transpired during my seventh and eighth grade years. Suffice it to say that we finished the year with heavier hearts than seventh graders should need to suffer. I did well in my subjects. I improved somewhat in math and looked forward to my eighth grade year. We had had industrial arts, art, music and home economics, too, but in small doses and I hated all of it except music. These classes were treated almost as after thoughts and seemed to be of little importance to both students and teachers.

That summer I began to spend more time with Joy and her family. I was a frequent visitor. So much so, that mom told me to stop bothering them. I didn't quite understand the attraction, but I knew that I felt happy being around them. Joy was kind to me. Her brother and sister-in-law tolerated me and even seemed to enjoy my company. They had a few beers or highballs on the porch in the evenings and, usually, started up a familiar song for us to sing together. They both chain-smoked and I coughed a lot. It didn't help my singing, but I think that Joy appreciated my youthful attempts at harmony. Little Pat, their son, made cameo appearances as a boy soprano. It was a good summer even though Mom began to complain of feeling ill almost every day. Dad was never there in the evening. I seldom saw him. The war effort often required that he work seven days each week. He was in bed until mid-morning and left for work about 3:15. I was in bed when he returned home.

Pearl Harbor changed the attitude of the country and its people. Everything revolved around beating Hitler and his gang. Rationing made getting food and gasoline very difficult. The older boys in the high school dropped out of school and enlisted. Casualty reports started coming back from the war zones. Our evening street games took on a more violent tone. The boys wanted to play war and have actual hand-to-hand combat. I joined in. It made me feel more manly and mature. We organized war games on Saturdays in a wooded area on the edge of town. It was called "Capture the Flag." We divided up into two armies.

The game required that we physically subdue an opponent and take his flag. That would make him officially "Dead." After two hours, the army with the most live men remaining won the war. I enjoyed this. I had become known as a kind of bookworm. This game allowed me to prove otherwise.

Summer ended and my eighth grade year was about to begin. Joy was, now, entering grade eleven. She was two and a half years older, but ahead by three grades. We spent more time talking. Neither of us felt that there was anything unusual about our friendship. After all, we were just neighboring friends.

Just before school began, Burt made a visit. He said that he'd like to talk to me. We took a walk up Sieber Avenue. He said that he'd noticed that the windows of Mrs. Smith's portable room were not being closed completely. He had disliked her last year for the frequent punishments that she'd given him. I thought to myself that this is not leading to a good place. I should have turned around and gone home. He asked if I would stand guard tonight outside her room after it had grown dark. He wanted to climb through the window and do something inside the room. I asked what he planned to do. He said that he wanted to play some jokes on her. I knew that Burt's idea of jokes could be destructive. He said that I wouldn't be involved but that I'd just be there to warn him if some one came.

To this day, I don't know why I agreed. Adventure? Excitement? I really don't know. But, when it grew dark that night, I told mom that I felt restless and just wanted to go for a walk before bedtime. She raised no objection. By that time, she was under a doctor's care and was on medications. She had become apathetic and listless.

Burt and I walked up the school's driveway and turned in among the portable buildings. The night custodians were in the high school building some thirty yards away. I saw two windows in Mrs. Smith's portable that looked a little open at the bottoms. Burt walked up and tried one. It opened easily. He said: "Just stand in the shadows and tap on the window if you see or hear someone coming." Like a fool, I did as asked. Burt climbed in easily and I heard him rummaging around inside. I wondered what he was up to. I heard drawers opening and closing. I heard something hit the floor. I grew anxious. I wished that he'd hurry up. Finally, Burt climbed out and we hurried away. We both went to our own homes. That night, I slept uneasily. What if someone had seen us? What had Burt done?

The next evening, I was on Joy's porch as usual. A police car drove up and asked to talk to me. Swallowing hard, I went down the steps and stood in front of the officer. He was not angry. He asked me if I had seen anything suspicious around the school last night. I said no and that I'd only walked through the school yard last night to get to the main street to Bryan's drug store to get a milkshake. He said that a neighbor thought they'd seen me on school grounds. He explained that a building had been entered and some destruction had taken place. I admitted that I'd been there, but hadn't seen anything bad. He seemed satisfied with that and left. Joy and her family had watched this exchange from the porch. I felt sick to my stomach. What had Burt done? He had said he just wanted to play a joke on her.

News travels swiftly in a tight-knit community like Ellet. Someone had broken into the school and wrote obscenities on Mrs. Smith's chalkboard. And, worst of all, had defecated in her desk drawer. Sweet Jesus! I had been the look-out for this. Had I known what he'd planned, I would have refused to go. But, I did. I hadn't seen Burt since the incident. I didn't want to see him again. Ever. When we did meet, I told him that he was a bastard. He didn't seem fazed by his actions and just asked me to keep my mouth shut or he'd implicate me, too. What an ass! I kept away from him until he and his family moved from Ellet later in that school year. Years later, I heard that he'd lost an arm in an industrial accident. Karma is a bitch.

I lived in fear of being found out for a long time afterwards. That incident marked the official end to my crime career. School started soon after. I had Mrs. Smith for math and science once more. Each time that I entered her classroom I sniffed the air and looked at her face to see if she showed signs of having found me out. But, that was the end of the affair. The culprits were never found out. Even today, I wonder if the statute of limitations has expired for the crime of pooping in a teacher's desk.

That incident is a prime example of how young people can be influenced by peer pressure and the thought of a moment of adventure and excitement. I had not wanted Burt to think that I was a coward. After being "good" all of my life, the thought of being a little "bad" had intrigued me. I lacked the courage and moral certainty to resist the temptation. I learned from that incident. I didn't want to feel the fear of getting caught ever again. We, as adults, should be cautious in labeling students who do "bad" things as being "bad" people. Most children are guilty of breaking the boundaries at some point in their development. It's our duty as parents and teachers to instill into their minds and spirits that they are guilty of only an act that society has deemed to be "bad." Let them know that they are worth forgiving and that we expect that they will not disappoint us again. Letting children know that they have worth is the key to influencing behaviors.

I had a new teacher for social studies, Mr. Allen. He was young and full of energy. He made his class into a fun time. We acted out historical events, made a lot maps and wrote original stories about historical figures. He was a good teacher. I realize that more fully now. He did the very things that I was taught to do in my education classes. He involved his students. He assigned some hands-on work. He used praise more than censure. He was a genuinely nice guy.

But, my favorite class was English with Mrs. Ellet. She taught Spanish in the high school, also. We were given a smattering of that language along with the basic language arts. It instilled in me a desire to learn languages. I look back to those little language lessons as being instrumental to opening a new world for me. I longed to visit those places that she talked about. She had traveled widely and was happy to share those experiences with her students.

But, what I remember most about the eighth grade was the Otis Beta IQ Test. It was given to all of us about half-way through the year. It was weighted heavily to measure one's reading and comprehension abilities. Mathematics was only a small part of it. I aced it.

In fact, Mrs. Smith asked me to stay after school the day of the test. She said that I had made a perfect score. I didn't miss even one question. My IQ turned out to be 140 on the test's scale. She said that no one had ever answered all of the questions correctly and there must have been a mistake. Then, she asked me if I had copied answers from other students. I said "No" rather emphatically. She pursued the matter by saying she would send me to Mr. Hyre's office to talk to him about this. I felt both elated and deflated. I did not cheat. I thought that the test had been very easy. It was right in my wheel-house. In retrospect, I criticize Mrs. Smith for accusing me without any basis for doing so. I should have been congratulated.

Mr. Hyre was a little more understanding, but seemed suspicious. He asked me if I had seen the test and answers before. He emphasized that this was very unusual. It had never happened in his many years in education. He said that he was not certain if the 140 IQ should be placed on my permanent record. I didn't know what to say. I was, almost, convinced that my high score had been an accident. I was too intimidated to argue with him or Mrs. Smith. I just left the office without rebuttal. All during my time at Ellet, I never asked to look at my permanent record. It was only after I'd begun teaching that I asked to see my records. There it was - Otis Beta - IQ 140 followed by an *. So much for motivation and support.

But, otherwise, the year went by smoothly and quickly. I felt that I'd learned a lot and had made a lot of friends, many of whom have remained friends down through the years.

In June, I felt ready for the high school and myriad of classes and activities which would be open to me.

On the home front, dad still worked hard and long. Mom became even more sickly. In the summer before I began high school, she was diagnosed with ovarian cancer. They operated, but closed her back up and declared it to be inoperable. They didn't give her long to live. But, mom proved stronger than that. Phyllis, my sister, grauated from business college and secured a job with J. Gordon Gaines Agency, a prominent insurance company. She continued to live at home, but was out at night so much that I seldom saw her.

Just before school started, my Grandma Jenny died of cancer. Granddad Joe came to live with us and slept in what had been the library on a day cot. The funeral procession from Akron to East Springfield, Ohio was one of the saddest occasions in my life. I had a huge lump in my throat during the entire fifty-five mile drive. The procession moved very slowly. It stopped in Amsterdam, Ohio for a service there before proceeding further south to the little cemetery in East Springfield where another service was held. I was a basket case by the end of the day. She was my mentor and my model. Even today, I can feel the lump and the hot, salty tears running down my cheeks.

Granddad, that lovable, bumbling alcoholic, cried like a neglected baby. He sobbed uncontrollably as he lay his head on grandma's coffin just before her internment. He cursed God and anyone else he could think of. It was almost too much for me to take in. I think about this scene often and have promised myself to spare my family scenes of this nature. I will be cremated and, if anyone desires, have a simple memorial service.

"Education is what survives when what has
been learned has been forgotten."

B. F. Skinner

Another September arrived and with it my first day of high school. Finally, I left those drafty, cold and dreary portable buildings and entered a two-story large brick building. Now, this is what a school should look like. In the main hallway were lists of home room assignments. I was listed on Mrs. Hall's roster. I had already picked up my class schedule the week before school opened. In the ninth grade, we had no electives. There was a general course of study and a college prep course of study. My classes were: English, algebra, civics, French, physical education and two study halls. I had wished that I could skip the algebra, but the counselor insisted that CP courses required my taking it.

Mrs. Hall was a short red-haired woman with a nice smile. Theoretically, home room was for taking attendance and listening to public address announcements by Mr. Hyre the principal. In reality, it was a time for talking to friends and catching up on the latest scuttlebutt. Later, when I became a principal, I did away with home rooms and lengthened the first period by five minutes to cover attendance and PA announcements.

Allow me to digress here. After all, it was sixty-eight years ago that I began my high school career at Akron Ellet. I am having some difficulty in dredging up names and faces from that time in 1946. I found my graduation class picture from 1949 and my four year books from each of my high school years. As I look at the pictures and words, the memories come trickling back. There were fifty-seven graduating seniors on that class picture. How smooth-skinned we looked. How free from worry-lines we were. It may have been the last time that we all smiled.

The boys all wore suits, white shirts and ties. The girls wore their best going-to-church dresses. Gene, Bill, Jean and I were the class officers. We were pictured front and center. Mr. Hyre, our principal looked stern and officious from his perch on the upper left corner. Mrs. Wilson, affectionately known as "Mrs. Wee," our class advisor, smiled down on us from the upper right corner.

The sobering thought was that almost half of us has passed away. By the time that you read this, more will have graduated to the great beyond.

The yearbooks helped me to remember details and to structure my thinking. Yes, those were the days, the halcyon days of learning and yearning. Those were the days when life seemed full of promise and hope. There wasn't anything that could prevent us from reaching our goals and achieveing our dreams. We said to ourselves, "I am an adult now. I can go to college or I can get a job. It's my choice. I know all about the other sex. I may or not get married. It's my choice. I can continue to live at home or move out. It's my choice. I will make a name for myself. I will be somebody to reckon with. I am the future."

Yes, that's what we thought. Little did we know what would lie ahead. And, that was a good thing.

Despite all our bravado, most of us were intimidated and a little frightened that first day in the high school. The older students pushed and shoved us in the halls during passing times. We had heard tales of freshmen being stuffed into lockers and trash barrels.

Just before homeroom began when I was putting my jacket into my assigned locker, I felt a presence behind me. One of the senior boys, a varsity football player, whispered in my ear: "I heard that you are going out for football. We like fresh meat. We eat freshmen for lunch."

With that warm welcome, I entered Mrs. Hall's room for the homeroom period. She called out our names for attendance. Most of us responded in squeaky soprano voices. Mr. Hyre's baritone voice came out over the public address system. He welcomed all of us back for the school year.

Mrs. Hall was, also, my English teacher. Nothing stands out in my memory about the class other than English remained my favorite and best subject. Miss Grandstaff was my civics teacher. Civics was dry, but we were convinced that all good citizens and patriots had to know civics. I day-dreamed through most of the tedious read and do the questions at the end of each chapter. There was little discussion of the intricacies of national, state and local government issues and policies. Looking back at that class, I know now that Miss Grandstaff was out of her element. She was a biology major and had little interest in the stuff of government even though she was certified to teach it. It's no wonder that, in later life, we would lack the fire and fervor that citizens should have in the governmental entitities that affect our lives so deeply. Also, in my later role as a principal, I tried to assign teachers to teach in areas in which they had sincere interest. It makes for much better teaching and for equally better learning.

I chose to take French because, even that age, I was interested in the cultures of other countries. It seemed to be a worldly, very suave thing to do. Movie stars who had French accents seemed to attract all of the better looking ladies. I did mangage to learn enough French to read and listen with some degree of proficiency, but the suave part seemed to escape me. In our French Club play, I played the part of the wolf in the French version of Little Red Riding Hood. My big moments came when I had to howl loudly at the appropriate times. At other times, I had to call out "Je suis le loup," Which meant "I am the wolf." The plaster of paris wolf's head made me feel invisable and hid any signs of stage fright. Those performances took me out of my comfort zone and helped me to handle many other things as my life unfolded.

Now, algebra was another matter. Mr. Snyder was a great teacher who had a dry sense of humor. He loved the beauty and dependable truths that mathematics has given to mankind. He tried very hard to instill that love in all of his students. He failed with me. While I loved the beauty and truth of the written and spoken word, the love of numbers escaped me completely. I really tried to understand the concepts of what was being taught, but my brain wouldn't cooperate. I managed to learn the formulae and the rules well enough to pass most of the tests, but I couldn't fathom why they were important for me to know and understand. It seemed more foreign to me than French. I couldn't imagine that I would ever need to know any of what was being taught. I couldn't apply it to my every-day life either then or in what I imagined to be my future. Now, I know that I wasn't wired for mathematics. It happens. Then, I was ashamed and embarrassed. Most of the other freshmen in my class had no problems with the subject matter. I faked it. I mangaged to pass the course with an average in the low 70's. My math grades throughout high school kept me off of the honor rolls and the National Honor Society. It, also, managed to keep me humble.

Physical education classes were taught by Mr. Scott who was, also, the head coach of the boys' varsity sports. He was a tough-looking and tough-acting kind of guy. I had signed up for football before school opened and we had had a few informal practices before school began. I'm certain that he didn't pay much attention to a scrawny, pimpled fourteen year old who weighed all of 120 pounds. So, when we had our first day of gym classes, he acted like he'd never seen me before. We had to wear gym shorts, white tee shirts and gym shoes. We had to shower after each class. My class was third period in the morning and it was a real hassel to change for gym, shower and change again for the next class.

In the warm weather of fall, we had class outside in the restricted area between the high school and the portable buildings. We started each class with jumping jacks, knee squats, push-ups, duck walks and wind sprints. I tried very hard to impress Mr. Scott with my blinding speed in the wind sprints. I, usually, came in second to Jimmy who had impressed the coaches with his all-around athletic ability. Later, that was to be my entree into the joys of varsity football.

In bad or cold weather, we had class in the small gym which featured a low ceiling and over-hanging balconies. That gym was the bane of opposing basketball teams who had to learn to shoot flat shots to avoid hitting the ceiling and the light fixtures.

The inside gym classes featured calisthentics, rope-climbing and wrestling matches with a little basketball thrown in.

I remember a lot about gym classes and Mr. Scott. They were both a test of my manhood. I wanted to impress him because I wanted to play football. But, my size was a negative. I had played sandlot football down at Rhodes Field behind the Chestnut Ridge Dairy with a group of Ellet students. We played tackle in the hard, grassless, stone-littered field against boys from Springfield and Mogadore. I had played one year with the East Akron Corsairs of the Akron Bantam Football League. I think that I was good enought to play high school football. But, I had played on the line as a guard. My size and weight didn't fit the requirements of playing that position in high school. At least, that was what Mr. Scott told me on the first day of regular practice. As a consequence, during my freshman and sophomore years, I only got to play a few minutes in each game and only if we were losing badly or were winning handily.

I should add that during my first two years we wore leather helmets and cotton uniforms. The helmets had no face guards. The first of my three broken noses occured when I was a sophomore and it was against our varsity who treated underclassmen as their personal punching bags. I had wanted to play basketball, but my badly broken nose precluded my playing immediately following the football season. By the time that I could breathe, it was too late. When I was a junior and senior, we

41

received plastic helmets with just a little webbing inside and new nylon uniforms that were difficult for opposing to hold on to.

A dramatic change occurred during the summer before my junior year. Coach Scott left for another job and Mr. Vinciguerra and Mr. Burks arrived at Ellet as our new coaches. During the summer practices, I impressed them with my speed during wind sprints. Coach Vinceguerra called me aside and said that he was looking for a pulling guard who was fast enough to lead interference for the running backs in his new offense. Would I be interested? Does a fifteeen year old have wet dreams? During those early practices I learned the intricate footwork necessary for a pulling lineman to be able to free himself to lead interference. And, even better, I was installed as nose guard in our five-man front on defense. I had shown quickness and arm strenghth in the early drills. The coaches wanted me to occupy the opposing center and guard so that our line-backers could make the tackles. I learned the sneaky art of jersey pulling, helmet slapping and verbal taunting. During my junior and senior years, I started every game and played both offense and defense. I was on the kick-off and punt teams, also. I never missed a play for two full seasons except for a few in the last game of my senior year in the title game against our arch rival Springfield. I had a very bad hip pointer and could hardly run. I had been receiving chiropractic treatments. The highlights of my football career were a touchdown against Wadsworth when I intercepted a pass and ran thirty-five yards and my several open-field tackles on Springfield's Tommy Pagna who later became an All-American player at Miami University.

I remember coming into the locker room in Wadsorth after scoring my first half touchdown. I was excited and began to loudly tell our team that we coud beat the highly favored Grizzlies. Mr. Bogner, our history teacher and faculty manager, came over to me and said quite loudly: "Don, don't let this go to your head. It was only a touchdown." Talk about how to deflate a young man's pride in his accomplishment! I don't think that I ever forgave him for that. The locker room became silent. The moment was lost. We ended up losing 12-6 by giving up two second half touchdowns.

Why do I remember this? It's because, in retrospect, I learned how important positive reinforcement and well-placed praise can be in a young person's life. I tried to do those things in my career as a teacher and administrator. I saw that it work wonders for the sensitive psyches of those young people with whom I had contact. Thanks Mr. Bogner.

I learned that sports can be a very important part of life. I learned that team-work is more important than individual accomplishment in determining success. I learned that the comraderie one shares in being part of a team makes one appreciate the value of friends and those who share common goals. I learned that there are valuable lessons to be learned from losing as well as from winning. I learned that sports' progams are and should be an integral and vital part of a school's total offering. I learned that a good athletic program enhances the self-esteem of both individuals and the school as a whole. I learned that the entire school community profits from a well-run student-centered program. Later, as an administrator, I took an active part in developing and nurturing athletic programs.

One more word about my football days. When I went out for football as a freshman, I had no football shoes. I was reluctant to ask my dad for money to buy a pair because he had said that football was a waste of time and that I should get a job after school and be a man instead of a boy playing games. Coach Scott said that there were some old used shoes in a locker in the dressing room. He told me to pick out a pair. I looked them over and all but one pair were far too big. That pair was too big, also, but it was the best of the worst. They were uncomfortable and my toes stopped about two inches from the front. When I ran, the front cleats didn't hit the ground. I had trouble getting traction . I'm ashamed to say it, but I wore those same shoes all four years of high school. I was too proud to ask for another pair from either my dad or the coaches. I think that there is a lesson or moral in this sad tale, but I'm unsure as to what it is. But, I do know that I was afraid to ask my dad for something that I needed badly and I was ashamed to admit this to my coaches. Later in life, I would have had no trouble in doing that. I did learn a few things.

During my freshman year, I would see Joy during class change periods and, sometimes, at lunch. I cast furtive glances her way in hopes that she would acknowledge me. Once in a while, she would see me and smile in her quiet unassuming way. When weather permitted, we continued to sit, talk and sing on her front porch. Something was growing. I didn't know until later what it was.

During this first year, I was elected to the student council and I joined the glee club and the French Club. For a student to gain the most value from school, he should be encouraged to take part in school activities. It is important for his social and emotional development to part of a group or groups.

I've tried very hard to reconstruct my freshman year in high school. The past is covered over with a fine layer of time-dust. It's strange what one does remember. I remember Bob who lived down the street from me. He was a scrawny, freckled face shy boy with red hair. He walked about looking down at his feet. He had a difficult time talking to people. He was considered to be a little "Strange." He didn't participate in any school activities and seemed unable to make friends. Now, at that time in my life, I didn't think much about the psychology of what made people different. I just knew that he seemed sad and lonely. Something made me try to make friends with him. At first, he didn't respond. He didn't even answer me when I said, "Hi" or "How are you doing?" He just looked down. This became a challenge.

I started to sit beside him during lunch time. At first, he ignored me. Finally, he began to look up and smile at me when I took a seat beside him. I asked him how school was going. He said quietly, "I'm flunking English." Well, that was my entree. I told him I'd be glad to look over his writing assignments and homework. He began to bring some of his work to show me at lunch time. I pointed out some errors and made some suggestions. He began to verbalize his thanks for the help.

My helping Bob didn't go unnoticed. Some of my friends and fellow football players began to tease me about sitting with this "Queer." Back in the day, being "Queer" was synonomous with being gay. My so-called friends began calling him a "Faggot" and a "Pansy." One of my classmates, Sam, was especially crude. He tried to organzize a group of guys to de-pants Bob during a passing time in the hallway. I objected and Sam called me a "Faggot-lover." Before I could act or respond, the bell rang for the next class and the teacher who was monitor during lunch time eye-balled us. I decided to save my response for another day.

I continued to help Bob when he asked for help. I continued to hear under-the-breath comments from young men who needed someone to look down on so as to make themselves look bigger. Bob became a project for me. I persuaded him to join the French Club. He had shown a natural ability to absorb the language. With a little push from behind, I talked him into taking part in glee club and the art club. He began to blossom, but only slightly. He continued to be painfully shy and reticent about talking with other students. He absorbed the constant comments about his virility and manhood without comment or acting out.

Because of my relationship with Bob, I remember two later incidents very clearly. When we were juniors, Sam happened to be in my chemistry class. So, was Bob. During a lab period, I observed Sam attempting to drop some hydrochloric acid down the back of Bob's pants. I went over and pulled his arm away. Sam said: "You're always sticking up for that fairy. You must be one, too." With that, I hit Sam very hard in his rib cage. He doubled over in pain, gasping for air. Mr. Smets, our chemistry teacher, saw this and rushed over and demanded to be told what was going on. I told him what Sam had tried to do. Sam said that I hit him for no reason. Mr. Smets was put in the difficult situation of deciding who to believe. No one else had seen what led up to my hitting Sam.

Mrs. Smets, being of a practical nature, told us that he'd meet us in the gym after school. He's get out the boxing gloves and we could settle it then. I said a quick "OK." Sam was still in pain and didn't say anything. It turned out that Sam had a broken rib and we never put on the gloves. Fortunately, society was not so litigious at that time, and Sam's parents never threatened me with a suit for medical expenses. As for Mr. Smets, he told me later that Sam had it coming. Secretly, he had believed my version of the story. Sam and I never talked much after that. It was his loss, I guess.

The second event happened many years later, 2011, to be exact. I was eighty years old. My wife and were attending the annual Ellet Alumni Association Banquet. During the social hour before the meal, a man whom I didn't recognize at first came up to me and said that he'd been wanting to talk to me for many years. He turned out to be Bob's older brother whom I had known only slightly. He told me that Bob had fallen on hard times and had become homeless. The past two years, Bob had been living in the woods in a tent as a complete recluse. Bob had died last year. But, Bob had told him several times over the years that I had been his only friend in high school and if it weren't for me he would have dropped out of school. As it was, he had graduated and had held a decent job for many years until paranoia and dementia took its toll.

I thanked Bob's brother for telling me this and expressed my condolences over Bob's death. I went back to our table to sit with Joy and our classmates. I sat silently for a while until Joy asked me what was wrong. I told her the story while choking back the emotion that had welled up in me. I am very glad that I had felt compassion at an early age for someone who needed compassion very badly. I am very glad that my friendship had shown Bob that someone did care for him. I'm glad that I helped him to get just a little enjoyment out of his high school days. I know that this brief relationship helped me to understand the quiet agony and pain that many students suffer alone and in silence. I am certain that this interlude in time helped me to be a better teacher and administrator. I take another look at our class picture. I see just the hint of a smile on Bob's face. I'd like to think that he is smiling at me.

I guess that I'd matured enough for Joy to look at me differently. I sure began to look at her differently. As my freshman year came to a close, I realized that she would be leaving Ellet High School and, probably, would be getting a job and that would mean that I wouldn't be seeing much of her. One day in May, she surprised me by asking me to take a walk with her. I wondered what was up. During the walk, she surprised me even more by asking shyly if I'd like to take her to the Junior-Senior Prom which was coming up in two weeks. I hardly knew what a prom was. By the time that we finished our walk, I had committed myself to not only going to the prom, but to a life time.

I realized after the surprise had worn off that she was running the risk of being talked about and, even, criticized for going to the prom with a lowly freshman. I would be the butt of gossip, also. We were breaking relatively new ground. I didn't even know if freshman were allowed to go to the prom. It turned out that we weren't violating school rules. We were just going against the established grain. But, we didn't care. Now, I had to learn to dance. I had to buy a suit. Would dad buy me one? Later, mom convinced him to do so. Neither of my parents knew how to dance. My sister, Phyllis, did, but she was hardly ever home and I'd be too embarrassed to dance with her. So, I got a library book that explained how to fox trot. I guessed that that was the dance of choice at proms. I studied the moves and prayed a lot.

The prom went fairly well. I managed to avoid stepping on her toes too often. But, I felt clumsy and I sweat a lot. We did get some amused stares from the juniors and seniors, but Joy didn't seem concerned. This was a new world for me. Dancing, the ballroom, the punch bowl, the girls in colorful gowns, the boys looking worldly and suave in their new suits. Some boys even wore tuxedoes. Joy had quietly told me that a corsage would be expected. I knew nothing about buying flowers. I asked a senior boy who lived on the next street where to get one and what kind to order. My next problem was money for the corsage and the possibility of going out to eat after dance. We had arranged to go with one of Joy's girl friends and her date. The date would drive. Little did I know then that I would go to four high school proms, two college proms and twenty-one more when I was a school administrator. I don't think that records are being kept for the number of proms attended, but I might place high up on the list.

I had two weeks to come up with some money. I had heard that one of the teachers wanted someone to mow and trim his lawn. He lived in Cuyahoga Falls. So, I applied and got the job. I took the bus to his home and used his lawn mower. He told me that two neighbors wanted lawn service, also. I ended up doing three lawns three times during the two weeks prior to the dance. I earned fifty cents an hour for the work. I ended with the grand total of $12.00 including tips. In those days, that was enough for my immediate needs. Even better, I worked all that summer doing the three lawns weekly.

We enjoyed the prom and the meal at The Waterloo afterwards. I was careful not to order more than I could pay for. It was close. In the car on the ride home, I sat very close to Joy. It felt good to feel my body against hers. Her friends dropped us off in front of our houses. I felt very strange. Was this the time to ask for a kiss or should I just kiss her? Her front porch light came on and her sister-in-law appeared in the door. I never had to make that decision.

Yes, I do remember our first kiss. That last week of school, one of her clubs sponsored a hayride. She asked me to go with her. I'd never been on a hayride. I'd never done a lot of things. We rode on the back of the wagon down some bumpy country roads and ended up going into a barn where we sat in and on the big stacks of hay. The purpose of going in there was to sing some country songs led by the owner of the farm. Joy and I found a spot up towards the top of the big stack of hay. The lights were dim and the music was soothing. We sat close to each other and held hands. As we grew tired of sitting upright, we lay back to be more comfortable. Then, it happened. As if by remote control, I leaned over and we kissed. I felt an electric shock. I didn't realize what a kiss would feel like. I caught my breath. I went back for seconds. I knew then that I'd never again experience anything like that. And, I was right.

You might ask what this story of young love has to do with education and teaching. Well, education takes many forms. We tend to forget how much love, personal relationships and the lack of those things influence our abilities to think and learn. The love-smitten young man thinks of nothing else except the object of his love. The rejected girl shuts out everything except her sense of loss. As teachers, we need to recognize those emotions in those whom we teach and make some allowances. We are teaching the whole person, not just the one who sits in front of us in room 207. That person has a life outside of what we can influence easily. We need to take the time to learn something about the lives of those whom we teach. Personal information if gathered with compassion can assist us to reach students who seem to us to be unreachable.

The summer moved in its predictable way towards fall and the beginning of my sophomore year. I continued to do yard work. It gave me a sense of accomplishment and the all-important spending money. My parents had never given me an allowance and I was loathe to ask for money. I saved up enough to buy a few clothes and some books.

I continued my almost nightly visits to Joy's front porch where we sang the old songs amid a haze of blue tobacco smoke. I have often wondered what her brother and sister-in-law thought of me. Did they suspect that they were witnessing the beginning of a life-long romance? I doubt it. I was just the skinny, crew-cut boy who hung around. As for me, I relished the opportunity to be near her and to enjoy a kind of family life which I had been missing. There was no music on my front porch.

Football practice started again and I was still considered by Coach Scott to be too small and too inexperienced to be anything more than a mobile tackling dummy. I tried mightily to show him that I was capable of playing. But, as it was last year, I was relegated to the practice squad. I was tempted to quit, but something told me that if I were patient, I'd get my chance.

Labor Day came and with it the beginning of my tenth grade year. On the home front, mom became more sickly. She tired easily and slept a lot during the day. Dad was working seven days a week from four in the afternoon until midnight. He slept until noon and when he awoke he was more grouchy than usual. Phyllis worked during the day and went out with her friends at night. I felt that I lived alone. I spent more time on the porch next door.

I went to school the week before school began to pick up my schedule. I knew that I would miss seeing Joy in the hallways at passing times. She had begun her new job at O'Neil's Department Store in Akron. We had an unspoken tacit agreement that we were a couple. I hoped that she wouldn't meet an older man.

School gave me a structure for my life. I looked forward to going back. I enjoyed learning. I sought the approval of my teachers. Educators need to recognize how many of their students need school, not just for education but for, possibly, the one thing in their lives that gives them stability and happiness.

So, my sophomore year at Akron Ellet began. In football, I was still relagated to the role of providing fodder for the varsity. Coach Scott was blind to my obvious abilities. My classes were English, geometry, biology, French II, phsical eduction and typing. Taking typing turned out to be one of my more fortunate life choices. It has helped me immensely in college and in my career. I feel strongly that everyone should be encouraged to take it.

Also, during my tenth year, I was my class' yearbook reporter, a member of the the glee club and French club and a national finalist in an essay contest sponsored by the National Advertising Council.

I continued to struggle with math, but I seemed to understand geometry more so than I had algebra. Mr. Snyder was patient with me, but shook his head often at my attempts to explain how I'd arrived at answers to his test questions. I seemed to get to the correct answer by strange and devious routes. That trait has followed me throughout life.

The year flowed on fairly smoothly and very predictably. My mother's health continued to deteriorate and my dad's impatience grew at the same rate. My relationship with Joy grew expoentially. I continued my nightly visits to their front porch. As the weather grew colder, I moved my visits inside to their living room. We took long walks when our schedules permitted. She was working regulary at O'Neil's Department Store in downtown Akron. On weekends, I'd take the trolley from Ellet to a stop near her store. Sometimes, I'd hang around and ride home with her on the trolley. That first hayride kiss had developed into almost nightly goodnight kisses. My life revolved around school and her. Not necessarily in that order.

Summer came and with it a change of venue. Joy's mother returned from Florida and moved into a series of rented rooms and apartments. Joy moved in with her. So, now, I had to travel to visit her. I rode a lot trolleys and buses during my junior and senior years of high school. Her mother looked at me with some degree of skepticism. I was two and a half years younger than Joy and looked even younger. To her credit, she didn't display too much criticism or anger. I think that she thought that, this, too, shall pass. But, it didn't

A big change occurred during the summer before my junior year. Coach Scott left for another job and the school district hired Eugene Vinciguerra and Joseph Burks as our two all-sports' coaches at Ellet High School. During the pre-school football practices, I tried really hard to impress them in the wind sprints and other fundamental drills. Coach Gene pulled me aside one day and asked me to learn the right guard assignments. He'd like to use me as the back-up to the senior who had inherited that position. That was encouraging even if I were only a back-up. The senior was big, strong and slow. I was small, somewhat strong and fast.

In a pre-season scrimmage with Copley, coach inserted me into the game at right guard. We used a lot of plays where the right guard pulled out of the line and led the interference for the running back. On my first play, I pulled, kept ahead of Jimmy and put a good block on the defensive half-back some twenty yards down field. Coach took me aside and told me that he was considering starting me at that position and moving the senior to a defensive tackle position. I went home that night feeling on top of that proverbial world. I told my mom who didn't really understand what I was talking about. I stayed awake that night to tell dad who wouldn't be home until almost one in the morning or whenever the Eastern Tap Room closed.

I met him at the door and told him the good news. He said: "What are doing up so late? Get back to bed! And, don't let me catch you reading." And, that was that.

The next evening, I told Joy who congratulated me, but, then, asked me what a guard was.

My junior year's classes offered a little more variety. Mrs. Wilson taught my English/Speech class. I almost failed the speech part because I was too nervous to talk in front of the class. But, I improved and the experience helped me tremendously in my college speech classes. I think that every student in high school should take at least one speech class. But, the teacher should be patient and kind. This class can be very traumatic for many students.

I started the advanced algebra/trigonometry class taught by Mr. Snyder after being coerced by the counselor. After one grading period, I asked him to let me drop the class. I didn't understand it and it was destroying my self-confidence. Surprisingly, he offered no resistance. I think that he was glad to get rid of me. My math classes with him had made him look like a failure.

"Five out of four people struggle with math."

Chemistry was taught by Mr. Smets. I liked him and I found the class interesting, especially the lab experiments. Psychology/sociology was taught by Mr. Bogner. He was interesting, but a little too full of himself and somewhat over-bearing. He was one of two teachers who asked me to grade our class' test papers.

The other one was Mr. Burks who taught the health class. The health classes were not co-ed. My class was all boys. He took the opportunity to tell some off-color jokes. His idea of sex education was to tell us to keep our peters in our pants. But, hey, it was fun for us testosterone infused boys.

I chose to take Spanish I, also. Mrs. Ellet was the teacher. She had been one of my favorite teachers in the eighth grade. Spanish was a little confusing after taking two years of French. They seemed to be too much alike and I mixed up a lot of the words. So, now I was becoming very cosmopolitan having a smattering of two foreign languages. In retrospect, I think that most students should be exposed to a foreign language, especially if the cultural aspects are emphasized.

Because I was, now, a varsity football athlete, I could waive taking a physical education class.

I became a member of the Varsity E Club, the choir, the student court, Hi-Y and was the junior class reporter on the school newspaper. Because I had a broken thumb and a broken nose at the end of the football season, Coach Gene asked me to be the basketball student manager because I couldn't go out for basketball. At half-times of the games,

Eddie, the other manager and I put on shooting exhibitions. I, carefully, avoided using my splinted thumb and kept my nose out of the way.

It was a good year at school. But, at home, not so much. My mother became more ill and my dad, not knowing how to cope with her illness, my sister's independence and my disinterest in anything but school and Joy, became more sullen and distant. He, often, didn't get home from work until two in the morning. I heard rumors that he closed up the Eastern Tap Room.

During that year, my grandma Smith died and my granddad came to live with us. Dad made the library, my favorite room, into a bedroom for him. He brought his spittoon with him and the house began to smell like his chewing tobacco. The spittoon was bad enough, but he often missed fire and the evil stuff fell onto the carpet. He had fallen into a deep funk over his wife's death. The friendly, funny old man whom I loved dearly, died towards the end of my junior year.

I continued to ride the trolleys and buses to see Joy whenever I could. And, that was almost every night. The ride took about twenty minutes and the walk from the bus stop another ten minutes. It was, usually, late when I got home and my homework suffered, I'm sure. But, my grades were good and seeing Joy regularly buoyed my spirits. In retropect, I wonder why my parents didn't object to my leaving almost every night and getting home at eleven or twelve each of those nights. They never questionned me or objected to my love-sick journeys.

The football team in my junior year had four wins and four losses. Our losses were close ones. I played both offense and defense and on the kick-off and punt return teams. I don't remember missing even one play during the entire season. I developed a stronger sense of pride in what I could do. I look back at that junior season as being a turning-point in the development of my self-confidence. I feel strongly that being on a team, becoming part of a group that has a common goal and purpose, is very important in a young person's total development. As a result of my experiences in athetics, I supported athletics and extra-curricular activities in my career as an educator. They don't detract from a school's quest to develop academics. In fact, they enhance and support it. It harks back to the early Greek ideal of growing both the mind and body.

During the summer between my junior and senior years, I worked as a page at the Ellet Branch Library. I spent many hours browsing in the stacks and acquainting myself with authors and book titles. That knowledge would serve me well in college and my later life as an avid reader. I loved the looks, smell and feel of books. I still do.

Also, during that summer, Joy and her mom moved to a little cottage on the grounds of The White House Trailer Park in Ellet. I, no longer, had to commute by bus to see Joy. I could walk. I became a regular at the park and got to know Mr. Lundy, the grouchy owner of the park. Later, he would become our still grouchy landlord.

That summer, I worked at a hardware store on Newton Street. I had gotten to know the owner because Grandad Smith had done some handyman work for him. I was the only clerk. I ran the store when the owner was absent. Much to my dad's surprise, I learned to recognize all of the stock of tools, nails, implements and all of the other things that a hardware keeps in stock. I, even, learned to cut and install glass in windows and doors and to replace mesh screens as needed. I was trusted to count and prepare for banking the day's receipts. I even offered advice as to how to repair and fix things. Sadly, this knowledge didn't transfer to my every-day life in later years. Except for glass and screens, my fix-it skills matched my math skills in futility. My brain just isn't wired for those things. I was and am smart enough to realize this. Instead of bungling those hands-on jobs, I just hire an expert to do them. When I was young, I worried that this lack of manual skills made me less manly. But, now, I know better. I think.

I looked forward to my senior year of football. We had several returning lettermen and the coaches had high hopes for us. But, as it turned out, we were, once again, a fifty percent win team. But, we went into our last game with Springfield tied for the league championship. We lost 14-7 to a team that featured several top college prospects including Tom Pagna who went on to be an All-American and a great coach. Our record is deceiving because we played schools that were much bigger in enrollment than us. We played such teams as Copley, Wadsworth, Hudson Western Reserve, Stow and North Canton. The win over North Canton was the first in our school's history. I scored a touchdown in our game with Wadsworth after intercepting a pass. My career personal highlight was my 12 tackles in the Springfield game. Even today, at age 83, I find myself thinking about those games. It is an example of how important athletics and other school activities can be in the life of impressionable students. As I write this, I am looking at the football team picture from my senior year. How young we looked. How full of life and hope. Sadly, of the twenty-six players, fourteen are deceased as are our two coaches. That's why I still attend football games each fall. I enjoy seeing the excitement and joy in the faces of the players. I see their will and determination to do well for their school and community. Their own pride is at stake. And, during those crisp fall days, I feel a resurgance of those same feelings - the feelings that I had when I was young, bold and fearless. It's good to feel that way again, if only for a brief sparkling moment.

I enjoyed my senior year. I took journalism with Mrs. Wee, Spanish II with Mrs. Ellet, physics with Mr. Smetts and history with Mr. Bogner. Again, I could skip P.E. because of football. I became the yearbook editor, class treasurer, a member the choir, a member of Varsity E and the writer of the class prophecy. At the end of the year, the class elected me as "The Most Likely To Succeed" and the winner of the Manhood Award. I still marvel at those awards. Also, I sang lead tenor in our male quartet, "The Elletaires." Mrs. King, our music teacher, booked many singing engagements for us in various church and civic groups. That experience is among the highlights of my scholastic career.

My school schedule gave me the afternoons off. I was to work on the newspaper and yearbook projects, but I had plenty of free time to leave the school grounds to go downtown to get a milkshake at Bryant's Drugstore and a hamburger at the Greasy Spoon. No one at school objected to my leaving school grounds. It was an era of trust and laissez faire. Those were the days!

My grades improved dramatically. I had no more math courses. All of my grades in years eleven and twelve were in the ninety percent range.

I had a lot of friends and many acquaintances. The teachers seemed to like me. For the first time in my life, I felt respected.

And, maybe, more importantly, Joy still liked me. Life was good. But, now, the future awaited me. I wanted to go to college, but how could I afford it? When I talked to dad, he just said: "Go if you want to. But, I can't afford to pay for it." My mother's parents, who had money, told me that I was on my own, just like they had been.

Graduation ceremonies were held at East High School. Ellet had no room for them. Our quartet sang two numbers. I received my awards. I didn't bother looking for mom and dad. I'd been told that they couldn't come. Dad worked and mom was too ill. I had come to expect these things. Dad never went to my football games. Mom could care less.

Soon after graduation, I secured a job at the A&P grocery store in Ellet. I hoped to earn enough to begin studies at Akron University. Joy and I began to think seriously about our relationship and where it would lead. She continued to work at O'Neil's and live with her mother at the trailer park. Gradually, the idea of marriage became a reality. If we combined our incomes, we could rent an apartment and I could work and go to college at the same time.

We planned to be married on June 18, 1950, one year after I graduated from high school.

During that year, we discussed the possibility of buying a house trailer at the trailer park where Joy's mother lived if one were to become available. We would need to make payments on the trailer and rent to the park. Plus, we'd need to pay utiliites. Already, I was feeling like an old married man who had financial problems. I might need to find another, better paying job in order to pull this off.

Joy's brother, Hugh, who was a supervisor at Goodyear, offered to talk to Mr. Wojno, the supervisor of a part-time progam called the "B-Squad." That conversation proved to be a life-saver. He arranged an interview for me with Mr. Wojno. If I passed the physical exam, I could begin work in January. The job started at seventy-five cents an hour with raises based upon merit up to $1.25 an hour. At the A&P, I made fifty cents an hour. I would work six-hour shifts on a shift of my choice and would be able to work double shifts when work was needed. Of course, I accepted.

I had a physical exam given by the Goodyear house doctor. He found that I had what is called essential hypertension. That is, I was born with it. It didn't come from any current stressors or new physical condition. He suggested that I arrange to be seen by an internist. So, I did. the doctor put me on a beta-blocker for the hypertension. I am still on the same medication.

It was exciting to be going to college. I was the first on either side of my family to do so. I visited with a college counselor to arrange my freshman classes. I planned to work at the A&P until January. Then, I'd begin my work at Goodyear. I requested night hours at both places so that I could spend the day at Akron University.

I worked at the A&P until January in the produce department. I kept the produce racks filled and watered. I worked in the basement of the store, also, unloading crates of ice-packed produce. Saturdays were my favorite days. I was given the job of announcing close-out sales over the loud speaker system. I developed a little humorous patter to help entice buyers.

In January, I began what was to be a five-year employment at Goodyear. Before my classes were to begin in the fall of 1950, I worked either six in the morning until noon or noon until six in the evening. I checked into the department and waited for an assignment to somewhere in Plant I or Plant II or, even, to the chemical plant or Goodyear Aircraft. I think that during my five year I worked in almost all of the departments in those areas. I built tires, I ran a mill, I operated a Banbury Machine and a calendar. I worked in the tube room and the belt room. I was sent into box cars to unload bales of crude rubber from the Far East. Sometimes, the bales contained poisonous snakes and spiders from exotic lands. I was sent down into tank cars to scrape off layers of latex, carbon black, sulfur or soapstone. I suffered from fumes in the chemical plant form the noxious benzine and other chemicals. At the end of each shift, I was given a bucket of hot soap to take to the showers to wash off the residue from the day's work. After I quit working there, my white shirt collars looked black after one wearing. That lasted for several months. I'm certain that my allergies originated there and that the pre-cancerous growths in my bladder were born there.

But, Goodyear was good to me. It allowed me save some money for our up-coming marriage. I worked a lot of double shifts when they were available. I value the experience that hard, dirty work provided me. I learned to appreciate the life of the working man. It wasn't easy. It was hard, monotonous work. I knew that I didn't want to spend my life in a factory. It was a difficult way to learn that lesson. But, I did have an interest in staying with Goodyear, possibly with Goodyear International. But, that would be after I earned my college degree.

Summer was approaching fast and with it, our marriage. The marriage would be at North Springfield U.P. Church in Ellet. The Reverend Earl C. Morgan would officiate. The reception would be in Joy's home in Ellet. We arranged for a week-long honeymoon in New York City. We would take the Pennsylvania train, the Akronite, to the Big Apple. We would stay at the Victoria Hotel on the corner of Seventh Avenue and Fifty-First Street.

I had never been out of Ohio. Joy had been only to West Virginia. We would sit up all night on the train in the coach section because we couldn't afford a bedroom. I'd waited a long time already, so one more night wouldn't be a problem.

June 18 arrived as scheduled. The wedding and reception went off without any problems. Ken LaFollette, Stanley Jaynes, Naomi Pratt and Ruth Dewalt were in the wedding party. I cried while standing in the receiving line after the ceremony. I don't remember crying for anything before that except at Grandma Smith's funeral. I was deeply touched that my coach, Gene Vinciguerra, attended our wedding. Later in life, I tried to emulate his thoughfulness in my dealing with students.

The honeymoon in New York City remains imbedded in my memory. After years of yearning, wondering, waiting and frustrations, we came together as man and wife. And, it was good. We arrived wide-eyed and excited in The Pennsylvania Station right in the heart of the city. We took a cab, our first cab ride, to the Hotel Victoria. I felt very manly as I tipped the bell hop after he took our bags to room 321. I had read about the attractions that the city had to offer and we managed to visit most of them. We went to Central Park, times square, Greenwich Village, the zoo, The Battery, Chinatown, took a boat ride to Ellis Island and the Statue of Liberty, ate at an automat, and attended a service at St. Patrick's Cathedral. I manged to get cheated by a pseudo sidewalk photographer who supposedly took our pictures, but really didn't. When I went to the store where the pictures were supposed to be, they had never heard of the guy. We saw the Rockettes at Radio City Music Hall and took the elevator to the top of the Empire State Building on our last day. Then, it was back on the train and home to Akron. We were Mr. and Mrs. Smith now. I was no longer a boy.

We had managed to buy a used house trailer in the White House Trailer Park. My mom persuaded my dad to loan us the balance of what we needed to buy the trailer. I was surprised that he agreed. The trailer had a living area with a couch that folded down into an almost double bed. It had a small kitchenette and a very small bathroom. There was a minute amount of storage space. But, it would be home until we could afford larger quarters.

I continued to work at Goodyear, mostly from six in the evening until midnight. I either took the trolley or hitchhiked to work. Some nights after work, I had to walk the two miles back home. We couldn't afford a car. I would be twenty-two before I could afford one. On Thanksgiving day in 1950, a huge snow storm hit the Akron area. During the Turkey Day game at the Rubber Bowl, I broke out with red splotches all over my face and body. It turned out to be chicken pox. I became very ill. Our house trailer was half-covered with snow. The door was blocked and the water and electicity shut down. The National Guard was called and a state of emergency was put into place. Tanks roamed the streets of Akron.

An ambulance from Hopkin's funeral home was dispatched to take us to my parents house until we could live in the trailer again. Yes, I remember 1950.

Part Four

Akron University -The Undergraduate Years

*"The direction in which education starts a man
will determine his future in life."*

Plato

September arrived and my freshman year at Akron U. was about to begin. I met with a college counselor to schedule my classes. I went to the burser's office to pay for my first semester. We had little left for groceries, rent and utilities. I began to realize the difficulty in gaining a college education. I wondered if it would be worth the time and sacrifices.

I attended freshman orientation day during the week before school began. We were given information about the university and the opportunities that it offered. After the lecture, we were swarmed by represenatives from fraternities and sororities. They had recieved information about our high school careers and were looking for worthy new members. I was approached by three fraternities and asked to pledge. I declined as I would be too busy with working and attending classes. A group of freshman asked me to go to lunch with them at a nearby restaurant. I went, but felt completely out of place. Their talk centered around dating, popular music and their up-coming course work. I was asked to meet them that evening for a social hour. I declined. I had to be at work. But, I didn't mind. I was no longer just a kid, I was a grown man with responsibilities. I had noticed that several had eyed my wedding ring and shied away.

My freshman courses at Akron U. were: freshman English, French II, Introduction to Humanities, ROTC and pysical education.

The counselor insisted that I take either French or accounting. I sure didn't want to take accounting. She placed me in second year French because I'd had two years of French in high school. The trouble was that I took French when I was in the ninth and tenth grades and had taken Spanish for two years after that. I had a foreboding. It was later proved to be justified. At that time, ROTC was required of all incoming male freshmen. The Korean War was rumbling in the distance and it promised to eat up a lot of second lieutenants. I had never thought of being an infantry officer, but it did sound adventurous. As for P.E., I thought it was kind of silly to require that of all freshmen. I had a choice of P.E. classes. I chose tumbling/apparatus and fundamentals of boxing and wrestling. Tumbling proved to be more dangerous to me than the martial arts.

ROTC required my wearing the issued heavy woolen winter uniforms on Mondays, Wednesdays and Fridays. In the Fall and Spring, they made our lives miserable. Freshman ROTC consisted of class room work and a heavy dose of marching drills on a field some four blocks from the classroom. Marching in formation seemed silly to me. Wars weren't fought that way any more. In the classroom, some of the material required the usage of higher math. Other lessons involved disassembling and assembling M1 rifles. I never mastered that completely. Anyway, I thought that officers carried side arms. The instuctors were arrogant and insulting. I learned quickly that the whole point of military instruction was to break down the individuality of the students. We were being forced to sacrifice our own needs and desires to benefit the common good. But, my low point was my choosing not to go to the required Armed Forces Day parade and deciding instead to work my regular shift at Goodyear. Rent was due and I needed the money. Anyway, I didn't relish the idea of marching down Akron's main street in my hot woolen uniform and silly looking cap.

I was called in to see the commanding officer. He pronounced me as being derelict in duty and that I would receive a D for the semester in ROTC. It was the only grade below C that I received during my time at Akron University. The commanding officer turned out to be the school board vice president in Mogadore when I was hired to be high school principal many years later. I don't think that he recognized me. He had kept his head down in his papers most of the time he was tongue-lashing me.

My French class proved to be interesting for a variety of reasons. The professor looked French, but he wasn't. He traipsed around campus wearng a beret and carrying an umbrella. He lisped when he spoke. Because we were second year students, he said that we would talk only in French and that we would be assigned famous French novels and plays as our textbooks. I was in over my head. I hadn't looked at the French language since I was a high school sophomore. The other students had taken high school French and French I here at Akron University. I struggled mightily with the reading assignments. Each day in class, the professor would question us about what we had read last night. He would look at me and in his squeaky lisp say: "Et vous, Monsieur Smith? I would say whatever I could in southeastern Ohio French He would look at me for a long moment and say: "Mon dieu! C'est terrible!"

I worked hard in French class to the detriment of my other subects. I managed to pass French I with a "C" for the semester and improved to a "B" the next semester. In retrospect, I should never have been forced to take French II. In my role as a counselor many years later, I tried to make certain that students were not put into a situation that would almost guarantee their failure. Challenging students is great, but too much of a challenge can be devasting to their self-esteem and future success.

Looking back at my undergraduate years at Akron University, I realize that my successes depended upon my level of interest in those particular subjects and my innate abilities in those areas. That comes as no surprise. My failures followed the inverse pathway. I did not like mathematics and I was, still, at that point in my development, a shy person who lacked self-confidence. So, I did not do well in my first speech class. It wasn't until I realized that I was just as good as most of the other students that I was able to stand in front of a class and talk naturally and effectively. Too often, we try to force students into doing things that are contrary to their interests and natural abilities. Sometimes, we need to wait until students come to realize the importance of stepping out of their comfort zones. Be patient, offer advice, show them the necessity and allow them to proceed at their own pace.

After my freshman year, I had to make some choices of subjects which would lead eventually to the career that I envisioned. Even though I had a degree in education in mind, I wasn't quite certain that I wanted to actually become a teacher. I thought that journalism might suit my temperment and abilities even better. Also, my work at Goodyear had made me think of the possibility of working overseas at one of their facilities in a management position.

So, during the next three years, my choice of courses was eclectic. I picked and chose among a variety of topics. I had no choice about taking ROTC. I, still, disliked, the obligatory marching drills and gun assembly routines. I hated those hot woolen uniforms. But, I accepted the fact that I'd probably end up in Korea as a second lieutenant in the infantry.

I continued to work at Goodyear at night and take a full load of classes during the daytime. Joy continued working at O'Neil's. I would get home from Goodyear about one in the morning after the two-mile walk. I slept until about six thirty in the morning and walked or hitchhiked to Akron U. I'd get home from classes about two-thirty, do some homework and head off to Goodyear again about five thirty. Joy and I were like ships passing in the night who seldom docked together.

During my junior year, we were able to move into a rented house on Brittain Road in Akron. My granddad Beresford owned that house, too. We paid him $55 dollars a month for the small two-story brick and stucco home which was a block from Resevoir Park. The basement was wet all of the time and the whole house smelled damp and moldy. But, our two children, Kathy and Michael were conceived there, so it wasn't all bad. We had docked long enough for this to happen. When she was eight months pregnant, she quit her job at O'Neils. I was, now, our only bread winner.

Because I had, finally, committed to getting a teaching certificate, I was assigned to do my student teaching at Barberton High School during their summer session between my junior and senior years. I was the only teacher of a class of 12 students who had all failed their English classes the previous year. I was given no course outline, no instructions other than I would be their teacher. I had only one visit during the eight weeks from an Akron University instructor. I was on my own. In retrospect, I wonder how the university got away with such loose supervision and control. I have no idea how I was graded or on what basis. No one knew what I was doing. Nor, did I, at least at first. Fortunatley, the students were an amiable lot. I assessed what they knew and didn't know and started from there. We did some grammar work, some writing and some speech exercises. I had fun and I think that they did, too. Our classroom was in the basement of the old Barberton High School. The walls were brick and seeped moisture out onto the floor. It reminded me of home.

All of the students showed up each day and did their assigned work. I was lucky. I passed all of them and we had a party on the last day. I heard from many of them for several years after that summer. I decided that I liked the idea of teaching. It seemed natural. Maybe, I thought, I could make a career out of this. Our daughter, Kathy, was born during my time as a student teacher. It was a busy eight weeks.

I graduated with a B.A. in Education in 1954. The diploma read: "With Distinction." I had received all A's and B's except for a "C" in my first speech class, a "C" in French II and a "D" in first-year ROTC. Drat, those Armed Forces Day parades!" My grade point average for the four years was 3.4.f

At that time, grades for the various classes were posted on the walls of the hallways in the classroom buildngs. Most classes were graded on the so-called "Curve." The class' highest grade set the top of the curve. The grades were, then, distributed according to the Bell Curve. The top 25% were A's and B's, the middle 50% were C's and the bottom 25% were D's and F's. My name showed up frequently as the highest grade. I got a lot of dirty looks from classmates for "Setting the curve." In later years, that practice of posting grades publicly was discontinued because it hurt the feelings of the lower scoring students.

I continued working at Goodyear with my plans for the future still in limbo. I was reluctant to apply for a full-time job at Goodyear and was uncertain as to whether or not to look for a teaching job. I had started to get a dual certificate so that I could teach all grades from kindergarten though grade twelve. But, I hadn't done student teaching in the elementary grades. So, I talked to the Akron University counselors and arranged to do student teaching in grade five at Robinson Elementary in Akron. I had already graduated, but it was not a problem. I would do my student teaching that fall and continue at Goodyear by working the six o'clock to midnight shift.

I soon discovered that I was not meant to be an elementary teacher. It takes a person of a certain mentality and disposition. I had neither. I perservered for four weeks. I, finally, admitted to myself that I not only didn't enjoy it, but I was very bad at it. My supervising teacher agreed, heaving a deep sigh of relief. She didn't need to fail me. I talked to the university and was able to drop out without penalty. I was satisfied with a secondary teaching certificate and my sanity being intact.

I worked long hours at Goodyear. I gained some self-respect by being able to do some very difficult and very tiring jobs. I came home from work tired and dirty, but with a feeling of accomplishment. It helped that I knew that I would not spend my entire working life doing this work. I applied to the Akron Board of Education for a secondary school teaching position in either English or social studies.

Part Five

SIMON PERKINS JUNIOR HIGH SCHOOL

"It is with children that we have the best chance of
studying the development of all kinds of knowledge."

Jean Piaget

In January of 1955, I received a call from the office of the superintendent of the Akron Public Schools asking me arrange a time for an interview with Dr. Martin Essex. The time had come.

Dr. Essex's office was on the top floor of the admistration building in downtown Akron. His secretary ushered me in. It was a very large office. I stood just inside the doorway . Dr. Essex remained seated at his large mahogany desk across the room, some thirty feet away. I stood there waiting to be invited to come in and be seated. He said nothing. I said nothing. I decided to take the intitiative and walk over, say "Hello," and introduce myself. He smiled and told me to sit down. He said that I'd passed the first test.

He told me that I had been recommended for a teaching position at Simon Perkins Junior High School in West Akron. It was the first junior high school in Akron and was being used as a pilot school to ascertain the value of housing seventh, eighth and ninth grade students in a separate building. It had started last year and had a hand-picked faculty. If I were accepted, I'd begin work the beginning of February. I'd replace a current teacher who had been having great difficulty in controlling her students and no longer wished to teach. I'd teach seventh and eighth grade social studies and science. "Was I interested?"

I took a deep breath and said: "Yes, sir, I'm very interested. I appreciate the opportunity." That was that. That was how it began. I was about to begin a thirty-two year career in the public schools. Dr. Essex looked up from his desk and said: "All right, then. Report to the principal, Sumner Vanica, as soon as possible to get acquainted with him and the school. You'll begin teaching on Monday, February third. Good luck, you might need it." He said his last words with just the hint of a wry smile. He looked down at his desk as a sign of dismissal.

His secretary greeted me with a stack of papers for me to read and sign. When I left the office, I was official. I was a teacher! For better or worse, I was a teacher. I was a twenty-two year old, crew-cut, clean-shaven, 145 pound teacher who was, more importantly, a husband and a father. I was all of those things and I felt proud.

Joy was proud of me, too. Maybe, things would improve financially. The salary was not great. I was to begin teaching at the princely sum of $3000.00 per annum pro-rated for the remaining four months. We decided that I'd continue working the night shift at Goodyear for a while. A while is not a finite number, but we had some bills to catch up with and I would need to buy a car. Simon Perkins was about fifteen miles west of our little house on Brittain Road.

There was one big problem. I had never gotten a driver's license. I had had one aborted driving experience with my dad and I had knocked the window seat off of our house in Ellet when I was seventeen years old. I hadn't attempted to drive since. But, first, I needed a car to practice with and to take the test in. Bill, one of my high school friends, had a 1948 Dodge sedan that he wanted to sell. It had a stick shift and an ugly, rusty body. He wanted $75 for it. He agreed to let me pay when I got my first school pay check.

He brought the car over to Brittain Road. It sat in the driveway until I got the nerve to try to drive it around the block a few times. He took the time when he brought it to explain the intricasies of the clutch, brake and gas pedals. Steering would come later. While it was sitting in the driveway, I painted it with black enamel using a sponge for a brush. The swirls added a certain panache to its looks.

After a few misguided attempts to drive the car, I decided to sign up for a couple of lessons with Sear's Driving School. After two lessons with them, I felt comfortable enough to take the driver's test using their school's car with the instructor in the back seat. We drove around for a while on a variety of streets and in a variety of situations. The state patrol officer looked at me and smiled. I was, now, a fully certified driver. I felt very proud. At age 22, I had finally reached the level of most sixteen year-old boys in America. The instructor drove me home. In the driveway, sat the sponge-painted black beauty. The open road awaited me.

Another important event occured just as I waited to begin my teaching career. I was notified that because the Korean War had ended and I was hired as a teacher, I could opt out of my ROTC committment without prejudice. I had mixed feelings. Part of me wanted the excitement and adventure of being a military officer. The other part of me wanted the chance to prove my ability as a teacher. Besides, we wouldn't need to relocate and adjust to a myriad of new situations. Little did I know, that teaching would provide some semblance to battle. But, I wouldn't have a gun as back-up.

I called Simon Perkins to arrange to meet with Mr. Vanica. His secretary answered the phone with a smile in her voice. After she consulted with Mr. Vanica, she said that he'd be glad to meet with me tomorrow at ten a.m. She told me that her name was Rhea and that she looked forward to meeting me.

I awoke early the next morning. I was excited. Joy was up already and feeding Kathy. I drank some coffee and managed to eat some wheaties. I went outside and started the old car to make certain that it was running today. Some days it was reluctant. It started on the third try and I left it running. I went back inside and said my goodbyes to the two women in my life. It was nine o'clock, but I wanted to leave early in case that any problems arose on my trip to my future. On my exploratory drive there, it had taken me about forty minutes. There were no expressways at that time, so the going was slow.

I arrived at the new school on Akron's west side. It was a two-story brick building just off of the traffic circle that connected Hawkins and Mull avenues. Nearby, was a large Catholic church and a Jewish synagogue. Just behind the school lay the third fairway of Good Park Golf Course. I pulled into the parking lot and looked at my watch. It was nine-forty-five. I sat in the car for another ten minutes planning on what I'd say to Mr. Vanica and how I'd answer his questions. I came up with nothing. I was nervous. What if he didn't like me and called Dr. Essex to say that this wasn't going to work? I knew that I looked younger than my twenty-two years and that I tended to talk in a low voice. Would my nervousness show? Would he think that I was too young and too weak to handle the rowdy classes that had caused the current teacher to quit? At five minutes to ten, I entered the front door and met my destiny.

Rhea was a tall, slim attractive young woman. She had a radiant smile and an enthusiastic manner. She looked up from her work and said: "You must be Don Smith. It's so nice to meet you. Mr. Vanica is in his office and expecting you." I felt much better. One can't overestimate the value and importance of a warm sincere greeting.

She ushered me into the principal's office. Mr. Vanica looked up from his work and looked at me with a smile. "Come in and sit down. We have some things to discuss and, then, I'll take you on a tour of the building. After that, I'll take you to meet Mrs. H whom you'll replace."

Sumner Vanica was a trim, solidly built man with a greying crew cut and piercing blue eyes. I know that it's a cliche, but he seemed to look clear through me. I wondered what he saw.

He asked me some questions about my background and personal life. He told me some things about him. He arose abruptly and said that it was time for the tour. As we walked around the building and looked into several of the rooms, I marveled at how quicky and energetically he walked. He greeted students and faculty with a smile and personal comments. Obviously, he was the king of his domain and he enjoyed the title.

We stopped at a room on the first floor and peered inside through the small glass window. He said that this would be my room and that he wanted me to meet Mrs. H. He seemed to hesitate a moment, but, finally, knocked on the door. He opened the door to a confusion of students who hurriedly took their seats. Mrs. H. looked up from her desk. She had been sitting there with her head down on the desk. The students, obviously, had been scurrying about the room doing nothing having to do with education.

Mr. Vanica stood in front of the class and stared them down for a few moments. The students grew quiet and wide-eyed. He commanded respect. He introduced me as being their new teacher beginning next week. Mrs. H. arose from her desk and greeted me with a timid, tired voice. She expressed her apologies to Mr. Vanica for having had her head on the desk and for the behavior of the class. Her eyes showed the results of crying.

I felt embarrassed for her. I felt the eyes of the students on me. Were they thinking that I would be another soft touch?

She showed me around the room briefly. She pointed out what was in the various file cabinets and cupboards. Mr. Vanica remained standing guard in front of the class.

On our way back to the office, Mr. Vanica told me that her classes had become accustomed to doing whatever they wished. He said that I'd need a firm hand and a resolute mind in order to bring them back under control. He stopped at the classroom next to mine and knocked on the door. A short, stocky blonde-haired man stepped out to greet us. He turned back to his class and said in a loud voice: "I expect you to sit quietly and do your work while I'm talking to these gentlemen." I didn't hear a sound coming from them as we talked. Mr. Vanica introduced Stan as being my neighbor and as someone from whom to seek advice and assistance in case I needed it. Stan is still my good friend sixty years later.

We returned to the main office complex and Mr. Vanica told me to look over the class materials that Mrs. H. had given me. He said that he'd see me next week and wished me good luck. I said goodbye to Rhea and nodded to the student secretary who worked next to her. I looked around the main lobby and the showcases before I left the building. I was going to be a Perkins' Panther beginning next week and I wanted to get a sense of what that meant. There were a few trophies in the showcase indicating success in track, basketball and softball. The school colors were blue and grey. A poster holding a picture of "The Student of the Month" was displayed prominently. The halls were quiet. No students roamed about. I remember thinking that this was a well run school and Mr. Vanica was a strong principal. Just then, the bell rang for class-changing time. I was engulfed in a wave of happy, talkative students. I was caught up in the moment and that moment was good.

When I arrived home, Joy and Kathy greeted me. Joy wanted to know how my meeting had gone. I told her that I thought that I would enjoy my new job, but that I had some concern about getting the wayward students in my classes under control. In my student teaching, I'd not had misbehaving students to contend with. But, I wanted badly to teach and nothing was going to interfere with that.

The remainder of the week went by quickly. I worked my usual shifts at Goodyear and, in my free time, read over my textbooks on student control and management. They were steeped in pedagological terminology and I wondered how well the rules and suggestions would work in real time. As it turned out, few of them worked at all.

The remainder of the week was taken up with family things. After I started to teach, I knew that family time would be at a premium. I stayed close to home and tried to spend quality time with Joy and Kathy.

When Kathy had reached the age when books began to interest her, I began to read to her each night before I went to work at Goodyear. When she seemed tired of the usual kiddie books, I began to make up stories each night about a fictitious little girl named Mary Ann. They were an instant hit. After a few weeks of this, I began to run out of plot ideas. I thought of hiring a screen writer. But, I managed to add to the on-going story each night until she realized that she might be getting too old for such kid stuff. Those nights remain firmly embedded in my mind. Even today, at age 60, Kathy remembers those stories and we mention that idyllic time frequently. When I began to teach, I worked for another year at Goodyear from six in the evening until midnight. Of necessity, the stories had to stop. But, Mary Ann and Kathy remain two of my favorite literary characters.

The big day arrived. I slept restlessly the night before. My opening remarks to my classes kept running through my mind. I knew that first impressions would be critical. If the students sensed my nervousness, I would be toast. I knew that fear emits some kind of pheramone or odor. I, even, practiced a few remarks in front of my bathroom mirror and looked for traces of fear or nervousness in my facial expression. I had worried, also, about what to wear. I wanted to look professional and mature, but, also, current. I wanted to look old enough to command respect, but young enough to relate. I decided on a plain blue sport coat, grey pants, white shirt and a red and blue striped tie. I passed muster with my wife and daughter after I'd eaten a hurried breakfast of oatmeal and toast.

The drive to Simon Perkins seemed shorter than it had before. Time seemed compressed. I parked the car and sat there. It was 7:15a.m. and the world stood still. Other cars began to pull into the lot. I saw Mr. Vanica's car pull into the parking spot near the building labeled "PRINCIPAL." Stan pulled in beside me and waved. He got out of his car and came over to my window. I rolled it down so that we could talk. He said, "You can get out now, Don, I'll walk in with you." He sensed my apprehension.

He showed me how to sign in on the faculty roster and led me to the faculty room where the teachers gathered before their classes began. The room was noisy and full of laughter. If teaching were difficult, the ambiance in there didn't reflect it. Stan introduced me to everyone. Most were welcoming and friendly. Some hardly noticed me at all and buried their heads in their newspapers or classroom work. A tall man walked up to me and introduced himself as "Bob." He said that he taught social studies, too, and would be glad to help me if he were asked. Bob said that he wanted to introduce me to "Buzz" who taught biology. Buzz looked at me quizically and said "Good luck, young fella. You'll need it."

I looked the around the room, smiled at everyone and started to my classroom I wanted to get there before the first students arrived. I opened the door, took a deep breath and walked in. I was walking in to what would be the beginning of thirty-three years of my life. The eastern view from the windows allowed the morning sun to flood in. The wall clock showed 7:50 and the ten-minute warning bell sounded. I heard students talking and laughing in the hall outside my room. I saw some of them looking in through the small glass window in the door. Girls giggled and boys talked in their best bravado. I heard one boy say, "He doesn't look old enough to be our teacher." I walked over to open the door. Opening the door proved to be a good metaphor for the next chapter in my life.

"Good morning! Please take your seats." The students either didn't hear me or were ignoring me. Again, I told them to take their seats. Slowly, they all sat down. Except one boy who sat on the radiator beneath the windows. My first test had come. "I said sit down!" My voice sounded very loud to me. I glanced at the class seating chart and saw that the empty seat belonged to Richard. I said: "Richard, sit down, now!" Richard just looked at me. Ok, I thought, what do I do next?'

The class looked at me to see what I would do. What I did was to walk over to Richard, grab him by his shoulders and pull him down from his perch. He muttered an obscentity under his breath and resisted my efforts. I pushed and shoved him across the room to the door. The door was closed and latched. I pushed him hard enough to break open the door latch and we both emerged into the hallway. Standing just outside the door was Mr. Vanica who had stopped by to see how I was doing. I thought that this would be the world's shortest teaching career. Instead of being questionned, or even worse, reprimanded, he smiled at me and said quietly: "Good job. I'll think that you'll do just fine. I'll take him from here."

I reentered the class to complete silence. I don't remember what I said to the class. I was too excited. I do remember Richard returning to the class looking subdued and shifting in his seat uncomfortably. I realized that the textbook suggestions for handling behavior problems don't always work with everyone. In the day, reasonable force, including paddling was permitted and, even, recommended for hard-core cases. Almost every day, as the year wore on, I heard the sounds of or was told of students being paddled by Mr. Vanica or the assistant principal. It was common and students and parents seemed to understand and accept the fact that it was just one of the tools that were used to control behavior. The school district even supplied the principals with flexible leather paddles or, if they asked, wooden paddles with holes drilled in them for better speed.

My class schedule consisted of two double periods of seventh grade science and social studies and one double period of eighth grade science and social studies. I had one study hall to supervise and one preparation period. I had thirty-five minutes for lunch. I had hoped to teach English. That was my favorite subject. Maybe, next year if all went well.

My other two classes seemed to go well. I was too nervous and preoccupied to allow my memory bank to register anything for later. The students seemed to be apathetic as I introduced myself and explained my plans for the balance of year. It was if they were just waiting to find a crack in my armor.

I shared study hall supervision with Miss Fifer, a no-sense English teacher who watched me closely to see if I had the right stuff. Study halls always seemed to me to be a waste of both students' and teacher's time. Later, at Mogadore High School, I would eliminate them in favor of longer class periods in order to allow time for lesson introduction and time for students to begin the work while the teachers were there to help them. But, I learned to stand in plain view of the students and look at them with an eagle eye so that I could prevent anything other than studying from happening. While doing this, Miss F. used her eagle eye on me.

My preparation period was shared by six other teachers. I entered the teachers' lounge quietly and sat down in a remote corner. I hadn't met any of this group earlier. They didn't seem to notice me until a lady with red hair and freckles walked over and said: "Are you substituting today?" I said that I was Mrs. H's replacement. She eyed me for a long moment and said: "You poor dear. I'll get you some coffee." Later, I came to know her as Miss K., the girls' phys. educ. teacher. Just then, Stan walked in, knocking against one of the tables and spilling Miss K's coffee. She admonished him with a smile and said: "Stan, you are like a bull in a china closet." Everyone in the room smiled and agreed.

Stan said that he had to hurry and that his class was working on a social studies project and he couldn't leave them alone very long. He nodded to me as he gulped down his coffee.

When I signed out for the day, Mr. Vanica came out of his office and asked me how things had gone. I said that except for the incident with Richard, things had gone very well. He smiled at me and said: "Welcome aboard. Don't forget to came back tomorrow."

On the drive home during the heavy rush hour traffic, I felt very tired and very relieved. I had survived the first day relatively unscarred. The old Dodge car groaned and rattled on its way back to Goodyear Heights and the little brick house. I hoped that the car would hold up long enough for me to afford a better one.

Joy and Kathy greeted me at the door. I felt like the conquering hero. But, I knew that that first skirmish was just the beginning of a major battle. After a hurried supper, I left for the third shift at Goodyear. When I came home after midnight, I spent over an hour preparing for the next day's lessons. That would be my ritual for the remainder of the semester.

The next day, I had no problem with the students not taking their seats when the last bell rang. Richard seemed subdued, but he still eyed me with a hint of malicious intent. I introduced a hands-on project having to do with medieval history. I divided the class up into groups of three and fours and let them choose a project to work on. It would involve a written report using at least four sources and a building project of some object having to do with that time period. I would allow some time in class for them to meet together and discuss the work. The other time I would use for my lecture and discussion. This would be for the seventh grade classes. For the eighth grade class, we would discuss the history of Ohio from its beginnings during our expansion to the West to the present day. Later, in the semester, I would develop some science units for both grades.

The days passed quickly. I enjoyed the students. Most of them enjoyed me, I think. I began to bring in motivational posters for the walls and arrange to use filmstrips and movies from the school district's large inventory. I learned to monitor my study hall without standing up the entire period. Miss Fifer warmed up and we used the study hall time to discuss things. She was the chairperson of the English department and I told her that I'd like to teach English at some point. She wondered if I could spell. I smiled and said that I was a good speller. Later, I learned that she had been the Akron area spelling bee champion in her youth. I learned, also, that she was a local tennis champion. She had achieved state and national rankings in various age groups.

Slowly, I grew to know most of the faculty members. We had teachers' meetings every Tuesday. Mr. Vanica ran tight, well-organized meetings. There was always a written agenda for each meeting. Some teachers grumbled about the necessity of having weekly meetings. They thought monthly ones would be sufficient. The following year, I wrote a parody of our meetings entitled "Tuesday's Children." It was well-received by the teachers, but Stan and Bob warned me that Mr. Vanica had a limited sense of humor when it came to his own actions. To my knowledge, he never saw a copy.

The staff could be called a motley crew, albeit a talented one. It was about fifty-fifty male and female and about fifty-fifty experienced and inexperienced. We had lively staff meeting discussions. Most of them had strong views and were not loathe to express them. I found the meetings and the informal moments in the faculty lounge to be informative and provocative. In retrospect, I think of them as being divided equally between liberals and conservatives. I learned a lot about life and about teaching. I couldn't have been placed in a better place to begin my career in education.

I remember some of the teachers very clearly after almost sixty years. Some, because they were dynamic, some because they were very quiet. But, all were good teachers and good people. Stan and Bob became and remain good personal friends. They both became my models for what good teachers should be. Mr. Vanica became a kind of role model although I didn't know it at the time. He was a good educator and a firm disciplinarian both with students and teachers. I think that all of us sought his approval and feared disappointing him.

Buzz had a perfect name. He did some funny, unusual things as he buzzed around, sometimes out of control. Jerry was the faculty comedian whose exterior actions belied a deep melancholia which, later, manifested itself in a tragic ending. Mike was smooth, charming and the consumate ladies' man. John was a gifted English teacher who looked and acted like the stereotypical English teacher. Gert and Janie made a lovable pair whom everyone loved.

Hal was the jock and the model of a gym teacher. I could go on, but it was a good group. It was a cohesive group. It was a group that was sincere about the job of teaching. We were honest with each other and with our students.

One other incident stands out as an example and a warning that young, especially male teachers should heed. One morning before class began, I was standing in the room in front of the windows leaning back with my hands on the heating unit. One of my students, Emily, looked in the door and asked if she could talk to me. I told her to come in. We were alone. She came over, smiled at me, and sat down on one of my hands. At that moment, I didn't know what to do. Should I ignore the fact that she sat on my hand and pretend it was an accident? Should I get angry and tell her to move immediately? I sensed the moral and legal problems which might develop from this. If I angered her, would she make up a story that I had molested her to get even? If I ignored her, would she think that I enjoyed it and make further advances at a later time?

It was a dilemna that I, now, realize many young male teachers have faced. I, very quietly, asked her to get up and move away. She smiled at me with a smile that indicated that she knew exactly what she had done and why she had done it. She left the room without saying anything. I left the room and closed the door. I walked to Mr. Vanica's office and told him what had happened. He took it in stride and said that these things happen and I had done the correct thing and he would support me if anything would develop from the incident. Lesson learned. Don't be alone with any female student irregardless of her age. Girls of Emily's age are beginning to feel their femininity and like to test the power that this has over the male sex. They can be provocative and very flirtatious. Young male teachers need to know this and take proper precautions. It can cost the careers of those who ignore the signs and warnings.

I, no longer, had doubts about my choice of careers. I enjoyed being a teacher. And, I thought that I was good at it. I worked hard at developing lesson plans and strategies for motivating my students. I picked up ideas from many of the teachers with whom I taught. I, especially, liked the teaching abilities of Stan and Bob. They loved their subject areas and they loved their students. I could hear Stan next door as he acted out roles of historical figures with great enthusiasm and gusto. On a couple of occasions, he invited me to come into his room and act out some historical scenarios with him. One time, I entered his room to ask a question and I found him standing on top of his desk wearing a pilgrim's outfit.

It was a good time. It was the best of times. I was doing something that felt natural and well-fitting. I came home from a day of teaching very tired, but strangely refreshed in spirit. Money was still a concern as my salary from both jobs barely covered our needs. But, I would make more next year. I never desired to be rich. I just wanted to do what I liked doing and, hopefully, do that nebulous thing called "Making a difference."

I began to think about getting my master's degree. It would mean a raise in salary and would open doors to possible advancement in my career. I would need to attend night classes and summer classes and, probably, quit working at Goodyear. Could I afford it? I'd make it happen some how.

The semester seemed to fly by. I experienced no more dramatic incidents. I tried very hard to master my craft. I looked forward to my next full year. I learned that my next year's class schedule would be more varied. I would teach one double-period of seventh grade social studies and science, one double-period of eighth grade social studies and science and one double-period of ninth grade English. In addition, Mr. Vanica asked me to be the school treasurer instead of having a study hall period. I accepted readily.

Bill, one of the social studies teachers, had bragged to me about his summer job working at a West Akron popular drive-in. He said that he made as much as fifty dollars per night working as a car-hop. I felt that to continue working nights at Goodyear was too tiring and it gave me little time with Joy and Kathy. I didn't much like the idea of serving food to the children and parents who lived in our school district. It seemed demeaning and embarrassing. But, the money intrigued me. We, definately, could use it. I went to talk to Walt, the owner of the drive-in. He said that he could use someone to take orders from the new booth that he proposed building in the entrance to the facility. I would take the orders, enter them in a kind of shorthand on a new-fangled machine which relayed the orders to the kitchen. By the time that the driver pulled in and parked, the order would be rushed out by the car-hops. He told me that I would share in the tip pool along with the car-hops. I could work up to five nights weekly if I desired. The new operation would begin when school was out for the summer. Somewhat reluctantly, I accepted his offer. As it turned out, I worked at this job for the summer between my first and second years at Simon Perkins and during the next winter. The money helped a lot with our finances. I made between thirty and fifty dollars each night that I worked. The parents and students whose orders I took never remarked about my working there. I think that they understood. But, I still felt a little embarrassed to having to be placed in this situation.

The summer went by quickly. I looked forward eagerly to the next school year. I was able to spend more time with Joy and Kathy. We took daily walks to the park which was only a block away. That summer, Joy and I drove to North Carolina to Pope Air Force Base and Fort Bragg. One of my classmates, Bill, and his wife lived on the base. He was an Air

Force Lieutenant and a graduate of Akron University's ROTC program. I had our old car tuned up and was able to buy four new tires. I, still, had grave doubts about it being able to make the 1500 mile round trip. While in North Carolina, Bill and I played golf at the legendary Pinehurst golf facility and at the officers' course on the base. I was able to witness what I'd missed by not remaining in ROTC. I didn't regret my decision, but I would have looked good in an officer's uniform. The trip home featured just one flat tire which I fixed with a lot of sweating and muttering. Joy's mother had stayed with Kathy in our home. It was our first time being separated from Kathy.

The next school year went by quickly. I felt more comfortable teaching science and social studies and, especially, enjoyed my new English class with the older students. I continued to learn some subtleties of my craft from the more experienced teachers. I wrote a little story for the school newspaper about my experiences as a new teacher. Miss Fifer approached me one day in the lounge and asked me how to spell "Separate." She said that I'd spelled it "Seperate" in the paper. At first, I was annoyed. But, she told me a tip about spelling the word. She said to remember that there is "a rat" in the word. I, n to this day, remember that little tip. During my time at Perkins, she would correct my spelling and grammatical errors, but, always, in a kindly manner.

At the end of the school year, Mr. Vanica asked me if, in addition to being school treasurer next year, if I'd like to be school assembly chairperson. I'd be responsible for selecting speakers for the monthly all-school assemblies. I'd contact those persons and arrange for transportation to and from the school. I'd be teaching only two double-periods daily and have two periods for the treasury and assembly work. I agreed and appreciated his confidence in me.

Stan had been working as a driver for Skippy Ice Cream Trucks, which was owned by The Waldorf Ice Cream Company on Beaver Street in Akron. He was making good money and told me frequently that I'd enjoy the work. The trucks plied the streets of Akron and surrounding communities from mid-afternoon until dark. Each truck had an assigned route. I had grown tired of working nights at the drive-in and decided to talk to Bob Sandberg, the owner of the ice cream company.

He said that he had an opening on one truck which had a route in North Akron. I could begin May 15 if I accepted the job. He said the pay was based upon sales. I would receive the difference between what it cost to re-stock the truck and what I'd taken in in sales each day. Stan had been making forty to fifty dollars daily based upon the weather and other factors.

So, it was that I entered the world of selling ice cream street to street. I had never driven a truck before. They were larger than I had thought and had hard-to-shift stick shifts. There were no rear-view mirrors, only two large side mirrors. Driving was bad enough, but backing them into the garage between two other trucks was really bad. They had to be plugged into outlets each night to operate the freezing units.

As you might remember, the trucks had record players and loud speaker systems. To the annoyance of many, the music would blare out loudly to announce our arrival on the streets of our routes. Those who were annoyed were not reluctant to let me know about their annoyance. But, to many children and their parents, the ice cream truck's arrival was the highlight of their day. I learned quickly that the poorer neighborhoods bought the most ice cream. The upper-class areas thought themselves too proud to buy from a street vendor.

I made many new friends that summer and learned of their individual likes and dislikes. I was able to call many children by their first names. My daughter, Kathy, enjoyed the fruits of my labors. I was allowed to bring home each night some of the damaged or partially melted delights. On a couple of occasions, I took her with me on the route. She operated the music system while we drove.

And, so, the summer went by quickly. I looked forward to the new year. One day, just before school was to open, Mr. Vanica called me at home. He apologized for the call, but he had a question for me. He wanted to place a young man who had just returned from the Air Force and had a teaching degree at Perkins as a student teacher. He wondered if I'd be interested in being his supervising and critic teacher. He would teach some of my classes as he was deemed to be able. At first, he would observe me. I would determine if and when he was able to take over a class. I felt honored. The next year would be only my third year of teaching. I agreed readily. It looked to be an interesting year with the assembly and treasury work and, now, with a student teacher who was older than me.

And, it was. Bill proved to be a competent quick-study. He was tall and commanded respect almost immediately. He was confident and articulate. He watched how and what I did and we discussed the day's events at the end of each day. Soon, he was ready to teach the eighth grade class. At first, I stayed in the room when he taught to monitor his work. But, very quickly, I felt confident enough in his ability to leave the room and go to the teachers' lounge. I'm certain that the other teachers wondered how I had gotten a student teacher so early in my career. To my surprise, the job of being a supervising teacher gave me credit towards tuiton for my planned master's degree work.

Bill would, later in his career, become a high school principal and the Director of Secondary Education for the entire Akron school system. Of course, I take pride in knowing that I played a small role in his success.

My third year of teaching was different. I had a student teacher and new jobs as school treasurer and assembly coordinator. I was busy, but the nervousness of being new and having to prove myself had vanished. The highlight of my being assembly chairman came when I arranged for Jesse Owens, the renowned black Olympic athlete, to visit our school and make a presentation at an all-school assembly. I picked him up at the Akron Airport after his short flight from Cleveland where he lived. During the ride to school, we engaged in small talk. He was easy to talk with and asked a lot of questions about our school and about me. I asked him about his Olympic experience in Berlin and about how the German people had treated him. He told me that he had had the impression that he was viewed as an oddity. They weren't accustomed to seeing many black people and Hitler's propaganda machine had brain-washed most people into thinking that blacks were an inferior race. It was a blow to most of them when he won his medals.

His presentation went well. The students seemed enthralled with his stories about the Olympics and his outstanding track career at Cleveland

East Tech High School and The Ohio State University. Before the day of the assembly, I had prepared a hand-out for home room teachers to distribute to all students which gave a summary of Jesse's life and career. They were quiet, attentive and had many questions for him. He answered all of the students' questions gracefully. On the ride back to the airport, he complimented our faculty and student body for the way in which he had been treated.

Being school treasurer was another matter. I had to remind faculty members constantly about filling out the proper forms for deposits and withdrawals. Each day, I took the day's receipts to the Akron Dime Bank branch which was some two miles away. The job did get me outside and enabled me to break up the day's routine.

Bill finished his student teaching at the end of the first semester. It had been a good experience for me to monitor and supervise a fellow teacher. It helped me in my later role as a principal.

The second semester went by without notable or dramatic incidents. I continued to arrange assemblies that featured local and, sometimes, nationally known individuals. A local blind pianist who had achieved international acclaim performed for us on two occasions. He was a consummate performer and artist. I would pick him up at his home and return him after the assemblies. He was a remarkable man. The students loved to hear him play and laughed with him as he laughed at himself.

With the money I earned driving the ice cream truck, I was able to begin to work on my master's degree by taking two night classes at Akron University. I enjoyed being a student again. I didn't enjoy the graduate school statistics course, however. It was that math again! But, I passed it. To this day, I don't know how. We had no calculators or computers to use. One standard deviation problem could take hours to complete. The other courses were a breeze.

The following summer, Bob, the owner of the ice cream company, asked me if I would like to work in the office to take his place. He was busy with his law practice. My job would be to check the truck drivers in from about eleven in the morning until about one or two in the afternoon. Then, I was to return in the evening about eight to collect their day's receipts and make out their orders for re-stocking their trucks. He said it was a salaried job. I would recieve one hundred dollars weekly for the seven days of work and a bonus at the end of the season in the fall based upon the amount of profit made during the season.

The days would be chopped up and I wouldn't get home at night until after eleven o'clock. I talked it over at home and decided to do it. As it turned out, on some days, I would accompany the various drivers and make out route maps for each route by marking down each street in the order that they drove the route. For those days, Bob paid me an hourly rate in addition to my salary for the office work. At end of the season in late Fall, I received the bonus check which was enough to pay for the next semester's courses at the university.

To this day, I thank Bob for his kindness and for the money which enabled me to complete my advanced degree.

I continued to work for Bob for a total of five years. One black spot remains in my memory. During my fifth and last year, Bob had noticed a rather large decline in net profit. We discussed the problem. The driver's were still selling as much, but the revenue was declining. Bob hired an undercover man to be a driver. It was discovered that the man who took the order slips for re-stocking and worked in the back of the facility on the loading docks was giving the driver's much more stock than the paid order slip called for. The drivers would, then, give the stock man a share of the additional money that they made by selling the "free" product. Bob had hired the stock man knowing that he had been a convicted felon. Now, he become one once again.

I look back at those years with wonder. Each night, I would take a bank deposit bag containing several thousand dollars to the bank's night depository. The ice cream plant was in a dark secluded area of town. At the rear of our facility worked a convicted armed robber who was, also, robbing us. But, I lived to tell this story.

During my fouth year at Simon Perkins, one of those life-changing things happened. Our well-loved guidance counselor, Fanny, died unexpectedly. We were without a guidance counselor. Mr. Vanica called me into his office after school of the day we heard the sad news.

He asked me if I would consider being named as her replacement. My masters' degree, when completed, would be in both psychology and English. I could be certified as a counselor when I completed the degree provided that I take a few additional school guidance courses. Mr. Vanica said that Dr. Essex would approve of my being the counselor provided that I complete the required course as soon as possible. I was both flattered and perplexed. I enjoyed teaching. The counselling job was full-time. I would no longer teach. But, the new position would pay more money. I asked for a night to think over the offer. I went home and discussed the situation with Joy. We wanted another child. She was no longer working. Money would be an important criterion. I would take the offer and the new job.

It was Wednesday. On the following Monday, I would begin a new phase of my career. I was twenty-six years old and my life lay before me. I looked forward to the challenge. Mr. Vanica arranged for a substitute for my classes until a full-time replacement was hired. I was to continue as assembly chairman, but not as school treasurer.

There is one poignant reminder of my teaching time at Simon Perkins that I have kept for these many years. It is note from a seventh grade girl that meant a lot to me then and means a lot to me now. The following is the note written by hand on an embossed note card quoted in entirety:

"June 9, 1955

Dear Mr. Smith,

So ends another year of my schooling and as my thoughts wander back, I think of my first day. I entered Simon Perkins seeing more men teachers than I had ever seen before. It startled me a little. I said to myself, "Gee, I didn't expect to see so many men teachers. This isn't going to be an easy year." Time passes and I'm beginning to get into the swing of things. It's now the end of the sixth grading period. I can't express my feelings in words about how much I have learned from you in social studies and science. I've gotten a big kick out of doing experiments, giving reports, having debates, not to mention the juicy tests.

I hope that your classes and students next year will enjoy you as much as I have. Good luck always and good health.

Your loyal pupil, Linda"

I am still touched when I read this note. Linda was very bright. She was a hard worker. She showed, even at age 13, that she had the potential to do whatever she chose to do. Linda was one of many such students at Simon Perkins. I had learned that she was from a well-to-do Jewish family. Her parents were college educated and contributed greatly to the needs of the school. But, Linda transcended her excellent upbringing. She was a genuinely good human being. My point is that I encountered many students like Linda. Several of them came from deprived homes and poor family situations. Linda was different in that she knew that writing thank-you notes was the proper thing to do when something pleased you. After meeting her parents, I knew where her ability and civility had come from.

The area that Simon Perkins served back in the 1950's was, predominantly, an upper class neighborhood. Upper class, that is, in terms of income and entitlement. There were many Jewish families in the area. It was my first exposure to the Jewish mentality. They were very cognizant of the necessity of having a good education. They supported our school both in word and deed. I was impressed with their children. They worked hard and were polite. I don't like to deal in stereotypes, but, almost without exception, the Jewish students were good students.

We had a few black students at that time, also. We had some caucasian students who came from a small section of our district who could only be described as coming from low-income families. Many of these students had truancy and behavioral problems. Their parents were not involved and seemed negative towards school and education in general. Again, stereotyping will seem apparent. But, to me these things became very obvious.

We had to do some ability grouping in our classes to compensate for these variances in motivation and background. Simon Perkins was a new school using the new concept of the junior high school. We had the freedom and opportunity to try new things and to develop new strategies in dealing with a diverse group of students. We had a dynamic principal and a talented group of teachers. I was lucky to have been part of this ground-breaking experiment.

I attended Fanny's funeral along with most of the Perkin's staff and other educators from Akron and surrounding areas. She had been loved and respected. I had to fill some big shoes.

Monday came and with it my new title as guidance counselor. I had come in over the week end to put my new office in order. Fanny's brother, Fred, who was Akron's director of physical education had come in the previous Friday to clear her things from her office.

I hung a picture on one wall and a motivational poster on another wall. The office was very small and contained only my desk, a filing cabinet and two straight-chairs. It had no outside windows. Next to it was a good-sized conference room with a large table, six chairs and two big windows which looked out on the front lawn of the school. When I became claustrophobic, I sat and worked in the conference room. I had my own phone line with connections to the other offices and to the outside world. I shared a secretary with the assistant principal. Also, I had an assigned parking space near the entrance door.

That afternoon, a worker from the maintenance department came in and removed Fanny's name from the door and replaced it with mine. I was open for business, but nobody came.

Should I be rounding up some students or should I wait for them to come in to ask advice? I decided to spend the day looking over student grades and compiling a list of those who were failing or who had had an unusual drop in their grades. It took most of the day.

Several of the teachers stopped by to wish me luck. A few of them came with suggestions as to how I should do the job. Two staff members were fully certified in guidance and had had hopes of taking Fanny's place. I could sense in their attitudes that they were unhappy. C'est la vie!

The next day, I started to call in those students who were failing one or more subjects. I attempted to use what I had learned so far about how to motivate unmotivated students. Some of them listened intently. Others, not so much. The effectiveness of what I did would be shown in the next grades of those students.

I had a few calls from parents who had heard that I was the new counselor. Most just wanted to wish me well, but a few came armed with complaints about how poor of a job the school was doing to help their child. I used all of the charm that I could muster. Mr. Vanica had impressed upon me that I was now a very noticeable face of the school. He emphasized that public relations were very important to help to ensure the success of this experiment in education. As for me, I just wanted to help each student to reach his or her full potential.

It became apparent soon that the job of a counselor is two-fold. It's fifty percent helping students with academic problems and fifty percent helping to solve behavioral problems. Oh, I forgot. It's another part trying to mollify irate parents. So, the job requires giving more that one hundred percent. It requires not just knowing the students in your own classes, but knowing most of the entire student body and the strengths and weaknesses of the teaching staff.

I enjoyed my new responsibilities. I was given a prominent role in our weekly staff meetings. I spoke at the monthly PTA meeings. Mr. Vanica and I talked frequently. The assistant principal and I became better acquainted. Before becoming counselor, I had thought of him as being rather cruel. He paddled a lot of students. Some, I felt, needed encouragement, not punishment. But, as I came to know him better, I realized that he had tried to use methods other than paddling with many students. When those other methods didn't work, he would give them a few swats. I never saw him do it with anger. I think he did it as a last resort. He had a quiet sense of humor. I came to see that most students actually liked him in spite of his role as "Hit man." Later, I was to use his philosophy when I assumed that same role. In simple terms, that philosophy was: talk, cajole, call parents, give detentions, assign manual work around school, talk again, use the paddle, suspend, expel. Not many students ever got beyond the fourth stage. On one occasion, I saw him tear up when he had to recommend expulsion for a chronic truant and behavior problem. I came to believe that "Firmness with a heart" should be the motto for those who work with students of any age.

I was on pace for finishing my guidance certification by the end of the coming summer session. I, now, had the ambition and hope of pursuing my doctoral degree. I was on a roll. I loved my counseling job. I made enough to live more comfortably and my summer job with The Waldorf Ice Cream Company provided enough money to take my graduate courses. And, then, there was the fact that Joy was pregnant with our second child. Life was good.

I remember putting up a poster on my office wall. It was a quote from Terrance, a noted Roman poet. It read: "I am a man, therefore, nothing human is strange or alien to me." By understanding those few simple words, I came to realize that all behavior, both good and bad, could emanate from me because I, too, was human. One shouldn't be so quick to judge others because you could fall prey to those very urges and actions. I tried to remember those words when I acted and interacted with students, teachers and parents. Down through these many years, I still remember.

That summer, I worked at Waldorf Ice Cream company and finished my last courses for my master's degree and my guidance certification. Now, I had to write my thesis to complete requirements for my master's degree.

What would be my topic? My thesis advisor was Dr. Mabel Reidinger, a full professor at Akron University and the president of the Akron Board of Education. She suggested that I do something practical, something that the school district could use. The district had become dissatisfied with the mathematics' test that was used to measure the growth of students in grades seven and eight. The results had become increasingly at odds with what classroom teachers perceived to be the actual growth rates. She suggested that I attempt to prove that the test being used gave false data and that I use tests from other sources to provide comparisons.

Well, mathematics is not my main interest as I've stated several times. But, when the doctor prescribes something, it is well to follow those instructions. Dr. Reidinger asked me to come to her home on Sunday afternoons for our thesis discussions. She was too busy on weekdays.

I presented her with my plans for developing the thesis. She gave me a few suggestions for gathering the data and I was on my way. Each Sunday, I would take my new work to show her for her approval. After three such visits, she gave me the go-ahead to complete the thesis and, then bring it to her for final approval. The result was that the Akron School District dropped the current testing program for grades seven and eight and adopted the program that my study had suggested. My thesis turned out to be 221 pages long. I sat up almost every night until past midnight working on it. I did my own typing and footnoting on the required margined thesis paper. I had gotten quotes from a professional typist to do it, but the cost was one dollar per page and I couldn't afford it. Joy had saved money and bought me a new Smith-Corona portable typewriter to do the work. With frequent sips of vodka and the use of copious amounts of White-Out, I completed the tiring task in time to recieve my Master's Degree in June, 1959. To this day, I believe that Dr. Reidinger persuaded the faculty review board to overlook some obvious White-Out smudges. Normally, those wouldn't be accepted. But, she didn't overlook my frequent dangling participles. I had to do those over.

My second as year as guidance counselor flowed smoothly. I was learning my craft. I was a frequent speaker at various school and civic organizations. My topics were, usually, concerned with student motivation and the techniques of counseling. I was a student of the Rogerian school of counseling named after its founder, a well-known psychotherapist. In simplistic form, it utilized the listening and reflecting back to the speaker what he or she had just said. When one hears what he's said, it is often self-revealing. It can show the speaker both his faults and his virtues. But, at other times, I just used the old-fashioned approach of telling the kid what to do in explicit language.

Both methods have their use. Toward the end of busy work days, the second approach became standard.

"That's your responsibility as a person, as a human being -- to constantly be updating your positions on as many things as possible. And, if you don't contradict yourself on a regular basis, then, you're not thinking."

Malcolm Gladwell

Part Six

MOVING ON UP

In May of that year, Mr. Vanica asked me to come in to see him at the end of the school day. If he wanted to see you after school hours, that meant it was something important or serious. Or, both. He said to pull up a chair and take a load off. He was blunt that way. He came right to the point. Our neighboring school in West Akron, Litchfield Junior High School, was growing in size. The principal, John Hagen, was near retirement age and in poor health.

Enrollment numbers would justify having an assistant principal next Fall. Would I be interested? I was completely surprised. I would be twenty-eight next February and had only taught three years and had been a counselor for two more years. I did have plans someday to be an administrator, but I hadn't planned on it so soon. I think that I acted shocked and didn't answer immediately. "Sumner," as I felt confident enough to call him then, "I guess that you took me completely by surprise." He smiled and said: "Good, now will you give me an answer? We need to move quickly on this."

I squirmed a little bit on the hard wooden chair and managed to squeak out a feeble "Yes, I am interested". I appreciate the confidence you have in me." "Good," he said. "I will tell Dr. Essex that you would like to be considered. I'll set up an appointment for you."

How had this come about? I knew that Mr. Vanica must have recommended me for the job. At our final PTA meeting for the year next week, I'll need to take him out afterwards to get him his favorite drink, a gin and tonic.

The appointment was for the next Wednesday at three-thirty. Appointments with "The Man" were always intimidating. He had a way of making you feel unsettled and not knowing what to expect next. I needed to convince him that I was old enough and experienced enough to handle this big job. Litchfield had the reputation of being a difficult place to work in. It was in Akron's highest-priced neighborhood and contained its most demanding parents. They expected quality work from their students and quality work from the teachers and administrators. Many of Akron's "Wheelers and dealers" lived in the district.

Once again, I was ushered into the office of the Superintendent of Schools. Once again, he remained seated, but this time, he motioned for me to come over to his desk. He invited me to sit down in a pleasant voice. I felt relieved that he was not going to play games or test me.

"Mr. Vancica recommended you very strongly for the job at Litchfield. I told him that no one that young could be that good." I looked down at my shoes. But, I knew that he admired confidence in his employees. Looking down was not a good thing.

I smiled at him and said: "Mr. Vanica is seldom wrong." I said to myself: "Self, you've acted like a smart-ass. You're ruining things."

Dr. Essex looked at me appraisingly and said: "Quick come-backs will be necessary in your new job."

Then, he smiled and said: " Welcome to the position of Assistant Principal . I know that you will do well."

With that, he looked down at the stack of papers and said quietly, "Arrange to see John Hagen as soon as possible to discuss his views of what your duties will be. That's all."

I felt both elated and deflated. Dr. Essex had given me the job, but his demeanor was rather dismissive. Later, I would learn that that was just his way.

The next day, I called Mr. H. and arranged for me to visit him at Litchfield.

John was a slight, dapper looking man in his late 60's. I could tell that he had been in poor health by his slow movements and sallow complexion. He had met me at front door of the lobby. He showed me into his office and asked if I'd like tea or coffee. I was experiencing his unfailing good manners and gentlemanly ways for the first time.

He handed me a copy of the school's class schedule. We discussed that for a short time. Then, he surpised me by saying: "This will be your office. I will take the assistant principal's office just behind this one. For all practical purposes, you will run the day-to-day operation of the school. I will handle the PTA programs, the glad-handing of those influential people who help us financially and the public-relation stuff. How does that sound?"

Well, it sounded strange is how it sounded. I knew he'd been ill and almost to retirement age, but I didn't expect his complete withdrawal from the normal routine of a principal. I had expected to handle discipline, attendance and other practical matters, but I hadn't expected to be de facto principal.

Further discussion revealed that he needed quietness and freedom from stress if he were to finish out his three years before he could retire with a decent annual stipend. I relished the challenge and the faith that Dr. Essex and Mr. H. had shown in me, but was this fair? I would be the principal but at an assistant principal's salary. But, that salary represented a large increase over what I'd received as a counselor. Another "But." I would have only six weeks off each summer instead of the fourteen I'd been receiving. Was it really a better job? I would have much greater responsibilities. The student body was larger. The staff was bigger. But, I would be a principal, a title that carried some weight in the world of education. In addition, if I did well, I might get my own school following this fast-track course.

Would I accept Mr. H.'s unusual terms? Of course I would.

That summer, I began my doctoral work at Akron University. Also, that summer, our son Michael was born. We talked about moving from Goodyear Heights and away from our damp little rental home. Bob S., my boss at the ice cream company, was a lawyer. He said that he would help us with any legalities that arose over financing, title searches and other things beyond my experience and knowledge.

Bill and Joanne, from whom I'd bought my old car, had bought a house in Mogadore. Our first and last house-hunting began there. A friend of ours from Ellet had a brother who wanted to sell his house in Mogadore. He wanted $15,000 for it. That sounded like a lot of money to us. I talked to Bob. He suggested an FHA loan, but said he'd do a title search first to look for any liens against it. He jacked up my salary (on paper only) from my summer work at the ice cream company so that my income qualified for the loan. Everything looked good. It was a big move for us. Our monthly payments would be $88.00 for thirty years. It made me sweat.

The house itself was not a mansion. It was a two-story Cape Cod house with a very small living room, kitchen, downstairs bath, two bedrooms downstairs and two bedrooms upstairs, one of which was unfinished. It had a full basement and a one-car ramshackle garage. The house had aluminum siding and metal storm windows. The lot was ninety feet by 150 feet. One of my first thoughts was that I'd need to buy a power lawn mower.

Out of courtesy, I informed my mom and dad of our intention to buy the house. His first reaction was asking if we could afford it. Actually, we couldn't.

We moved into our new home in Mogadore during the summer before I began my job at Litchfield. Moving is always a chore and this one was no exception. I rented a truck and our friend, Bill helped us move. But, finally, just before school opened, we were in and mostly settled. Kathy and Michael enjoyed playing in the lush back yard. There were many neighborhood children and they soon had many new friends. Our neighbors were neighborly and we adjusted quickly to life in suburbia.

Part Seven

LITCHFIELD JUNIOR
HIGH SCHOOL

*"The best teachers are those who show you where
to look, but don't tell you what to see."*

Alexandra K. Trenfor

My job at Litchfield began the week before school opened. I had to adjust to a different school environment and a new group of teachers and students. Being an assistant principal posed a new set of problems. The assistant is known as the "Heavy." He is the enforcer of the school's policies and rules with both the students and the teachers. He is the one to mete out the punishments if those rules and policies are violated. So, it was one sunny September morning that I put on my most stern expression and entered a new phase of my career in education.

We had had a staff meeting on the day before classes began. Mr. H. introduced me to the faculty and support staff. I still had my crew cut and was clean-shaven. I think that I was the youngest member of the professsional staff. Mr. H. announced that I would be using the principal's office and would be assuming most of his former duties. The teachers exchanged glances and raised some eyebrows. Several nodded as if they had expected something like this. Rumors had had it that Mr. H. had lost a step or two and was biding time until his retirement. But, he was well-loved and respected so there were no smirks or "Told you so's" involved. It seemed to them that this passing of the torch was a well-earned reward for his many years of loyal service. I gave a brief presentation of my background and my thanks for the opportunity to work in this fine school. Every one seemed to accept the change and appeared to be anxious to begin the new year.

Dr. Essex had been correct. This was a different kind of school and a different kind of student. My first proof of that came when one of the English teachers came into my office an hour into my new job and demanded that I do something to punish a young man who came to school each day wearing pants without a belt. I asked her if the school's policy book and/or dress code demanded that boys wear belts. She said that the school didn't have a written student policy book or a written dress code. But, she knew that common decency and common sense required that boys wear belts. I was kind of a belt man myself so I told her that I'd look into this serious situation. I hope that my attempt to hide a smile didn't fuel more anger.

To prove my concern, I called the young man into my office and told him of his teacher's visit. I said that it is advisable to keep one's pants up in the school environment. He said nothing. He just pulled out his shirt tail and showed me his suspenders. His pants were in no danger of falling down. I said that it was unusual for a young boy to wear suspenders. He told me that he had a bad rash on his stomach and his doctor had advised to not irritate it more by wearing a belt, at least for a while. Well, I could't argue with that.

I sent him back to class with my apologies. I told him that I'd talk to his teacher. I did and received an icy look and the comment: "It just doesn't look right for a young man not to wear a belt."

Because of that incident, one of my first jobs out of the box was to assemble a committee of parents, teachers and students to discuss the writing of a school handbook so that questions about dress, grooming and general behavior would have a solid basis on which to answer them. By the end of the school year, a printed handbook was placed in the hands of all faculty and students.

The summer between my first and second years at Litchfield found me working for The Burch City Directory Company. I went door to door gathering information that would be published in the new directories. I was assigned to some of the so-called worst areas of Akron. I met a lot of interesting and, sometimes, scary people. It broadened my understanding of people and how they lived. When my seond year began, I felt that I had a better and deeper knowledge of human nature.

As it was at Perkins, I was privileged to work with a great teaching and support staff. As I'd been advised, the parents were very involved, mostly, in a positive way. Our PTA meetings were the scene of lively discussions. When Mr. H. or I articulated a need for the school, that need was, usually, met quickly without going through mountains of red tape and bureaucratic decisions. We needed new stage curtains for the the multi-purpose room. A few weeks later, a delivery truck pulled with the curtains. Men showed up to install them. Done! Many of the parents were successful business people and community leaders. They were accustomed to making decisions quickly and acting upon them quickly.

But, that involvement could be annoying, too. I found myself being questionned and second-guessed about my actions on numerous occasions. If I disciplined a child, often, I would receive a phone call. The parent or parents would want to know all of the circumstances and why I chose to handle it the way in which I did. I tried to stay calm and give a reasoned response to all such inquiries. It made me more patient about my own responses to students' actions. I began to sift through possible courses of action instead of simply a knee-jerk reaction. It made me a better administrator.

Mr. H. was very kind to me. He became a mentor. We talked often about my work as we sat in his back office. He never told me what or what not to do. He just offered advice from his many years of experience. He showed up for work almost every day even when it was obvious that he didn't feel well. I learned a lot during the three years that I was there.

The long commute from Mogadore to West Akron took a toll on the old Dodge. One cold winter day, it died on the Tallmadge Avenue Parkway. I called AAA and had it towed to my mechanic. The tow-truck driver drove to me to work and a fellow teacher drove me home that evening. It was Friday and I would have the week-end to handle the car situaton. My mechanic told me that the patient had died after he had made a valiant effort to save it.

So, it happened that I came to buy my second car, a two-year old Chevrolet with a small v-eight engine. I test drove it and was amazed at the response when I stepped on the gas. I perspired when I signed the papers that obligated me to three years of car payments. I was not certain that we could afford car payments on top of our newly-acquired house payments. But, we needed reliable and safe transportation. I'd find a way. Besides, the car had large tail fins and it was pink and white.

At Litchfield, I learned how to become an effective administrator. I learned how to balance and juggle my roles as both student advocate and teacher advocate. Sometimes, the two positions were very far apart. Then, throw in the wishes of parents and the downtown administrators and you have a, sometimes, volatile mix. I found myself along with John's advice, making a lot of big and important decisions. It was a heady, exciting time as I learned my craft.

I need to mention Margaret, our guidance counselor, who was of great help to me, also. She was a wise, mature lady who lived in the neighborhood and had been on the staff from the beginning. She and her husband owned a profitable business and were members of the near by country club. She helped me to navigate through the rough waters of the privileged mind-set. It was obvious that I was not accustomed to the perks and niceties that most of our parents enjoyed and expected.

She helped me to polish my manners and appearance - a little patina on the rough spots, if you will.

Her husband invited me to play golf with him at the country club on several occasions. I had played a little golf before, but I was lucky to break a hundred for eighteen holes. I, certainly, had never had a caddy before or locker room and dining room privileges.

My first round with him was a true learning experience. My caddy was patient, but I'm sure he had tales to tell his fellow caddies after our round. I found most of the bunkers and all of the water hazards. The out-of-bounds markers became familiar friends. I was cowed and subdued as we sat in the plush dining room eating our filet and drinking top-shelf red wine.

But, I began to understand much better the mind-sets of our school's parents and children. It wasn't as if they were demanding. They expected quality in not only what we did, but in what they and their children did. I grew to understand and appreciate that. To them, education was a top priority and it should be that way for everyone, including me.

Litchfield fed into Firestone High School, widely considered to be the top Akron high school because of its advanced placement programs and emphasis on the fine and performing arts. Over ninety percent of its graduates attended college. As the feeder school, Litchfield was expected to prepare its students for the rigorous academics at Firestone. When any of our students entered grade ten they were programmed to succeed. If they didn't, we heard about it from their parents and from their high school teachers. The pressure was on us to perform.

Our teachers prepared difficult lessons and difficult tests based upon those lessons. Copious amounts of homework was routinely assigned. Making the honor roll was expected of almost everyone.

I began to grow uneasy about our few students who didn't have the ability or motivation to keep up with their goal-oriented fellow students. We, by catering to the best and brightest, were setting them up for failure. Litchfield had not had classes grouped according to ability. It had been assumed that all of its students were among the best and brightest. I set about to persuade Mr. Hagen, our counselor and our teaching staff that we needed to better provide for those students who had limited abilities. During my second year there, we scheduled one group in English, social studies, science and math in each grade to be composed of lower ability students. I was careful to assign teachers for each of those classes who agreed with this philosophy. Also, I was careful to not label those classes in such a way as to stigmatize or embarrass the students who would be in those classes. It was a difficult sell, but the effort paid off. Most of those students improved not only their grades, but their attitude towards school. They, now, could compete on a level playing field.

I began to tire of the long daily commute from Mogadore to West Akron and back. My days were long and I wanted more time with home and family. It was especially annoying when I needed to be at school for evening activities or PTA meeings. I either had to stay over after regular school hours or go home and come back.

I sent a letter to Dr. Essex saying that if an opening in adminstration were to occur in a school closer to my home, I'd like to be considered for it. It didn't seem likely as I'd not heard of any resignations or firings. But, it was worth letting the downtown office know of my interest.

The summer before my third year at Litchfield found me working at a different job. I became an insurance investigator for Retail Credit Corporation. I learned a lot about human nature while doing this work just as I had by doing the previous summer's directory work. This new job forced me to dig a little deeper into that human nature. I was assigned to check on the health, character and morals of people who had applied for new life insurance policies. I was trained to talk to those people who might know something about the life of the applicants. I talked to neighbors, friends, store clerks, gas station personnel, ministers, teachers and anyone willing to talk about the lives and habits of those seeking the policies. I learned a lot. I learned that your life is more of an open book than you might imagine. I learned that people are quite willing to talk about and gossip about even their best friends. I heard some very juicy stories about infidelities, drug usage, perverted habits and anything that had made their ears and eyes perk up.

I know that I heard some lies, exaggerations and fantasies, also. My job was to try to sift out the truth from reams of minutiae and write reasonably accurate reports to the home office. I enjoyed gathering the information, but not typing the reports at the end of very long days. I was paid by the number of reports that I submitted.

I was glad when the school year began. I enjoyed being at Litchfield among the group of gifted and dedicated teachers. I enjoyed working with the students. The discipline problems were, usually of a minor annoying type. Tardiness, gum-chewing, arguments between students and talking too much in class were the main offenses. I seldom did more than talk or assign detentions to the offenders. Once in a while, fighting or smoking caused me to levy more severe penalties. The school

Donald E. Smith, Ph.D.

district's policies stated that those type of offenses could cause a student to be suspended. Rarely, in my three years at Litchfield did I need to use the board -approved paddle. If I did, it was because nothing else had worked. We discussed discipline procedures not only at staff meetings, but at the PTA meetings so that parents could express their opinions.

Part Eight

HYRE JUNIOR HIGH SCHOOL

"The best teachers are the ones who remain students at heart, the ones who keep learning from their students and the world around them."

Charles P. Pierce

I am proud of my efforts at Litchfield and I was sad when I was notified by Dr. Essex that my request to be assigned closer to home would be granted beginning the next school year. The situation was eerily similar to my placement at Litchfield. I would be assigned as an assistant principal at Hyre Junior High School in the Ellet area of Akron which was only three miles from my home in Mogadore. I had mixed feelings, but I accepted the assignment. The similarity was that the principal, Charles Querry was, also, near retirement and had health problems, too.

In my interview with him during the summer, he told me a story similar to Mr. Hagen's. He was growing tired, had bad digestive problems and just wanted to segue quietly into his retirement years. He would leave the basic operation to me and he would provide advice and handle the PTA. I could do that. I had already done so.

The similarities didn't stop there. The two buildings were identical having been built on the same architectural plans. A third building, Innes Junior High School in Kenmore was, also, of the same design. The grand junior high experiment at Simon Perkins had proved so successful that Akron had built three more of them.

So, when school began in September, I felt right at home except for a new staff and a new student body. The Ellet neighborhood was once part of Springfield Township and had been annexed to Akron in the 1930's. It still retained its small-town flavor and sense of being separate from Akron City itself. When asked, people usually said that they lived in Ellet, not Akron. I had graduated from Ellet High School and had lived there from age twelve until I was twenty-two. So, working in Ellet was like coming home.

Just a block away from the school was Eastgate Shopping Center which was a big attraction for the students at lunch. There had been a lot problems with students leaving the campus and marauding around the stores in the center. Merchants had complained. The school lacked enough supervision to handle the problem effectively. The school's rules prohibited students leaving school grounds during lunch time, but the lure of the mall was strong and each lunch time some students would manage to get there. Mr. Q. briefed me about this problem when we met the week before school. Another problem was that the school lay adjacent to a large wooded area where I had played war games when I was the age of the school's students. Sneaking off into the woods at lunch time was another favorite student activity. So, the staff was attacked on two fronts. Students of warfare know that that is almost impossible to defend with limited resources.

I was told that this would be my first problem to solve. Events followed a path that I had become accustomed to. I was introduced to the staff. To my surprise and dismay, some of the teachers at Hyre had been my teachers when I was a student at Ellet High School. It would be a challenge for me to supervise and evaluate my former teachers. Would they take kindly to my role as their boss? Fortunately, I had gotten along well with the teachers whom I had known previously.

The students at Hyre were what might well be called "Average." I use that term in a good way. To me, it means that there were some excellent students, some poor students and a lot of average students. The parents were a mixture of working class people whose jobs were in the tire factories and retail stores and those who had various professional jobs. Some houses were modest and some were quite luxurious. Some supported schools and teachers and some were suspicious and, even, hostile towards education and educators. So, all in all, it was a very typical school.

As at Litchfied, I occupied the principal's office and Mr. Q. took the assistant's office. My duties matched those I'd had the previous three years. Just the cast of characters was different. My former teachers accepted me without any negativity. I think that they took pride in the role that they had played in my development.

Two incidents stand out in my memory. One was tragic and one was semi-humorous.

The one with humorous overtones took place during the first week of school. Two of the men teachers had had numerous arguments during the previous year. Most of them occured in the teachers' lounge during their shared "Free" periods. It didn't matter what the subject was. They disagreed on everything - sports, politics, women, teaching methods and life in general. The disagreements started again when they met during the meeting that we had the day before school opened. I had devised a plan for supervision during the lunch period that would allow more teachers to be available for supervision. Without knowing the background, I had placed those two men together to patrol the perimeter of the school grounds. One of the men, a math teacher, said loudly: "I am not working with him!" The other man, the physical education teacher, responded: "No way!" I told them that we'd work this out, but, for now, that was the assignment.

The second day of school, I heard a loud commotion in the main lobby just as the lunch period began. Students were laughing and cheering. My secretary rushed into my office, and said: "Mr. Smith, you'd better get out in the hall. Two teachers are fighting." I thought to myself that this is going to be quite a year.

In the hall, the two men were circling each other in semi-comical John. L. Sullivan poses. They feinted, bobbed and weaved. Punches were thrown, but few were landing. The students gathered from all corners of the large main lobby. Other teachers had arrived. They were enjoying the spectacle, too. As the only administrator on the scene, it was up to me to intervene. I told them loudly to break it up. They were too involved in their own emotions to listen to anything. I stepped between them while ducking wild swings. I think that both of them were relieved to stop before real damage might be done. I told them to follow me into my office. As they cooled down, I tried to decide what to do about this breach of protocol and common sense. The other teachers and the students would be anxious to see what I would do. And, it had to be something other than just talk to them.

I told them that I was sending both of them home for the balance of the day. Before they returned tomorrow, I wanted them to call me at home tonight to tell me that they had composed themselves and that the disagreement between them would not result in any additional problems for them or for the school. I would enter a report of this incident into their personnel folders. It would be removed at the end of the year if no other problems occured. If they did, I would suspend them indefinately and send them for conferences with the superintendent for his decision as to whether or not they could continue in their current jobs. As for their afternoon classes today, I would assign teachers who had free periods to cover those classes.

They left my office looking both embarrassed and subdued. Mr. Q. had been in his office eating a bland lunch and drinking Maalox. He had not been aware of the incident. I gave him a complete report later in the afternoon.

The "Fight," as it became known, was the talk of the school for a long time. It will go down in the annals of Hyre Junior High School as a the highlight of the year with one very sad and tragic exception.

The next incident wasn't really a highlight. It was a very sad lowlight.

I was in my office talking to a young man whose behavior had been giving his English teacher nightmares when my secretary called on my intercom. "Mr. Smith, please go out to the running track. There's been an accident." I left hurriedly hoping that someone had just scraped their knees on the cinder track. As I approached, I saw a group of students and the physical education teacher standing around a boy who lay flat on his back on the track. I told the students to step aside so I could kneel down beside him. The teacher looked pale and frightened. I asked him what had happened. "He just fell over while he was running the laps."

I felt the boy's chest and could not detect any breathing movements. I knelt closer and felt for a pulse in his neck. Nothing. I opened his mouth and pulled his tongue out, checked for obstructions, pinched his nose shut and began artifcial respiration. I breathed in his mouth while compressing his chest. I asked the gym teacher to take over the compressions. We did that for almost ten minutes before I admitted to myself that it was too late. He was gone.

Other teachers had gathered by now and I sent one into the office to call the paramedics. I said nothing to the assembled crowd other than telling them to return to the building and go to their assigned classes. After the emergency squad had taken the boy to the hospital, I asked the gym teacher to come with me to talk to Mr. Q. . During that discussion it was revealed that the gym class had been instructed to run their usual two laps around the class before the calisthentics began. It was determined that all of the students had submitted health records to the office as required. We looked at the boy's record and nothing on it would preclude his taking part in physical exercise.

I called the boy's home and told the mother that her son had been rushed to City Hospital and that she should go there immediately. I decided to let the attending physician tell her that he had died.

I asked the gym teacher if he had noticed anything unusual about the boy while he was running the laps. He said that the boy usually complained about running and he'd done so today. He complained about being out of breath. But, he always did that.

I sent for three students who had been in the same class and asked them if they'd noticed anything strange about the boy today. They all said that he always complained and that everyone just ignored him. He was not the athletic kind and complained about most everything that the class did. To me, it was apparent that this was a classic example of "Cry wolf."

The next day, both parents came in. Their attitude was both of grief and anger. They were in shock from their son's death, but were angry at the teacher for forcing their son to run laps. I told them that unless his health records showed he should be dismissed from physical activity, we would have had no reason to excuse him. In the discussion, it came out that the boy had had rheumatic fever at a very young age and they had neglected to record that on his health record.

Later, the autopsy would show that there had been heart damage due to the fever. But, that didn't allay the parents' anger at the teacher and the school in general. The father was irate and became verbally abusive to me and anyone within earshot. He demanded to see the gym teacher. I refused. His wife and I had to make him sit down and cool off. Before they left the school, he said that he was getting a lawyer and that he would make all us pay and that we would lose our jobs.

When the funeral arrangements were announced, we had a special staff meeting to determine who should go to represent the school. The gym teacher wanted to go, but I tried to dissuade him for fear of violence. He insisted. We, finally, decided that he, our counselor and I would attend. Anyone else could go if they wished.

We met at the school and I drove the three of us to the funeral home on Exchange Street in Akron. There was a big crowd gathered inside. When we walked in, I heard a loud voice say: "That's the bastard who killed my son." The father walked over to us accompanied by two other men who turned out to be his brothers. I told the gym teacher to keep quiet and sit down. Fortunately, cooler heads prevailed and other friends and relatives managed to diffuse the situation. The service proceeded without incident. But, as we were leaving, I heard one of the brothers say: "He hasn't heard the end of this."

Over time, the situation calmed down. The school was not found to be at fault. The gym teacher was exonerrated, also. But, unfortunately, he decided that teaching was not for him. At the end of the school year, he resigned. The incident did have the effect of putting more emphasis on making certain that health records were up-to-date and accurate. It was a lesson learned in the very hardest of ways.

The balance of my first year at Hyre went by smoothly without drama or trauma. I continued to learn on the job. Even though Mr. Q. kept a low profile, I learned a lot from him as we talked each evening about the day's events. I honed my skills doing the multitude of tasks that is required of a building principal. I constructed the next year's class schedule, edited the student handbook and handled most of the discipline. I led most of the staff meetings and attended all of the PTA meetings along with Mr. Q. I approved all of the purchases of textbooks and educational supplies and refereed squabbles among custodial, kitchen and teaching employees. I tried to be in the hallways during all passing times. I helped Mr. Q. to visit the teachers during their teaching periods and write the required evaluations.

I devised a schedule for available teachers to be outside during lunch time to prevent students from sneaking off to the shopping center and the wooded area behind the school. I made a schedule for teachers to share supervision of restrooms during passing times. Because the teachers considered these duties to be extra work above and beyond their teaching duties, they demanded, through their union representatives, to receive additional pay. After the obligatory arbitration, it was decided that these duties were part of what a teacher should do during the school day without expecting to be paid extra for doing them. A teacher is not just a classroom teacher. He or she is expected to accept reasonable assignments other than teaching if they fall within the contractual hours of their work day. Supervision of students falls within the scope of that obligation.

For a while, I was not the most popular man about campus. But, soon, most teachers realized that Mr. Q. and I couldn't do all of the required supervision by ourselves. The ones who rebelled, by reflex, rebelled against everything. I didn't lose sleep.

Towards the end of the year, Mr. Q. announced that, do to poor health, he would retire as of June 30. I felt a little flutter of anticipation. Would I be named principal? I learned very soon after that that Dr. Essex had other plans for me. I was notified to make an appointment to see him.

Once again, I entered the holy of holies. He beckoned me over to take a seat opposite him. He began by saying that he hoped that I wouldn't be disppointed by not being named principal at Hyre. But, I was. He went on to say that Mr. Ault, who had been the principal at Akron East High School, was planning on retiring soon also and wanted a less strenous job during his last one or two years. As a reward for his long and meritorious service, he was being assigned to replace Mr. Q. at Hyre. I kept a stoic expression, but thought, "How nice for him."

Dr. Essex went on. "You've done a fine job at Hyre, but you are still very young. I want you to get some senior high school experience. If you accept, I will assign you to be a unit principal at John R. Buchtel High School in West Akron. I have no doubt that, very soon, you'll have your own school. How does that sound?"

Well, it sounded like a combination compliment and criticism. I was doing a good job for a young guy is how it sounded. I could do nothing but accept his offer.

Dr. Essex went on to say that Buchtel was a very large school, almost 2000 students in grades ten, eleven and twelve. Mr. Tucker was the principal and Mr. Coberly was the other assistant principal. I would have my own office and share a secretary with Mr. C. Tentatively, I would handle school-wide attendance and part of the discipline with Mr. C. I would help to supervise athletic events and other activities. As time goes by, my duties might change according to needs.

He emphasized that Buchtel had a long history of academic excellence and offered many advanced placement courses. The sheer number of students and the eighty plus teachers presented an enormous challenge for adminstrators. Then he added something that proved to be prophetic. There is change in the air. South High School will close in the near future and those students will, probably, come to Buchtel and many of its students will transfer to Firestone High School which is only partially full.

What he meant was that Buchtel will receive an influx of black inter-city students and we will lose a big portion of our caucasion students. It would be a dramatic change for everyone, students and staff alike. How true that proved to be.

So, it came to pass that I said goodbye to Hyre and prepared to enter another new phase of my career. I had never worked with senior high school students except during my student teaching. I imagined that they would act more mature and be easier for me to relate to. I still looked very young or least that's what I was told. I hoped that my age and appearance wouldn't prove to be a problem.

Part Nine

JOHN R. BUCHTEL
SENIOR HIGH SCHOOL

"Education is a progressive discovery of our own ignorance."

Will Durant

Working at Buchtel meant another long daily commute. But, it, also, meant an increase in salary. All things are relative I told myself.

That summer, I continued working as an insurance investigator. I was offered a full-time position with Retail Credit Corporation, but I was going to ride the education horse to see where it would take me.

Where it took me was to Buchtel High School on Copley Road in West Akron. It was a large facility, really three buildings connected by a maze of corridors. The main building had two floors and the others had three. Behind the buildings were the football stadium and the track. The Buchtel Griffins had a long history of athletic excellence to go along with their academic excellence.

I arranged to meet with Mr. T. the week before school began. He was a tall, thin bespectacled man who had trouble smiling. He seemed very business-like and professorial. He had been a long-time math teacher. That, in itself, sounded an alarm. He told me about my duties and what he expected of me. I didn't think that keeping track of attendance and sharing in discipline sounded too challenging. I asked if I would have part in the academic life of the school. He just nodded and said: "One thing at a time. Time will tell."

He showed me my office or, rather, my cubicle. It was very small. It held my desk, one filing cabinet and one straight- backed chair. I had no room for any personal things to make it more inviting. The door opened off of the main office area and an opening in one wall to the outside lobby allowed students to talk to me without their coming ino the office. That opening onto the school's main lobby became my portal to the life of the school. Had I not kept that open, I would have been entombed, sealed away from all living things.

At the opening staff meeting, Mr. T. introduced me to the staff. I felt one hundred and sixty eyes giving me the once-over. Most of the eyes appeared skeptical. I had heard rumors that I was considered to be Dr. Essex's fair-haired boy and a possible snitch. I would need to allay such rumors very quickly by trying very hard to be just "One of the gang."

Being one of the gang proved to be difficult. It was a close-knit kind of clannish group whom I found to be less than open about change. Many of the teachers had been there for years and didn't see any reason for doing things differently from what they'd done for those years

At one of our first staff meetings, I suggested a minor change in keeping class attendance. Someone called immediately for a vote. I lost by a healthy margin. I resigned myself to going slowly if I wanted to change or improve anything.

Mr. T. ran the meetings like a drill sergeant. He didn't brook any deviations from his printed agenda. Eventually, I was able to get some things on the agendas by telling him well ahead of the scheduled meeting. He stayed in his office most of the day. Mr. C. and I provided supervison at passing times and before and after school.

Mr. C kept high-powered binoculars in his office which he used to search the perimeters of the school grounds for escapees and interlopers. I found this amusing and made the mistake of telling him so. It took him a long time to accept me as an equal assistant principal because of my penchant for proposing new ideas and making light fun of some of the old ones.

During my first year at Buchtel, I began working as an evening college counselor at Akron University. My main job was to interview new transfer students from other colleges and universities and determine how much, if any, of their previous course work could be transferred to Akron and how much credit could be given. I had to determine if the content of the course work they had taken matched the content of the courses that Akron required. It was tedious work and the lack of concrete guidelines made most of it a matter of my judgment calls. As one might imagine, I had to make quite a few students angry. But, it was an entree into college level teaching which I aspired to do one day.

My first year at Buchtel was boring. Attendance and discipline didn't do much to excite me. However, there were a few exciting moments. I broke up a lot of fights. The girl-fights were the most exciting. They occured mostly in the restrooms. A student would come into the office screaming: "Fight, fight!" I would follow her to one of the restrooms to find two bald girls pulling and tugging each other while their wigs lay on the floor like road kill. I would wade in between them, trying to avoid their flailing arms.

Mr. T had a policy that after a student's third tardiness to school, the student would receive two swats with the official paddle. I tried to talk to him about my ideas about the policy. I told him that I'd rather reserve paddling for more serious offenses and, then, only when nothing else worked. These were high school students in grades ten, eleven and twelve. They were practically adults. Some of the students were as old as 20 and were military veterans who had been permitted to return to earn their diplomas. Mr. T. told me in his best stern voice without looking up from his paper work, "Just enforce the policy as written"

My premonition of doom came to pass. Lonnie, a big, burly veteran with a perpetual scowl, reached his third tardy mark and the secretary escorted him into my office. I asked him if he knew about the three-strike and out policy. He looked at me with a twisted grin and said: "Yeah, let's get it over with." I told him that I thought the policy was silly for mature students, especially 20 year old veterans. He said if that were the policy, that I should enforce it. He told me that he was working nights at a fast-food place and didn't get to bed until after two a.m. He tried to be on time, but didn't always make it. I felt sorry for him. I got the feeling that he was sorry for me. Before, I could continue the conversation, he bent over and grabbed his ankles. "Just do it. I need to get to class." So it was, that I swatted this hulk of a man for being a few minutes late to school. I felt both silly and embarrassed. To Lonnie's credit, he didn't argue or resist. He was accustomed to following orders. Me, not so much. In spite of the policy, it was the last time that I used that paddle for minor offenses like tardiness. Mr. C. made frequent use of his. So much so, that the PTA brought up the paddling policy in one of their business meetings. Mr. T. reprimanded me in private after I had told the members that I didn't think that paddling was appropriate for high school students. I had begun to question it for any students, but it was the 1960's and it was a common and approved method of discipline.

Sometimes, outsiders would sneak into the building through one of the many doors. Usually, a student would open one for them having had advance notice. The outsiders, sometimes, had weapons of various kinds and I'd have to notify the police. At that time, we had no security guards. Just me and Mr. C.

We had students attacked with knives and a girl raped during the school day during my time at Buchtel. The boy-fights often ended with serious injuries requiring medical attention. Oh, yes, senior high school proved to be a barrel of laughs.

I need to tell you about Captain Dave our boy's physical education teacher. He was ex-military and everything about him exuded that fact. He ran the gym classes like basic training. The boys' white tee-shirts and shorts had to be spotless. The calisthenetics were run like clock-work. Anyone who loafed had to run countless laps around the gym He had to be addressed as "Coach" followed by a loud "Sir!" The boys couldn't wear rings or other jewelry to class. If they did, he would confiscate the item and keep it locked up in his office. He wouldn't give them back until the school year ended. This policy caused me countless problems. The students complained and their parents complained. I asked Mr. T. to back me in persuading the captain to modify or soften the policy. He agreed with the policy. So, I had to try to explain the efficacy of a teacher stealing the rings and necklaces. It happened several times that the kept items were lost or misplaced. The captain and I never had a meeting of the minds over his methods of discipline. Gym classes should be fun. At Buchtel, they were not. They were a thinly disguised form of torture. For some reason, I usually ended up handling the complaints. The girl's gym classes were a little more humane. A little.

Actually, one incident, not in gym class, did provide a small barrel of titters. In the three-story section of the school, there was an open stairwell reaching all three floors. For some time, teachers and students would report seeng puddles of a liquid on the first floor beneath the stairwell.

We didn't know with certainty what the liquid was, but it smelled suspiciously like urine. I took a sample to our chemistry teacher. He verified that it was.

We tried in vain to catch the secret pisser, but he or she continued to avoid our sighting. Finally, Mr. A. happened to be walking nearby and felt a drop of liquid hit his partially bald head. He, being a veteran and of quick reflexes, looked up and saw on the third floor a rapidly escaping figure. Mr. A. saw him enter the room assigned to the educationally challenged students. He ran up the stairs, entered the room and saw a boy trying to zip up his pants. It was circumstantial evidence at best, but through the gentle persuasion of his teacher, he confessed to the dastardly deed.

He lost some privileges because of his acts, but because of his condition, the punishment went no further. He will go down in the annals of Buchtel lore as "The Phantom Pisser of the Third Floor."

Because of chronic truancies, I made a lot home calls in order to find the truants and talk to their parents if possible. I learned much about the home lives of these part-time students. Some just didn't get up and no one was there to awaken them or prod them. Some were hung-over or still intoxicated. Some ran and hid from me. Some students and/ or parents wouldn't answer their doors or, if they did saw who it was and slammed the door in my face. I had the law on my side, but tried not to use it if at all possible. Some parents were apologetic and said they'd given up trying to get the student to go to school. I explained the alternatives. Either get to school or get a verifiable job with a working permit if they were sixteen or older.

If they did neither, the student faced time in juvenile court for delinquency by virtue of truancy and the parents faced fines or even jail time for aiding and abetting said truancy.

I was considered to be an arm of the court and was authorized to use whatever means at my disposal to get those truants back in school. I had been warned that doing this work could be dangerous. If I so desired, I could be licensed to carry a side-arm. Well, I did get licensed, but never had to use the gun.

I did get cussed at and did chase a few miscreants down with my old fooball tackling skills, but, all in all, the assignment was more frustrating than dangerous. I was invited inside for a lot of food and the occasional drink. On one occasion, I was offered a "Doobie" to smoke along with the truant and his parents.

Mostly, those attendance calls were made in what was known as "The Little Farm" area on the extreme western edge of Buchtel's district. If Buchtel had a "poor" section this was it. There were a lot of basement homes and some trailer homes. In many cases, the student had no father figure in his life. The mother was, often, out of work. This area and these students were in sharp contrast to the norm in this district.

During my second and last year at Buchtel, we had a rash of faculty cars being vandalized. We were advised to park in a lot rented for the purpose that had been surrounded by barbed wire and guarded by a rent-a-cop.

Some days, I wondered what I was doing here. Mr.T. never involved me in any curricular educational plans or decisions. He did all those things on his own behind his closed doors. We seldom talked. He seldom talked with any staff members about any topic of substance. Many students remarked that they didn't know the principal and never saw him. He didn't speak at assembies. Students introduced any guests that were the speakers.

I never heard either praise or censure. I received no written evaluations. I ran my little world and the other staff members ran theirs. Seldom, did we meet to share any ideas or thoughts. I felt that my career had reached an impasse. I was not growing. I was suffocating in my little cubicle. I did come out to help with crowd control at athletic contests Our home basketball games in our over-crowded gym were noisy wild affairs. We had some physical altercations occasionally and the police on duty had to call for back-up. The football games were more subdued due to the big distance between opposing fans. My job was to roam the perimeter of the field and look for disturbances. It was difficult watch the game while I watched the crowd.

Near the end of my first year at Buchtel my mother became very ill. She had been suffering for over five years with ovarian cancer. My dad and health care workers had been taking care of her in my old home on Sieber Avenue in Ellet. She spent most of the days in a hospital bed in the living room. I went to see her after school, but she was barely awake and I don't think that she knew me. The next day, Saturday, I went to see dad before he went to work. We called Phyllis and over the phone we decided it was time to put Mom in a nursing home where she would receive around the clock care.

Within a few days, we picked out a nursing facility located in South Akron. Mom didn't live long after that. I received an urgent call at work from the nursing supervisor saying that I'd better go see her as soon as possible. I left from work almost immediately. When I arrived, she was lying in bed with her eyes closed. "Mom, Mom!" She opened her eyes and smiled weakly and said, "Donald Duck, quack, quack!" Those were the last words that she spoke to me. She died early in the morning on the next day. After years of suffering quietly, she died quietly. My memories of mom are muted and dim. She seemed to be ill most of my life. It didn't seem to be a great shock when she died. She just faded away silently. A service was held in Akron. The funeral procession wended its way slowly some fifty miles south to East Springfield, Ohio where she, my dad and all four grandparents had been born and raised. Another service was held there in the little chapel on the grounds of the country grave yard.

My dad was stoic throughout. It was difficult to see emotion if any were there to see. But, that was dad. The tiny cemetery had received one more occupant. You know, the circle of life and all that.

Dad would re-marry some five years later to a crotchety old retired school teacher. We never really connected. That's enough to say about that.

During my second year at Buchtel, we had the influx of black students who came from the recently closed South High School. Our teachers had a difficult time adjusting their teaching methods and materials. Many had been teaching mostly A.P. courses and, now, they had to adjust to teaching in a more basic, conventional manner. The teachers, in their defense, had received no training or advice as to how to make this big adjustment. It was an upsetting year. Many teachers were frustrated and many students failed. The students became more unruly because they had been placed in a situation where they were almost guaranteed to fail. The teachers wanted new and different books and help with this new breed of sudents. The administration said that money was not available for new books or for in-service training. I sensed the frustration that permeated the school. It could have been avoided with more careful and compassionate pre-planning for this major change. I attempted to talk to Mr. T., but his attitude was that the students would need to adjust. Some of our best teachers planned to retire earlier than they had planned. They became disenchanted with how the entire problem was being handled and had little hope that it would get better.

I felt powerless. I was locked into a big, unbending bureacratic system which, if it changed at all, would change very slowly. So, when I was approached by the superintendent of the Mogadore schools to consider applying for the high school principalship, I listened.

I had been home-schooling the boy next door. He had very debilitating muscular dystrophy. He was confined to a wheel chair with no use of his legs and limited use of his arms. I had been asked to do this as a favor to his parents, our long-time neighbors. The school board approved my doing this and I went to his home every evening when I returned from school. I tutored him in all of the subjects necessary for his high school graduation. It was a rewardng experience. One of my proudest moments was when I was asked to push him in his wheelchair across the stage to receive his diploma. He died a few years later from complications of the dystrophy. His lungs had been comprised along with most internal organs.

So, I was known to the Mogadore Superintendent and the school board. I agreed to an interview with board, but withheld my actually applying until after the interview.

The interview went well. The five member school board asked some probing questions about my experience and my thoughts as to how I might adust to a small-town high school after working in a big city district. The board was composed of a good mixture of professional business men and some home-spun local men. I was impressed by their knowledge and sincerity. I guess that my answers pleased them as I was offered a two-year contract at just slightly above what I'd been making at Buchtel. I took into consideration that I would have no assistant principal, only one counselor and 700 students in grades seven through twelve. It was called Mogadore Junior - Senior High School. It would be a big responsibility with very little non-teaching assistance. I told them that I would give them an answer the next day. I wanted to talk to Joy and give the matter some deep thought.

The school board had promised that, barring any horrendous actions on my part, I would run the high school and they wouldn't interfere. The superintendent, Mr. Cordier, agreed. I would be given the freedom to turn the school into the area's best. I would receive four weeks paid vacation, a car allowance, a paid-up life insurance policy and a stipend annually for professional growth.

It was near the end of the school year and it was a busy time at Buchtel. I was involved with graduation plans for a class of 800. The logistics were staggering. We had a dress rehearsal scheduled for tomorrow and I had promised the Mogadore board an answer. That evening, Joy said that I should do what I really wanted to do and she would support whatever I decided. It was typical Joy.

The next day was hectic. The students were difficult to control during the rehearsal. The faculty sponsors for the senior class did little to help Mr. C. and me. At the moment that the class president opened his shirt and displayed body paint that said, "Screw Buchtel," I made my decision. I would accept the Mogadore job. I would be able to control most of my own destiny in a small school and the promise of the school board to let me do it.

At the end of graduation rehearsal, I returned to my office and composed my letter of resignation. I had enjoyed my time in The Akron Public Schools, but it was time to move on, to have my own school.

Before I left for the day, my secretary brought me a postcard that had arrived while I was at rehearsal. It was from Prince Washington, a black student who had had some academic and behavior problems while at Buchtel. We had several occasions on which to talk because he seemed to enjoy being chronically tardy to school in the morning. He told me with a smile that he just did it to be able to talk with me. The postcard was postmarked from Fort Benning, Georgia. I quote: "Dear Mr. Smith, how is school, or should I say how are you and the student body getting along? Well, here I am in the army. I just thought about school and how it seems whenever I think about school, I think about you (smile)."

Pvt. Prince Washington, Jr.

I had met a lot of students like Prince. They had had little attention from parents, especially their fathers. I realized that I'd miss the interaction with students such as Prince. Was I making a mistake? In later years, I learned that Prince had become an Akron police officer and had received citations for bravery and community service.

On the day of graduation, Buchtel's first black homecoming queen came up to me and gave me a quick little kiss on the cheek and said: "Thanks for being so nice."

When I had learned that I was to be assigned to Buchtel, I had had some apprehensions. I had never worked or associated with many African-Americans. While growing up, I had heard a lot of nasty racial comments about black people. My grandparents and parents made many of them. My high school classmates and teammates made them on a daily basis. People advised me not to go there as it would be dangerous.

I vowed to withhold judgment until I had my own experiences to call upon.

As I prepared to leave Buchtel, I had only good memories about the students and bad memories about my growth as an educator and the way things had been run. The students were, warm, aloof, funny, sad, emotional, stoic, excitable, smart, sly, dependable, undependable, physical, trusting, suspicious, lazy, ambitious and totally human. In other words, they were just like all other students regardless of race or family background.

Can you imagine that?

So, I left Buchtel and the Akron Public Schools with mixed emotions. I felt sad to leave those needy, sensitive and loving kids whose actions, sometimes, hid their softer sides. Their emotions were out there for all to see. If they liked you, they showed it. If they didn't, they showed that, too. I was privileged to have been part of their lives.

The following pictures show me at work from 1954 to 1984. They depict my change from a crew-cut wide-eyed boy to a somewhat jaded and aging man.

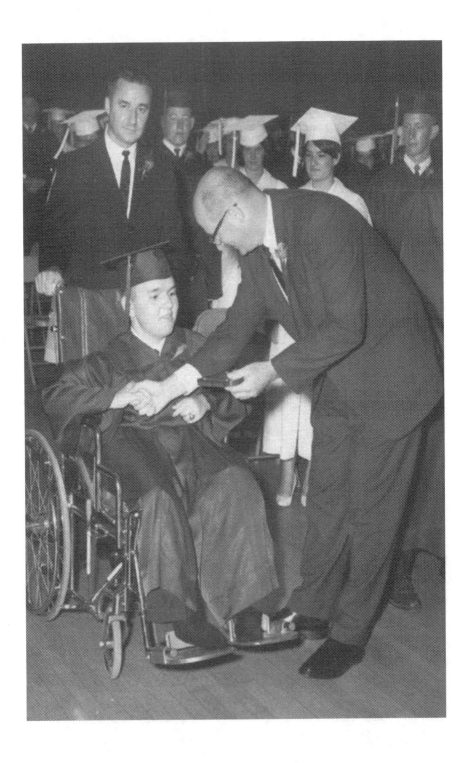

Part Ten

THE MOGADORE LOCAL SCHOOL DISTRICT

"Education is the single most important job of the human race."

George Lucas

A staff meeting was scheduled for the day before students were to return. Teachers and principals from both the elementary and high school were to attend. The superintendent led the meeting. Two school board members were in attendance to welcome the staff back for the beginning of another school year. I had stayed up late the night before preparing a few remarks that I'd give after being introduced. Yes, I was nervous. It was my first appearance as the new kid on the block.

After Mr. Cordier had made some opening remarks and the school board members wished us well, I was introduced with comments about my background and experience. I remember looking out at the eyes looking at me with veiled skepticism. I was young, had no experience as a full principal and had been chosen instead of one of the three high school faculty members who had applied. One of whom chose to resign in anger and disappointment.

I arose to speak. I heard my own voice say in an unnaturally high pitch, "My name is Don Smith and yours is not." Well, I thought that it was funny, but no one laughed. In hindsight, it was not a good idea to start with lame humor. The board members shifted uncomfortably in their chairs and Mr. C. rolled his eyes. One blonde middle-aged lady gave me a smile of encouragement. Later, she introduced herself as Miss Read, the guidance counselor. I forged on with some general comments as to how much I anticipated working with all of them and how I'd heard so many good things about the Mogadore Schools. I told them that working here would seem like coming home. After all, I'd lived here for the last eight years. I didn't mention that I still felt like an outsider.

Mogadore, like Ellet, is a close-knit community of, mostly, long-time residents. It's history dates back to the early 1800's when it was part of the Western Reserve land grant. It was called Bradleyville when it was first settled. It was named for Ariel Bradly, who, as a young boy, had scouted for the colonials against England. It was renamed Mogadore after a Mid-Eastern town of the same name. In Civil War days, Mogadore was a station on the underground railroad which enabled slaves to escape to Canada. Its history includes having been a hotbed of KKK activity and one of their Imperial Grand Dragons once lived here.

The residents were proud of their town and its heritage. It had a mayor, village council and its own police and fire departments. For the most part, the homes and lawns were well-maintained with very few vacant lots and homes. The annual wage of the families was close to the national norm. The educational level of its citizens was close to the national norm. In summation, it was a very typical, very normal suburban village.

I told the assembled teachers and administrators that I would like to raise the high school above its average standing on the standardized test scores. I would like to see more of its graduates go on to college or technical trade schools. As I looked into the eyes of the audience, I saw a kind of collective look that said to me: "Yeah, right! Good luck with that."

I spoke of one more thing that had bothered me a lot. During the past football season, Mogadore had had a game televised over local television. It was a big deal. A first. To the shame of the team and its fans, it was a debacle. Mogadore was penalized for over 200 yards. Many of the penalties were for unsportsmanlike conduct, fighting, cursing, taunting and other egregious actions. To top it off, one Mogadore adult fan had run onto the field and punched one of the officials. It was televised all over the greater Akron area. As a result, Mogadore was placed on probation by the Ohio Athletic Association.

I would be inheriting this problem and this mind-set that seemed to permeate our players, coaches and fans. I vowed to the audience that things would change. Not many of those who attended that meeting thought that it would happen.

After the general meeting of all staff members, each building principal was to have a meeting with his own staff. I had been introduced to Mr. Adams just prior to the first meeting. He had been at Somers Elementary for a few years before I arrived. He was friendly, affable and volunteered his help and advice if I were to need it. As it came to pass, I did on several occasions.

Between meetings, the staff was furnished with a picnic-style lunch by the combined PTA groups. I sat with my fellow administrators and the two school board members. I don't remember what we ate, but I do remember my queasy stomach. I was nervous about the up-coming high school staff meeting. I realized how important it was that I make a good first impression. I had sensed a kind of aura of negativity coming from the high school teachers when I was introduced earlier. I understood its origin. Some of their own had been by-passed in favor of a young man who had had only big-city experience. They knew from their own experiences how different working in a small town could be. The teachers, the students, the parents and the townspeople were all woven together very closely. New people were looked at often with suspicion before they could earn their right to be considered one of them. My first job would be to win the opportunity to prove myself worthy of being considered for inclusion.

I stood before the assembled high school staff without notes and without the use of the provided lecturn. I paused a moment and looked out at the blurred sea of faces. I spotted the one smiling face that had given me courage when I had been introduced. Miss R. gave me a slight wink and nodded her head. I will always remember the kindness she showed me, not only on that first day, but in the many days that we worked together before my retirement.

I took a deep breath and began the first of many MHS teachers' meetings. My challenge was to highlight some of the things that I would like to either change or introduce. It was risky business. It would alienate the staff if I criticized either them or the last principal. I didn't want to suggest that they hadn't been doing a good job, but, from what I had observed, read about, been told about and sensed, I knew that I had been hired to correct some of the obvious faults and shortcomings. The school board and the superintendent had said as much.

I would move slowly. I would involve the staff, the students and the community. They needed to buy into those planned changes or they would fall flat. And, so would I. So, at my first meeting with the staff, I dealt in generalities, not specifics. Suggesting specific changes would come later after I'd learned more about the teachers, students and support staff. I was very well aware of the importance of secretaries, custodians, bus drivers and kitchen staff. We needed to form a more cohesive group that would all work towards common goals.

Speaking of secretaries. I had been introduced to Ruth, my secretary, just before the morning meeting. She was a middle-aged little bundle of nervous energy. Mr. C. said that she had been there a long time and had served two previous principals. She knew all of the students and most of the parents. He said that if I wanted something to get done, Ruth was the one to do it.

She greeted me warmly and said if I needed anything, just ask her. Just then, a parent came into the office and asked if her daughter could change her English class from the last period of the day to an earlier class of the same subject. She had a job and wanted to leave school early. Without hesitation, Ruth told the parent that she would take care of it before tomorrow's school opening. I was taken aback. Normally, this type of change would need to be approved by the counselor or principal. Mr. C. didn't bat an eye at this obvious breach of protocol. I said to my self: "Self, this needs to be addressed very soon. I hope that it doesn't start a turf war." To prevent suspense, I'll just tell you that it did.

The meeting went smoothly, mostly because I dealt in banalities and generalities. Ruth had prepared the necessary forms and lists that the teachers would need to open school. After I had finished my remarks, I dismissed the teachers to go to their rooms to prepare for tomorrow. It was a full day of work for them. I noticed that the office did not contain a sign in or sign out chart. I asked Ruth for the beginning and ending times of the teachers' work day. She told me that they are just to arrive in time for their first class and can leave just after their last class. Well, I'd see about that. Later.

That night at home, I stayed up late making a list of the things that I'd look for during the first few days of school. I ended up with "Everything."

I arrived very early the next morning. Only the custodians were there. The high school head custodian, Paul, was in the hall outside of my office. He didn't speak until I had said "Good morning." Then, it was just a raspy grunt. He had been within earshot when Mr. C. and I had toured the building and had heard me say that the floors and lockers looked dirty. I knew that the custodial staff had all summer to make the buildings shine. I said "Buildings" because the junior-senior high school occupied two separate buildings about ten yards apart. Students had to walk outside in inclement weather when they had classes in the two different buildings. It wasn't the best of situations.

I entered my office. I had taken pains to make it look inviting to students, teachers and parents. The overhead lights were turned off and the only light was the lamp on my desk. The draperies were closed to keep out the harsh sunlight. I had brought some paintings for the walls and some memorbilia from my family's summer vacations to place on my desk and the two tables.

I had prepared some comments for the morning public address announcements. I planned to make daily annoucements of coming events and things of importance to the staff and student body. Later, I would begin to use the student announcers. It would be a good experience for them.

I had found some chimes in the storage room to begin the announcements. I wanted to standardize a lot of things so that everyone would know what to exect. I took a packet of green note paper from my coat pocket. The school's colors were green and white. I planned to always write notes to staff members on the green note paper so that they would know that that note in their mailboxes would be important.

I looked up and down the empty hallways. I felt a sense of pride. This will be my school. I will put my stamp on it. I will spend as much time as necessary to make it a place in which we can all take pride.

The first thing that I planned to do was to improve its appearance. A school that has pride will not have trash on the floors or graffiti on the lockers and walls. I vowed to set an example. I will tell Paul that he and his crew had to sweep the hallways mid-morning and just after the lunch periods are over. I will assign teachers to supervise the restrooms during the class change times. I wanted my first changes to be obvious and easy to notice. I wanted to let everyone know that a new sheriff was in town. I will set an example by picking up any trash that I see on the floor. I want the pupils and teachers to see me doing it. Maybe, they will take the hint and start doing it themselves.

It was 7:30. Ruth came in with a cheery "Good morning!" I decided to wait a few days before I approached her about what I felt that her duties entailed. And, more importantly, what they did not. A secretary can make or break you. She appeared to be someone to handle with care. She had earned that courtesy. The teachers began to straggle in. Some arrived only a very few minutes before the tardy bell would ring. I felt strongly that all teachers should be in their classrooms at least fifteen minutes before classes began. Students should have the opportunity to talk with them before school. I felt the same way about the end of the day. Teachers should stay at least fifteen minutes after school ended so that students could talk to them. I would address those problems and the sign-in, sign-out chart a little later.

I stood outside of my office door and watched the students come by on their way to home room. That was another issue that I intended to tackle. I planned to extend the first period by five minutes so as to include public address announcements and eliminate home room periods.

My experience in the four Akron City schools had convinced me that study halls were, largely, a waste of both students' and teacher's times. Starting the next school year, I planned to lengthen the class periods to one hour instead of the current 45 minutes. It would allow teachers to teach a lesson, give an assignment and give time at the end for students to begin the assignment with the teacher there to answer questions and elaborate on what they had assigned. I would eliminate the study hall periods on a trial basis.

I had, even, toyed with the idea of eliminating the bells. I had alway been annoyed by the bell ringing to end a class and the students getting up and leaving instead of my dismissing the class. What if no bells rang and the teachers dismissed them when the period ended? Of course, all of the teachers' watches and the classroom clocks would need to be carefully synchronized. It might be worth trying.

I had been told by the school board and the superintendent that it was my school to run as I saw fit unless my actions caused serious problems or upheavals. I'd like to think that they meant it.

The students filed by. Some smiled and said "Hello." Others whispered to each other about the new principal. Some didn't notice me. A few gave me a look that they hoped would indicate to me that I didn't scare them.

Some teachers came into the office to check their mailboxes. Most, apparently, went directly to their classrooms. I hoped that they all had gotten to school on time. I wouldn't know. A few stopped to wish me good luck.

I hadn't told them that I planned to visit all of them in their classrooms very soon. Mr. C. had revealed that teacher evaluations had been few and far between during the past few years. I would add that to my list of corrections and changes. My mind had been racing about what I planned to do. Maybe, I should bide my time and let things come to me instead of being so pro-active. But, that wasn't my style.

The tardy bell rang. I saw a few students running across the parking lot and entering the school's side door. They, apparently, went directly to their home room. Later, I would inisist that tardy students report to the office before going to their classes. In that way, we would know who and how many were tardy each day. Maybe, I was just being a stickler for rules. But, I just wanted conformity and for every one to be treated equally. I had heard that some teachers had not been marking students tardy while others did.

I went into my office and prepared for my first public address announcements. The items were just routine, mundane items. But, I began by saying: "Good morning! Here are your news and announcements for today, Tuesday, September 4, 1966." This beginning would be repeated daily for the next eighteen years. This would always be preceeded by the NBC chimes. I wanted my actions, mannerisms and peculiar quirks to be predictable, something that students and staff could count upon. For better or worse, I determined to be dependable. In the mercurial world of teenagers, they and the things around them change rapidly and without obvious patterns. I wanted to be a small beacon of stability in a world that, often, defies attempts to make it stable.

That first day went by without any incidents that stayed in my memory. I do remember going home about five thirty feeling exhausted. It wasn't from physical effort. I had spent most it standing outside my office watching students go by during passing times and sitting in my office organizing my thoughts for next Tuesday's teachers' meeting. A few teachers had asked if we would have a meeting so soon because we had just had one yesterday. I smiled and said that a lot of things needed to be discussed.

I awoke several times during the night. Each time that I awoke, my mind was on things that I wanted to do. Some things required immediate attention and some things I would introduce in measured amounts over an extended period of time. My goal would be to ladle out the changes in small doses in order to lesson the shock value. I knew from past experience that too much change coming too quickly can be a turn-off rather than a harbinger of better things to come. Human nature tends to resist change unless that change is seen clearly as making things better. I planned to involve students, teachers and parents in the development and implementation of many of my proposed changes. I wanted them to take ownership of those proposals so that they felt that they had played an important role in making them come about. A few changes, due to immediate need, would be by executive order.

I sensed that the faculty had a built-in aversion to accepting new ideas. Many of them had been at Mogadore High School for a long time and had become enamored with the status quo because of their length of service, tenure, union loyalty and a "We've always done it this way" attitude. I would need to be careful not to offend individuals or the reputation of the school itself. I realized that by recommending changes, I would be criticizing what they had accomplished over the past many years. I would take every opportunity to praise the many good things about the school, its teachers and its students. But, at the same time, I recognized that, in several areas, the high school had fallen below acceptable state and national standards. Painful or not, some things would be changed, added or eliminated.

Yes, I did consider myself to be an agent of change. But, more importantly, I considered my self to be an enabler. An enabler of students and of teachers. My job would be to provide a safe, clean environment in which students could reach their maximum potentials. My job would be, also, to provide teachers with the tools and environment that would enable them to teach with maxium effectiveness. If I could provide all of that, then, I would be an effective principal. Any changes that I would propose would be to enable all of us, students and staff alike, to be the best that we could be. Changes for any other reasons, would be doomed to failure.

One other problem had caused my fitful night of tossing and turning. Last night, just before we said goodnight to our daughter and son, Kathy and Mike, they had voiced some concerns about my being a principal at Mogadore. They had been thinking about it and were concerned that their friends would tease them or make fun of them because they were the principal's kids.

It was a valid concern. Kathy was in the eighth grade in my building and Mike had entered the fifth grade at Somers' Elementary. At a point in the future, they both would be in the junior - senior high school building with me as their principal. I had wondered how they would handle the possible teasing, taunting and bullying. They were of two very different personalities. Kathy was rather shy and sensitive. She was a good student and wise beyond her years. She would take her peers' teasing very seriously. Mike, one the other hand, was outgoing and boisterous. He would either ignore the comments or join in on the fun. I knew it would be difficult for them irregardless of how they handled it. It was something else for me to worry about.

The alarm clock sounded at six a.m. I wanted to be at school by 7:15. I ate a hurried bowl of oatmeal and gulped down a cup of coffee. I took a quick shower and said goodby to Joy and the kids. Day two had arrived. I planned to talk to Ruth about her duties and have the teachers' meeting during the lunch period. Several teachers had questionned the need for one so soon after the meeting we'd had last Friday. But, it was Tuesday and that was the day for my weekly teachers' meetings. I had made a concession to have them at lunch time instead of their usual after school time. I hope that they had remembered to bring a lunch today instead of eating in the cafeteria.

I drove the two blocks to school instead of walking through the backyards. It seemed more professional.

I greeted Paul, the head custodian as he walked by when I was getting out of my car. He was still angry with me about saying that the buldings were dirty and not maintained well. Soon, I would need to have a conference with him. He returned my "Good morning" with his trade-mark grunt. Heavy lies the crown.

I took my position in the hallway just outside the office door. I wanted to establish the habit of saying good morning to the students and staff when they arrived each morning. I, also, wanted to make certain that the teachers would sign in before going to their classrooms. The ones who taught in the separate annex building had been accustomed to just going directly to their classrooms. They had grumbled the most about this new policy. Later, after I'd grown certain that teachers were arriving fifteen minutes before the first period began, I'd consider not requiring morning sign-ins. My new policy of having teachers sign out in the office before leaving at the end of the school day had met with similar grunts of disapproval. I felt strongly that teachers shouldn't rush to leave immediately following the end of the last period. Students should have access to them for questions and concerns.

After I made the morning announcements, I closed my office door and requested that Ruth fend off any visitors or phone calls for the next thirty minutes. Little did she know that I was preparing my remarks for my meeting with her that would follow my alone time. This meeting would be touchy. Ruth had become an institution and was considered to be the voice of the high school. Principals had come and gone, but Ruth had remained. She was good at her job. She was personable and well-liked. But, only one person could be in charge. And, that would be me.

When the early morning rush had subsided, I asked Ruth to come into my office. She appeared with notebook in hand expecting to take dictation. I told her to sit down and that I wanted to talk to her. She looked at me with a hint of suspicion. I began by telling her how many good things I'd heard about her work and her devotion to the school and its students. Her face softened and she said that she loved her work, the students and the staff.

I told her that I was surprised on my first day here when I heard her agreeing to change a student's schedule and grant that student an early realease. I told her that it should be the duty of the counselor to change a schedule and an early release needed to approved by me. Ruth looked surprised. She said that the former principal had not objected to her making those kind of decisions. I smiled and said, "Ruth, you're working for me now and I do object. I value and appreciate your abilities and experience, but I am in charge now and I want you to understand what I expect so that we have no misunderstandings in the future. I know it's difficult to adjust to new bosses and new policies, but this is what I expect." She looked at me for a few seconds and said, "Yes, sir. Is that all? I should get back to work and do the day's absentee list." I told her that she could go back to work. When, she left, I had to wonder if it really were all finished. I hoped that we wouldn't have a power struggle I knew, already, that other power struggles were on the horizon.

FACING THE PROBLEMS

"This is how it is today: The teachers are afraid of the principal. The principals are afraid of the superintendents. The superintendents are afraid of the boards of education. The boards are afraid of the parents. The parents are afraid of the children. The children are afraid of nothing."

Milton Berle

The superintendent had warned me that a group of parents would be coming to the next school board meeting to object to a pregnant student and the father to-be being permitted to remain in school and, worst of all, being permitted to take part in school activities. He told me that some of the board members agreed with the parents. He wanted me to attend the meeting and explain my position on this very sensitive topic. The current policy stated that the pregnant student be placed on home instruction and that the young man be barred from taking part in any extra-curricular activities.

I wanted to meet with the two students before I made any statement about what I felt should be done.

I had been informed that the school's dress code was under fire, also. Another group of parents had said that they would address the board about what they condidered to be a too lenient dress code. They wanted it to be stricter and to be enforced more evenly. I had been asked to come up with what I considered to be a better code.

Those two big issues along with enforcing some new faculty rules and making peace with the custodial staff would make my first several weeks interesting if not entertaining.

At the staff meeting today at noon, I planned to introduce my policy of having each teacher submit lesson plans for the following week before leaving school each Friday. I knew, from my past experience, that if a substitute were needed, most teachers leave no plans for them to follow. By submitting weekly plans, there would be guidelines for the substitutes and no instructional time would be lost. I knew that this plan would meet with both vocal and quiet resistance. I was so correct.

I hadn't wanted to move too fast with new policies or changes to old ones, but I sensed that some things should be changed quickly, resistance or not. I left my office and walked by Ruth's desk. She didn't look up or acknowledge me. I knew that I had hurt her feelings, but better now than later in the year. I had to establish quickly that I was in charge. It wasn't that I wanted all of the power, I just wanted to correct an obvious fault and do what I knew to be proper. I had disliked the way things had been run at Buchtel. I wanted to avoid making those same mistakes. I hoped that I could make the changes that I felt were necessary without alienating people and hurting feelings. Sometimes, that isn't possible. Status quo is a powerful enemy. It's not overthrown easily.

At noon time, I faced a sea of faces that featured mouths chewing the food from their sack lunches. This was a new thing for the teachers. Instead of after-school meetings, I wanted to try lunch time meetings. I wanted to give them a break from staying past school hours as a peace offering for having weekly instead of monthly meetings. Several had already complained about ruining their lunch time. Some had complained about ruining their smoking time as I had said I didn't want smoking in the classroom where the meetings would be held. I told them that I'd try to leave five minutes in the alloted time for lunch so that they could go to the teachers' lounge for a quick smoke. It seemed that more Mogadore teachers smoked than did the teachers I'd worked with in Akron. I was curious about that and planned to try to try to find out why this was the case.

The bell rang for the start of the lunch period. I noted that some teachers had not arrived. I waited a few minutes before I announced that I expected all them to arrive on time. That was met by an icy silence. One by one, four stragglers appeared. I told each of them that I wanted them to be on time as we had a lot of business to cover. Again, silence.

So, the meeting began on a somewhat negative note. I had written an agenda and passed out copies to each teacher. I gave them a few minutes to familiarize themselves with the topics that we would discuss. Later, I learned to put the agendas in the teachers' mail boxes the mornings of the meeting days to give them time to digest them.

I began with my reasons for having them sign in each morning and sign out each evening. Most of them just gave me blank expressions, but Jim spoke up and said: "We are not students, we are professionals. We should be trusted to arrive on time and not leave too early." Heads nodded in agreement. I replied: "That's a good point, Jim. But, I want to see if my policy of arriving at least fifteen minutes early and staying at least fifteen minutes after the last bell is being followed. It's all for giving the students access to each of you for questions, comments and concerns. I have been told that in past years, some of you arrive just in time for the opening bell and race out when the last bell rings. And, if you have a last period preparation period, you leave during that period. If, after a trial period, you are following the new policy, I might eliminate the signing in and signing out."

A few heads nodded in silent agreement, but most just continued chewing their food.

The next topic on the agenda was the matter of lesson plans. I had been told that there never had been any plan to require that teachers make them and, if they did, they were only seen by the maker of the plan. My concern was two-fold. One concern was that substitutes would have some idea of what and how to teach. The other concern was that by making lesson plans, it forces the teacher to actually plan ahead and would provide a written history of what the teacher had been doing and what he planned to do. I told them that they should submit their written plans to me before leaving each Friday. After all, they were given daily preparation periods to do planning and preparation. It wasn't given for smoking in the lounge. These comments were met with some muttering among themselves and some raised hands. I nodded to Jack who spoke up saying: "I just leave a one-page list of things a sub can do such as silent reading, do homework for other subjects, or have a spelling contest."

I asked if it wouldn't be better if the sub could continue with the work you've doing and move ahead as you had planned? Jerry said: "Those subs don't really teach, they just try to keep order." "That's my point," I countered. "Wouldn't it be great if the subs were given something so that they could actually teach."

The same few heads nooded in agreement. I needed to know the names of those people who agree with me. I needed to cultivate support. I knew that I'd need it in the coming days.

While I was talking, I noticed two male teachers exchanging glances and making some quiet comments to each other. They smiled a lot and it was obvious that they were suppressing laughter. I looked at them and held my gaze for a few long seconds. They smiled at me and, once again, exchanged knowing glances. I thought to myself that they would require my watching them closely. Later, I found out that they were social studies teachers and Mogadore's version of Abbot and Costello.

Much later, I came to know Fred and Denny as two of the high school's very best teachers.

The third item was the need for faculty supervision during passing times. I wanted all teachers to stand by their doors to help with supervision. Most problems in a school occur during those hectic times. I wanted a man and a woman on each floor to supervise inside the restrooms during those passing times. And, I meant "inside," not outside. I wanted students to know that there were faculty members on duty. Mr. C. had told me that smoking had been common at the high school, especially in the restrooms. Smoking by students was against school board policy and I was a strong supporter of not smoking because of health reasons. I would reserve comments about the smoke from the teachers' lounge permeating the building for another time. This third item caused even more mumbling and rumbling than the first two items. I told them that I would accept volunteers for the restroom supervision, but would assign teachers if I received none. I would rotate the assignments over the six grading periods so that all would share equally. I said that I could not supervise everthing and everyone by myself. I needed their help and I expected it. Jim asked for recognition. He stood up, faced the group and said: "As union president, I'm not certain that requiring us to do this type of supervision is in violation of union rules. I will bring it to the attention of our union leaders."

I told Jim that that was fine, but that the superintendent and board members had given thier approval to assign teachers those duties and I expected you to do them. If I am informed otherwise, I'll comply with whatever I'm told.

I stood in front of them and paused while looking out over the assembled group. They were good teachers and good people. I didn't want to alienate them. The things that I'd suggested had been for the good of the school. It wasn't my personal power trip.

I spoke slowly, "Some of the things I've outlined for you may seem like extra work and some of it might seem unbecoming to a professional person. But, we are in this together. I don't expect you to do anything that I don't expect for myself. I will arrive early and stay late. I will plan my work dilligently and with an eye for the future. I will help to supervise during each passing period and while you are in class. I will take my part in the rotation of restroom supervision. But, I need all of you to take ownership of the idea that all of us share in helping to make this a school in which we can all take pride. I've been a teacher. Yes, teaching was my main job, but I shared in other things that were necessary to do in order to make it a school that was safe, orderly and a place where substantive learning could take place. I expect nothing less from you. I hope that you understand my reasons for making these few changes. I promise that I won't make unnecessary rules or policies. I promise that I won't make knee-jerk decisions. I want the students to succeed and I want you to succeed. My success, if any, is a very secondary motivation. I ask for your cooperation. If what I've asked you to do turns out to be either illegal or wrong, I'll reverse my position without hesitation."

I paused again. I looked at the audience. The group had stopped chewing and looked at me. I hoped that they liked what they saw. Sensing that enough had transpired for this meeting, I dismissed the teachers with a wish for a good afternoon. I had planned to bring up a few more topics, but I knew it was time to quit. There would be many more Tuesday's.

After the meeting, I went back to my office. I asked Ruth for last year's school yearbook. I wanted to be able to recognize and call by name the thirty-two members of the teaching staff, the six members of the cafeteria staff, the three custodians and the two bus drivers. I looked at their pictures and hoped to be able to link names to thoses faces when I met them in and around the school.

The teaching staff was a good mixture of young and old, experienced and inexperienced. Mr. C. had given me a general idea of some their strengths and weaknesses. I asked Ruth for the confidential evaluations that had been made over the past years for each teacher. To my surprise, not many were available. It appeared that the previous principals had not made many classroom observations or had entered any sort of evaluation into their folders. It was a school board policy and a state mandate that principals make classroom visits on a regular basis to each teacher to ascertain the quality of their work. Most teachers had less than one such evaluation per year and some had none. To make it worse, the evaluations that were on file were very generic and contained very few specific comments about strengths or weaknesses. Maybe, the shortage of past records was a good thing. It would mean that I would be making evaluations based upon just my own assessments and have little background information to influence my judgments.

I looked at the faces and tried to read into their souls. I knew that all of them had entered the teaching profession wanting to make a difference in the lives of their students. I hoped that they had had the satisfaction of knowing that they had done so. I knew, also, that life often gets in the way of realizing one's dreams. If they had fallen short because of their own inadequacies, had they dried up and become bitter and cynical? Had they realized that not all students really want to learn? Had they suffered indignities from parents and their superiors? Had they lost the spark that they once had had? Were they just treading water until they could retire? Or, did each new day present a fresh and exciting challenge? Did they look forward with anticipation to each class and to each student? I would learn these things soon enough. I hope that

I'd find that the majority of the teachers came to school each day with open minds and open hearts. I hoped that the majority could say, in honesty, "I love to teach."

The support staff would be more difficult to read and assess. I would not be able to have the same bond with them as I hoped to have with the teaching staff. It would be another case of "Town vs. Gown." I would be their boss, but I would need to work hard to earn their trust because of our presumed differences. I would be considered to be someone who had never done a decent day's work in his entire life. I would be that prissy, over-educated guy who hadn't a lick of common sense. The worst part of that was that it just might have been true.

Looking at the pictures helped me to match names and faces, but the in-depth knowledge of each them would come only from working with them on a day-to-day basis.

I closed the book and went out into the main office. I told Ruth that I would keep the yearbook in my office to refer to as needed. She didn't look up, but said: "Yes, sir." This silent treatment had to stop. If anything can ruin a principal's working life, it would be a poor relationship with his secretary. I asked Ruth to come into my office and told her that we needed to talk.

I said, "Ruth, I value you and I value the work that you do. If I offended you earlier, I, certainly, didn't mean to. I just wanted to let you know, that administrative decisions are to be made only by administrators. I'm new here. I will ask you for your advice and opinion frequently. You know more about this school and this town than I do. I need your help. But, I don't have the same attitudes and policies as did the previous principals. There can be only one principal. If that upsets you, I'm sorry. We need to be able to work together. I don't want to spend my time here with my secretary giving me the silent treatment. And, I won't. If you'd rather work for someone else, so be it. I don't plan to leave. Can we make this work?"

After a long silence, Ruth looked up and gave me a half-smile. Well, I thought, a half-smile is better than the blank stares that I had been getting. I stood up as a sign of dismissal. As she turned to leave, I saw that her eyes were moist. As she left the room, I heard a faint, "Thank you."

I remember a lot about this incident because Ruth became, over the eighteen years that I worked with her, not only a competent and loyal secretary, but a trusted friend who assisted me in many ways. Well, there was the time that I banned her from attending our home basketball games because of her abusive language towards the officials. But, that was just her way of showing school spirit.

During my first two years at Mogadore, I continued to be an evening college counselor at Akron University. I worked three evenings each week from seven until ten. Those were long days, but we needed the extra income. During my third year at Mogadore, I began to teach evening college classes. I taught creative writing in the English Department and education courses in the Education Department. I taught three evenings each week during the school year and five days each week during the summers. I continued teaching at the university until my retirement from public education in 1984. After I retired, I continued teaching and supervising student teachers throughout a three-county area for the next two years.

The next school board meeting was coming soon. Mr. C. reminded me that many parents were expected to attend to complain about the pregnant girl and the young man. I needed to organize my thoughts for my presentation. This could prove to be a very volatile meeting with feelings running high. My arguments would need to be persuasive and based upon common sense and logic. Mogadore was a conservative community with small-town values. I would not win the hearts and minds of its citizens with if my approach to this problem if I didn't make my appeal based upon those values.

I had heard already from a number of people who felt that having a pregnant girl attending school would be showing that the school district not only condoned promiscuity, but flaunted it. And, wasn't that boy just as guilty? The attitude of those from whom I'd heard seemed to be: "Kick them both out. They are a bad influence on our naive and innocent students."

The days before the school board meeting flowed by smoothly with one glaring exception. During the noon-time lunch period, I was standing in the main lobby talking to the police chief who had stopped in to say hello. Out of the corner of my eye, I caught a glimpse of a boy chasing another boy in the parking lot. They were running at full speed toward the plate glass door which led into the lobby. The boy who was in pursuit gave the other boy a big shove and the boy came through the glass door causing a shower of broken glass that fell on the chief and me. Momentum carried the boy who did the shoving into the lobby and into me. Instinctively, I reached out and slapped the boy very hard across his cheek. He looked at me with big eyes and ran back out onto the parking lot and disappeared down the street. The chief looked at me and sighed. "Well, I'm sure glad I stopped in today. I imagine that we'll be hearing from Bob's mother. I know her and she's a hand-full."

We checked out the boy who had been shoved. He had only a few minor scratches from the broken glass.

I did hear from the boy's mother and, also, from his father. They appeared before the school board at the next meeting to complain about my brutality. Fortunately, the superintendent and board members backed me and my reflexive action. The blame was found to be with the chaser and shover. That hearing was held in executive session prior to the big public meeting about the pregnant girl and the baby's father. Talk about double headers! I had serious doubts before those meetings about my career in Mogadore.

I looked out of the window of the classroom where tonight's meeting was to be held. The administration office was too small for the expected crowd. The parking lot was beginning to fill up. Most of the seats in the classroom were already occupied. The board members and superintendent went into a huddle and decided to switch the meeting to the gymnasium. The night custodian was summoned to begin setting up chairs.

I hoped that the meeting wouldn't turn into a raucous circus atmosphere. I hoped that tight rules would be enforced to limit speaking times and that speakers would be required to state their names and to be respectful to each other. Prior to the meeting, community feelings had been running high. Both sides of the issue had been promoted and expressed in the bars, restaurants and private homes throughout the town. I had not expected such polarization of viewpoints. I hoped that people, irregardless of how they felt about the issue, would recognize that the important thing was the future of the two young people who were involved. Hope. As Emily Dickenson said in one of her poems, "Hope is the thing with feathers." Hope has little substance. Actions have permanence and value. I hoped that tonight's meeting would result in actions that would benefit those two young people who had become the focal point of so many strong feelings. I felt strongly that they needed an advocate if they were to going to be able to have happy and productive lives. I would be that advocate.

The school board president called the meeting to order. It was a special meeting for the express purpose of discussing the issue of permitting pregnant and/or married students to remain in school and to be able to participate fully in the school's activities. He spelled out the ground rules for people who wished to speak. Each speaker would be given five minutes and the use of profanity and personal or degrading comments would terminate a speaker's time. Each speaker must identify himself by name and address.

The president explained the current board policy in regard to the issues being discussed. While he spoke, I replayed in my mind the meeting I'd had with the two involved students. I had sent for them to come to my office a few days before tonight's meeting. They were ushered into my office by Ruth who introduced them to me. They looked at me shyly and were obviously embarrassed to meet me. After they'd taken their seats, I told them that I wanted to meet them personally and reassure them that I felt that they should be in school and be able to take part in any activities that they chose. I warned them that they had a lot of critics in the village and that they would hear a lot of hurtful comments from both parents and students. The students who would be critical were those whom had been brain-washed by their parents.

I promised to help them through their remaining time at Mogadore High School in any way that I could. I told them that at the school board meeting I would support them one hundred per cent in their efforts to remain in school and to retain their status as full-fledged students. I applauded their committment to each other and to their stated goals of graduating and, possibly, going on to college. Both had been involved in several school activities, including sports. I told them that I hoped that the school board would revise its policy that prohibited students in their circumstances from participating in those activities.

They both seemed very mature and goal-oriented. They thanked me politely and seemed to feel reassured that I would support them. As for me, I felt very good about helping these two fine young people. Maybe, in the eyes of society, they had made a foolish mistake, but shouldn't a school do everthing in its power to help them through this situation? It's at times like this, that young people need help and support, not punishment and admonitions.

The school board president, Mr. Fry, had set up the meeting at the request of the board's vice president, Mr. Carpenter. The president opened the meeting by explaining the current board policy. He told the audience that board policy permits married students to attend classes but are barred from participating in sports or other extracurricular activities. Each case would be judged on its individual merit by the high school principal.

Mr. Carpenter interjected that he would like to see the policy "Firmed up." He pointed out that a recent court action had upheld an Ohio school board that had barred a student from playing on the high school basketball team. He went to say that this is not just a Mogadore problem. It's happening all over. It's a sign of moral decay and it's undermining our whole society. He stated: "Something has got to be done about it. It leads to disrespect for authority on all levels."

Board member Tompkins disagreed. He said that this kind of punishment solves nothing. It comes too late. It's after the mistake has been made. " I think our policy should try to help these kids to become better citizens."

One teacher arose to say: "This is a parental problem. They aren't getting pregnant in the school halls. It happens away from school while under the supervision of their parents."

Mr. Tompkins cited a court opinion which prevented school boards from barring married or pregnant students from taking part in extracurricular acivities. The opinion did state that unmarried pregnant students could be barred.

Tom Murphy, a teacher, half-time counselor and coach who had just been approved to be my assistant principal, arose to ask: "Are textbooks and the classroom all that education means here in Mogadore? Doesn't education also encompass sports and social activities? If not, why does the school sponsor and fund them? Allowing a student to use his God-given abilities can help him."

Superintendent Jack Cordier responded that the State of Ohio requires that all school systems provide a program of extracurricular activities.

Bill Evans, teacher and coach, said: "I don't know the answer, but I can't see punishment for getting married."

Earl Davis, parent, said: "Every place you there is sex - in books, movies, television, everywhere. We are going to have to help the students. Why just punish them?"

Ken Wolfe, teacher, said: "We speak about protecting the 99 percent and helping the one percent. The 99 are safe and the one percent needs our constant care."

Brad Carleton, teacher, spoke up: "Morality is based on the Christian faith. By punishment, you might be denying getting scholarships and graduation."

Mr. Fry asked me to speak as I would be the one to enforce the board's policy. I stood up and looked around the room. Some were smiling. Some were frowning. It was to be expected.

I defended the current so-called flexible policy that Mr. Carpenter said needed "Firming up." "In cases that have come before me in recent years, I've felt it to be in the best interests of the students to allow them to lead a normal school life which would include sports and other activities. They have made many worthwhile contributions to the school. More importantly, they have benefitted themselves. Instead of being punished and ostricized, they have been accepted. They have graduated and gone on to become responsible and productive citizens. I would like to think that we help all students, both those who are model citizens and those who fall short of that. I am pleased with the current policy which permits married and pregnant students to remain in school and to take part in the activities of their choice."

As I sat down after speaking, I heard some murmerings from the audience. One women stood up and said that she and several other parents objected to the current policy. She said that they objected on moral grounds. They felt that pregnant or married students had a detrimental effect on the other impressionable students. More pregnancies would result if these students remained in school. Several heads nodded in agreement and the murmering continued.

A man stood up and said that his daughter had seen the married couple hugging and kissing in the hallway between classes. In a louder voice, he said: "What kind of example does this set? You should be ashamed of yourself to allow this to happen!"

Mr. Fry asked if anyone else wished to speak. There were more murmerings, but no one asked to speak. He concluded the meeting by saying: "We thank you for attending and expressing your views. We wanted to hear what you are thinking. We feel that the public should have a say in the decisions that we make. We will vote on this at our next board meeting. We will decide whether or not to keep our present policy or change it to a new one."

At the next meeting, the board voted to retain the current policy. The vote was 4-1 with Mr. Carpenter dissenting.

Donald E. Smith, Ph.D.

I was relieved. My over-riding belief was that if there were any time that students needed help, guidance and normalcy, it was during times and situations like the ones being debated.

The things that stand out in my memory of those first days at Mogadore seem to involve problems. I prefer to think of them as situations that needed to be resolved.

Another situation involved complaints and concerns about the school's dress code or lack of same. A group of concerned parents had approached some of the board members about what they considered to be too much leniency in regard to students' dress and grooming. As it had with the married students' policy, their concern evolved into a group of the parents attending a board meeting and demanding that something be done about the perceived laxity. The board members, through the superintendent, empowered me to look into the situation and determine if changes were, in fact, needed.

My first step was to look closely at our present policy and determine if it were worded in such a way as to be fair to the students and strong enough to curb dress and grooming that would be detrimental to the process of learning and the image that we wanted our school to display to the community. Those two goals might just be mutually exclusive if not worded properly.

After reading the current policy carefully, I decided that changes needed to be made. In order to make those changes work, I would need students, parents, faculty and the school board to buy into them. There is no better way to do that than to involve all concerned parties in the decision-making process. I wanted everyone to feel that he had a voice in the procedure.

I believed firmly that we didn't need a lot of rules. I didn't want to have rules on the books that couldn't be enforced uniformly and fairly. Common sense and common decency should be the main criteria.

When school opened, I had informed parents via the school district newsletter of the few rules that had been enforced in the past . There

156

was no student handbook and no dress and grooming guidelines that were board-adopted. The building principals had been the sole judges of what was proper and improper. I wanted to firm this up by having clear guidelines adopted by the school board and given to all parents and students.

I met with the high school student council and told them to think of reasonable guidelines for a student dress code. I planned to have the council meet in an open forum along with the school board, teachers and parents at the earliest convenient time. Mr. Cordier and the board president concurred with this plan.

Out of this open meeting with a free flow of questions and answers, hopefully, would come some clear direction for this on-going problem. I asked for volunteers from among the student council members to model examples of inappropriate and appropriate dress and grooming styles. I had no shortage of volunteers. I could sense that the students appreciated being involved in the decision-making process.

I had strong faith that their innate common sense would prevail and not make a travesty of this procedure.

The combined meeting was held on September 22. A large crowd showed up. I wondered if a similar crowd would show up if the meeting concerned curriculum. I knew the answer. Dress and grooming was a touch-point. It involved the actual lives of the students and their parents. Yes, they were interested. I moderated the meeting along with the Student Council president, Keith Shiflett. He told the audience that the council members had recommended the following guidelines: girls would be allowed to wear slacks in cold weather, boys' hair could be shoulder length in back but not to cover the ears, boys could not wear just plain white tee shirts, skirt lengths should reflect common sense and decency.

He stated that more work would be done and, possibly, other guidelines would be recommended. I opened up the meeting to comments and questions from the audience. They had many of both. Following, are some of the ones that I wrote down: Dave George said: "We are here tonight as students to express our own tastes. But, as students, our main reason is to be here to learn."

Frank Housley said: "Our parents were told what to wear and how to wear them. Maybe, they lacked the backbone to defend themselves." His comment was met with a mixture of applause and groans.

Donna Fisher claimed that 95 percent of the girls would like to wear slacks to eliminate the boys' stares.

Shelly Yorgey was in favor of nice slacks, but not blue jeans.

Ken Holcomb responded to that by saying: "Boys would pay more attention to teachers if girls wore slacks." This drew laughter from the audience.

Teacher Marjorie Walt said that nurses and waitresses wore slacks and students should be permitted to wear them, too.

Sue Calentine said that it doesn't matter what you wear, you come to school to get an education. Loud applause was heard.

Jeanne Bauhart requested that the shirt tails of blouses be worn out during hot weather. Teacher Hugh Laughlin replied: "Shirt tails look sloppy. Only shirts designed to wear out should be permitted."

He went on further: "You cannot legislate a student dress code. The principal has to decide what is acceptable. A boy with long hair doesn't bother me, but it might influence my of opinion of him." I groaned inwardly.

Parent Mrs. Shiflett said that dress code should be up to the parents. If the school doesn't like a student's dress, they can take action.

Teacher Grace Fleming said: "I've noted the decline of student dress over the years. What we decide now will determine the dress code for this school in the future."

Teacher Jerry Reller added: "I would hate to be a student and have to carry around a list of rules. I think Principal Don Smith should set the rules and he should enforce them." Thanks a lot, Jerry.

Larry Wilkens, counselor, opined that this is a disagreement between the young and the old. If students are neat and clean and don't wear anything disruptive, they're okay with me.

Teacher Brad Carleton said that surveys show that the more neatly dressed a student is, the better he performs scholastically.

Parent, Mrs. Moore said: "I am impressed with the comments of these students. We had fads back in our day. We had peg pants, duck tail haircuts, and sweaters buttoned backwards. School officials disagreed and cracked down on us. I like this open discussion among all concerned parties."

Board member, Jack Clevenger, said: "Part of what you are saying is what I'm feeling. The comments from this meeting will help me to reach a decision when the Student Council's recommendations come before the school board."

I was pleased with the results of the meeting. At the next open meeting, we would have the style show with student models showing both the good and the bad. The Student Council Committee will hold additional meetings during school hours to complete their recommendations. Those will be presented to a special school board committee headed by Jack Clevenger. That committee will make a recommendation tp the five member school board. The wheels of change turn slowly. But, hopefully, the result will be a workable dress and grooming policy - one the students can live with and one that I can enforce with a good conscience. I've always disliked suspending students for how they look. I'd rather overlook.

Tonight's meeting showed me that students, even those who rarely speak up about anything, can get up before a large audience and express themselves adequately. It shows how meaningful issues can empower people. All teaching should be based upon that.

The next open meeting was held on December 1 in conjuction with the monthly P.T.A. meeting. Several students modeled acceptable and unacceptable examples of clothing, jeweley and facial hair. Among the presenters were, Mike Adams, Delese Wear, Cindy Ward and Vicky K'Meyer.

I told the audience that, in addition to developing a dress code, we were working on the writing of a student handbook. Students Deb Early, Alan Morckel, Deb Rosato, Mike Adams and Karen Caldwell were working with me. It was to be printed commercially in January and distributed to students. It will explain all school policies and rules including dress and grooming, student activities, attendance, grading and a description of subjects offered.

I told the group that, in order to have workable school rules, the students must have a part in developing them. Our pupose is to encourage self-government, thinking and responsibility.

The high school faculty favored the new guidlines and agreed to abide by them themselves.

Superintendent Jack Cordier complimented the students as being of high caliber. They have received compliments from state inspectors on their appearance and behavior. He attributed this to the guidance of their parents.

At a school board work session prior to the December 21 board meeting, board member Clevenger said that the dress and grooming guidelines presented by me were acceptable and should be approved at the board meeting. I told them that the guidelines might seem somewhat liberal, but that I was more concerned with attitude and behavior than I was with appearance.

Prior to developing the new guidelines, Mogadore High School had never had a formal policy. Decisions had been made by the building principal based upon his own personal viewpoints. I wanted to change this. And, I did.

During the next few weeks, other meetings were held with student council, the P.T.A. and at board work sessions. The O.W.E. teacher revealed that a senior boy had been suspended for having a beard. Four other students were sent home to change clothes for various violations. I continued to tell everyone that the school has no authority to dictate dress unless the clothing or grooming is harmful or obscene. Student Dale Arehart complained about teachers having beards if students are prevented from having them. Teacher Tom Haskins said that, in the future, we'll need to look at a dress code for teachers.

Jerry Butcher, the O.W. E. teacher, made a survey of Akron City and Portage County schools and revealed that most schools are open about hair, somewhat divided about beards and sandals and that most Akron schools have no dress code at all.

Teacher Vicki Falb said: "I'm not ready to say that students can function without guidelines at all."

And, so it goes.

At the regular board meeting, the recommended guidelines were approved after some lengthy and heated discussion. Mr. Carpenter said that they were far too lenient. The other members approved, but cautioned that if the policies led to too many problems, the matter would be reviewed again and some changes might be necessary. So, after several months and several meetings, the following guidelines were adopted by the school board:

1. Girls will be permitted to wear slacks. Shorts and bermudas will not be allowed.
2. Students will be permitted to wear sandals without socks. Other footwear will require socks.
3. Skirt length and dress length should reflect common sense and decency.
4. Tee-shirts, intended as underwear shall not be permitted to worn alone as a shirt or blouse.
5. Clothing with inflammatory or profane symbols, pictures or writing will not be permitted.

6. Sideburns and moustaches shall be permitted if neatly trimmed. Beards will not be permitted.
7. Hair should be neat and clean and boys' hair should not exceed the base of the collar.
8. In special program such as O.W.E., the program's coordinator shall have the right to regulate dress and grooming.
9. All situations not covered in these guidelines shall be judged and/or enforced by the administration of the school.

In summary, a student's dress and grooming should, not only, reflect his individual rights and tastes, but should, also, reflect pride in himself as a person and a member of the school, but, in addition, as a representative of our community.

These guidelines were to be printed in our new Student Handbook. Whew! It was a difficult and lengthy process, but it needed to be done.

Another on-going problem had to be corrected. Paul, the custodian and his intrepid band of henchman continued to resist my efforts to make the school more presentable. I had told him to sweep the hallways mid-morning and after lunch time. Well, he took some cursory swipes at doing it. But, on a more personal note, my office was not being cleaned. He said that he only vacuumed and dusted once weekly. I told him that I wanted it done each night after school. He did instruct Mr. Beckley, who worked nights, to do so. But, "Igor," as he was known, had hands like ham hocks and the mentality to destruct, not clean. The building was a mess. I couldn't work, let alone thrive, in such an environment. Again, things had to change.

I requested a meeting with Mr. Cordier and Paul. I said that our building gave a terrible impression to visitors and was unsuitable for faculty and students alike. I said that the floors needed scrubbing and waxing, the lockers needed repainting, and a new cleaning policy needed to be drawn up and enforced. But, my big request was for a lady custodian to be hired to clean the offices of the counselors and administrators. We needed a woman's touch to do those things properly. Paul almost lost his dentures. Never, had the school system had a lady custodian. Paul said that she couldn't do the work of a man. I said that I was glad of that, especially, of our men. Any hope to be friends with Paul died with that last remark.

Mr. Cordier said he'd take these things under advisement. The school board would need to allocate additional funds for most of the requests.

I suggested that Jan Yorgey, wife of one of our current custodians, be hired for the new job. She had applied a long time ago and was shot down. Mostly, because she was a woman.

Moving ahead in time, the funds were allocated. The floors and lockers were renewed. My requests about the cleaning schedule were approved. Jan was hired. The offices sparkled. I was happy and Paul was livid. He began to mumble about retirement. I didn't dissuade him.

Jan continued to thank me for hiring her almost everytime that I saw her. She served faithfully and well until her retirement many years later.

Not much after these events, Paul did retire and Steve Conklin replaced him.

Speaking of custodians, I need to relate another memory that just popped into my frontal lobes. I had taken it upon myself to broadcast our home basketball games. I made the welcoming remarks, announced the starting line-ups and did a little patter during the games. I didn't do a play-by play. At halftime, I had insisted that the custodian on duty mop the entire gym floor. Reese, the other night person, did the duty. After seeing how well that he mopped the floor and picked up litter throughout the game, I announced during one game that he had just made the first team all PCL sweeping team. The audience arose as one and gave him a standing "O." He beamed with delight and became an audience favorite at all of our home games. He began to sweep with little flourishes in time with the music from the P.A. system. He would wave to the crowd and bow when he finished. Kids even asked for his autograph. A star was born right there in our tiny, cramped gymnasium.

Our little gym with its low ceiling and shorter-than-regulation floor was worth at least five to ten points each game. The visiting teams had a hard time adjusting to it, especially during fast breaks. They would run out of room before getting off their last pass. The railings on each side created a danger zone for them. They, often, hesitated going after loose balls in fear of being injured. One other danger was Ruth, my secretary. On several occasions, the referee would come up to me at halftime and ask who that lady was who sat in the front row and yelled insults at me. I feigned ignorance until I couldn't ignore the problem any longer. I told her that she'd have to keep quiet and not cause any more disturbance. She responded by not coming to any more games. I guess she knew that keeping quiet was not in her bag of tricks.

GETTING ON WITH
IT - ANECDOTES
AND VIGNETTES

*"Education is what survives when what has
been learned has been forgotten."*

B. F. Skinner

It was obvious that our little school was having difficulty in competing
with the much larger schools in the Suburban League. We were getting
beaten regularly in most all sports. That first year that I was at Mogadore,
we won two football games out of eight. We weren't playing on an even
field (or court.) I brought up the subject at a board meeting after the
football season. I suggested that I might talk with principals in the
Portage County area which had a number of schools more similar to us
in size. I was given the go-ahead to do so.

I contacted principals in Waterloo, Windham, Garretsville, Southeast,
Field and Woodridge in northern Summit County. I suggested that the
principals and athletic directors of each school meet and discuss the
possibility of forming a new league. The superintendents and school
board members would be brought into the mix if the new league seemed
feasible. It was decided to include Streetsboro in the conversation, also,
even though the system was a little larger than the others.

As a result of several on-going conversations including school boards,
The Portage County League was formed. During the first three years
of competition, we won 32 consecutive league football games. I served
as president of the league for the first seven years and wrote most of the
league's constitution. It proved to be a good move. We, along with the
other schools, prospered in the new league. The competition was fierce
but it was among similar sized schools.

It was during this formative time that I instituted monthy athletic councel meetings which included all of our coaches, our athletic director, the superintendent and myself. At first, we met at night in the school and, sometimes, in a near-bye restaurant. Then, I had the idea of meeting in Sanginiti's Restaurant in downtown Akron. The restaurant had a spacious meeting room called the Rose Room. I arranged for the strolling violin group of Miles Battalini to serenade us during our meals prior to the meetings. Coaches, being coaches, had had little exposure to the soothing melodies played by violins. There was grumbling and vulgar criticism of this affront to their masculinity. They blamed me for trying to bring a little culture to this group of testosterone infused philistines. Actually, I think that most of them liked to be serenaded by the strolling musicians. But, the culture didn't stick to most of them.

The football team, after the formation of the new league, was very successful during my entire time as principal. In 1979, we won a state championship. All told, we've won four state championships and several runner-up trophys. Because of that, we had several occasions to go to Columbus prior to our appearances in the post-season play-offs. We had to pick up information and meet with officials of the OHSAA. We made those trips in the school district van. Back in the day, most of our coaches smoked. Several smoked very bad cigars. I am very allergic to smoke of any kind. By the time we'd get to Columbus, I'd be in need of an oxygen tank and a respirator. Finally, I began to wear an army surplus gas mask during the trips there and back. Ah, those were the halcyon days. It was the best of times.

As has been mentioned, this was Mogadore Junior-Senior High School. It housed about 700 students in grades seven through twelve. The students were housed in two separate buildings about twenty yards apart. The high school had two floors and the junior high building had three floors. It was a lot to supervise and mangage. To make things worse, we couldn't all fit in at the same time. I had to devise a class schedule that had three starting and ending times in order to accomodate all of us. We coudn't all be in class at the same time. I had to arrive at school before 7:15a.m. and I didn't leave until after five p.m. When we had night activities, games, meetings, etc., I had to stay over or come back after a quick supper at home. When I was hired, we didn't have an assistant principal to share the supervisory load. I began to talk to Mr. C. about getting some additional help.

Tom Murphy was the likely choice. He had been serving as a half-time teacher and half-time guidance counselor. He was certified in administration and had expressed a desire to get experience in that field.

Tom gave the appearance of being a burly jock. He could be loud and aggressive. But, as I began to know him better, I discovered another side. He was intelligent, knowledgeable about the field of education and had a warm, sensitive side which he tried very hard to hide.

He had the reputation of being a firm disciplinarian. He would be the perfect Yin to my Yang. We could play "Good cop, bad cop" to perfection. I told Mr. C. of my recommendation and he and the school board agreed to give him a new contract as half counselor and half assistant principal. On the surface, that might seem to be a strange combination. But, Tom made it work. He fit into his new role quickly and well. He, also, remained as an assistant football coach and head wrestling coach. Later, he would be hired as a full-time assistant principal. When I retired, he replaced me as principal

But, there were a few bumps along the road. Tom did retain his temper. It did surface openly on several occasions. Sometimes, when I heard his loud voice penetrating the walls of his office, I would check in to calm things down. One incident stands out. It made the newspaper and an executive session of our school board.

The parents of a male student met with the Akron City prosecutor to discuss pressing charges against Tom for allegedly striking their son as he and Tom were discussing the theft of silverware at the senior banquet. The boy reported the incident to the Mogadore Police. No charges were filed after the police investigated.

The boy's parents asked Mr. Cordier to take disciplinary action against Mr. Murphy. Mr. Cordier and I met with Mr. Murphy to discuss the incident. Teachers Brad Carleton and Sue Bendict were witnesses to the occurance. After talking to Tom and, later, to the boy, we determined that the discussion between the two had evolved into a minor scuffling when the boy refused to cooperate in his questionning and became belligerent. The physicality had started when the boy attempted to leave the room without being dismissed. The two witnesses agreed that no blows were struck. We decided that no formal disciplinary action was necessary. Fortunately, so did the city prosecutor.

Being a school disciplinarian is not an easy job. I knew. I had been in that role in three Akron City schools. If you're too lenient, you're accused of being soft. If you're too tough, you are labeled as being a bully and one who loves to inflict punishment.

Tom was a stickler for following the rules and for insisting that our students be courteous and polite to the school staff and to other students. When students disobeyed the rules or displayed bad behavior, it was not overlooked.

In the wake of the incident with the Akron City prosecutor, I advised Tom to take a deep breath and count to ten when the inevitable daily problems began to pile up. I told him to take his time in making disciplinary decisions. Don't make gut-reaction decisions. Think of the long-term consequences. Do what you think is proper, but be certain it was decided by rational thinking, not anger.

Tom took my words to heart. He became a somewhat softer and mellower version of his former self. Somewhat being the operative word. We, still, talk about a later incident when I heard and saw Tom in the hallway holding a male student up against the wall and berating him for some misdeed. I advised Tom to let the boy go and calm down. The boy had said some crude things to Tom and calming down was not his priority.

When I saw that Tom was really upset, I told him that it would be best that he go home for the remainder of the school day and think of quiet mountain streams and fields of purple flowers. To this day, Tom likes to remind me of the day when I "Suspended" him.

Mr. Murphy was first and foremost an educator. He was responsible for many of the new and creative things that we were able to do as a school during our years of working together. He had the respect of our staff and the respect of the student body- - all of whom could see through that "Tough" exterior and recognize him for being someone who had a true love for education and young people.

In thinking of Tom, I am reminded of the great contributions made by the entire Murphy family to the youth of Mogadore. Tom, his father and his ten siblings contributed heavily to the success of many athletic and academic programs in Mogadore. Tom's dad was on the school board when I was hired. He had a wise and steadying influence on the board. I respected him greatly. Tom's brothers were all great athletes and, later, became coaches in various school and community athletic programs. Tom's sisters were active in many community and school support programs. But, many other Mogadore families served the community well down through the years. I think of the contributions of the Adorni, Raddish, Calcei, Pollock and Tompkins' families. I hesitate to name names because I will leave out many other very deserving families. Those families and others like them are what makes Mogadore a great place to live in and raise a family. People know that their children will be treated well and be mentored by great role models.

> *"The main aim of education should be to send children out into the world with a reasonabaly sized anthology in their heads so that, while seated on the toilet, waiting in doctors' offices, sitting on stationary trains or watching interviews with politicians, they may have something interesting to think about."*

Sir John Mortimer

I was not immune from being accused of excessive discipline either. I remember well the thumbtack caper. The home economics' teacher had complained to me that a boy in her class had placed thumbtacks on some girls' chairs. One girl had received a puncture wound. I called the boy into my office and told him that this was very dangerous and it had to stop. He agreed and he left my office with three evening detentions.

A few days later, he struck again. The teacher brought him to my office and said that another girl had been butt-stuck. That didn't sound right, but I knew what she meant.

I admit that this angered me. I said, "Ok, if you like to hurt someone's back side, then, I'll hurt yours!" I told him to bend over and put his hands on my desk. I gave him three swats with the leather paddle that I'd brought from Akron. It was flexible and conformed to back sides. I didn't wait for a witness to observe the ritual.

He winced at each strike, but seemed to accept the punishment as being justified. I sent him back to class with the admonishment that a future occurance would result in a three-day suspension from school. I told him that he'd be lucky if the girl's parents didn't want him prosecuted by the local police for felonious assault. I didn't realize then that I'd be facing the same charge.

The next day, the boy's mother went to Mr. Cordier's office to state that she'd contacted a lawyer and she was pressing charges against me for causing physical harm to her boy. To prove it, she showed him poloroid pictures of the boy's nether region. The pictures showed faint discoloration of the butt cheeks. Mr. C. called me and informed me of the pending charges. As it turned out, the local police declined to press charges and her lawyer decided to drop the matter. The police chief said that the boy was lucky to have gotten off with only purple marks on his butt. The boy never employed thumbtacks again as weapons of ass destruction.

It's interesting what one remembers about his life. As I try to think back to my days at Mogadore High School, the things that remain embedded in my psyche are mostly problems. Scattered among the problems, are a few moments of triumph and elation. I guess that problems reign supreme because they caused the most community uproar and emotional reflex. The good things that we accomplished didn't cause that kind of response. In writing this book, I fear that when it's published I will remember many things that I should have included. It's called writer's remorse. I not only fear not including things that should be included, but it brings back some guilt about not doing things that should have been done and doing some things that should never have been done. But, that could be true of everyone who has reached those final few years of life. To channel Old Blue Eyes, "Regrets, I have a few."

Ah! A memory spoke to me. I was accused of sexual harrassment by a young art teacher. Before you find me guilty, let me explain. A male art student asked to speak to me. During the conversation, he complained about the lack of subject content being taught and the teacher's obvious flirting with other male students. I thought to myself, "Was this sour grapes speaking?" He went on to describe in some detail some of her actions. His account was enough for me to ask the teacher to come into my office during her preparation period.

When she arrived, she smiled at me and sat down in the chair in front of my desk. She crossed her legs slowly and asked what it was that I wanted. I told her of the boy's comments and accusations. She became loud and accused the boy of lying to get even with her for giving him a bad grade the last grading period. I told her that I hoped that the boy's accusations were not true. I told her to be certain that her conduct was above reproach and that I hoped that this was all a misunderstanding. She became more angry and accused me of believing the boy and not her.

I knew that her loud voice could be heard in the outer office and I told her to calm down. She didn't. So, I said that she should leave and return to her class room. She stood up, but didn't move towards the door. She continued to speak in a very loud voice. I took her by the arm and escorted her to the door. As I opened the door, she said in a loud voice: "Mr. Smith, you are hurting my arm and you touched my breast!" Ruth and two students in the outer office looked on in amazement. The eyes widened and their mouths opened. The teacher said she was reporting this to the union representative and that I hadn't heard the last of this.

A few days later, Tom Haskins, business education teacher and Teachers' Union building representative, asked for an appointment with me. As we talked, he was apologetic. He had talked to other teachers about the art teacher and had found out that she was doing a lot of flirting in the teachers' lounge and they had had other students complain about her teaching methods and flirtatious ways. He said the incident with me would not go farther. Neither would the teacher. Her contract was not renewed at the end of the year. But, she continued to eat bananas in a provocative way in the teachers' lounge. Yes, I do remember this.

Not all of my memories have that tinge of humor that, in hindsight, makes them the stuff of light-hearted banter over a coffee or a beer. Some are hurtful and some are poignant. Some are best forgotten.

One such memory involves one of our students who was convicted of supplying drugs to another student. The other student later died from a drug overdose. The convicted student was removed from school and supplied, at board expense, with home instruction. He was not permitted to take part in or attend any school activities. His relatives tried to get him reinstated as a regular student with full privileges. But, the school board didn't relent. It was a sad case as the expelled student had been, to students and staff alike, a nice young man with a bright future.

The times, they were a'changin. It was the time of the Vietnam War, beatniks, peaceniks and protests of all kinds. It was the time of the Kent State shootings which caused a wave of increased protests among students of all ages and those who opposed the war. Drug usage was rampant even among school-age children. I had to send students home for extended periods of time until they received drug counseling and proof of being drug-free. Several students over-dosed durng the school day and had to be removed from class struggling and kicking. I had to restrain physically several who became violent.

New policies and laws had to be put into place to cover new problems and violations. The older generation predicted that this was the end of our civilization as they had known it. School behavior and decorum were being tested as never before. Students challenged the policies and rules. They questionned everything and every one. They no longer trusted adults to make wise decisions. After all, hadn't the adults screwed up the world and all within it? It forced me to reconsider our policies and to make certain that they were necessary and in every one's best interest. It was no longer just "Do it. Don't ask why." "Because I said so!" no longer flew. Students wanted more say in the making of school rules. I knew that that wasn't a bad thing. We should be teaching students to govern and control themselves. That should be part of the curriculum.

I convened a meeting of Tom, the assistant principal, our guidance counselors, our department chairpersons, and student respresentatives from each grade level. I presented the idea of forming a Faculty-Student Senate. It would be the governing body of the school. I suggested that the Senate be composed of a representative from each grade level elected by students from each grade, an equal number of faculty members elected by the entire faculty, the assistant principal and the counselors. I would preside at the meetings and vote only in case of a tie. In proposals that I would deem detrimental to the school and/or in violation of school board policy, I would retain the right to veto. Any member had the right to make proposals. We would meet weekly or in special meetings when necessary. We agreed to the format and I presented it to Mr. Cordier and to the school board for their approval. They liked the idea, but Mr. Carpenter, who was now board president, cautioned that the Senate might approve some dangerous policies. He urged caution. I said that I would practice due dilligence. Whatever that meant. The board approved the plan.

The Senate proved to work well. I admit being surprised by how conservative the student members were. They took their duties seriously and the student body seemed satisfied with having a voice in how the school would be run.

"Education is not to reform students or amuse them or to make them expert technicians. It is to unsettle their minds, widen their horizons, inflame their intellects, teach them to think straight, if possible."

Robert Maynard Hutchins

BREAKING UP IS HARD TO DO

One of the most difficult jobs of a school administrator is removing a long-time volunteer or employee from his position. This is true especially when they've become icons in the community and have legions of friends and supporters. In my case, it was doubly difficult because I was new to the job and hadn't developed a group of loyal supporters.

I'll begin with the G. Lynn Pugh, local minister and long-time public address announcer for our home football games. He was well-loved and respected by all who knew him except for opposing football fans. Putting it mildly, he was pro-Mogadore and in no way bi-partisan or impartial.

I had attended Mogadore football games prior to becoming the high school principal. G. Lynn was funny, caustic and, often, questionned the officials' calls over the public address system. Sometimes, he made fun of opposing players and fans. I wondered how he could get away with some of his antics.

During my first year of being principal, I began receiving phone calls and complaints from visiting fans, school officials and coaches. I talked to the fiery little red-headed minister and asked him to cool it down and just make the announcements and not inject personal comments. He agreed, albeit reluctantly. We made it through my first season.

When my second football season began, I had the same discussion with G. Lynn. But, he just couldn't resist the temptation to cheer for Mogadore and help to officiate the games. At the end of that season, I asked him to step down as our announcer. He was hurt but not angry. He said that if I didn't want him, he'd resign. When the news leaked out, I heard from angry adult fans and from our faculty. They accused me of being insensitive and caving in to the complaints of opposing schools. I did it in the name of good sportsmanship and keeping peace with our opponents. It was difficult for me to remove him from his long-time job. To this day, I feel guilty about doing it.

The second such incident was even more painful. I had recommended that the school board not renew the head basketball coaching contract of a long-time coach and teacher. The board approved my recommendation by a unanimous vote of 5-0. That was only the beginning. When the news hit the streets, I was deluged by phone calls, letters and in-person visits from angry parents, students and teachers. They wanted to know how I could recommend the firing of the coach who had been the head basketball coach for 15 years, most of which had been very successful.

But, there was more to the story than the won and loss record which was 178 wins and 115 losses.

In my first two seasons at Mogadore, he had gone 10-4 and 17-1. Everyone, including me, was happy with the team and their coach. The only problem that I had was one trying to build school spirit. In spite of the winning records, the student body seemed disinterested in supporting the team. Few students attended the games and those who did didn't follow the cheerleaders attempts to make a lot of noise to encourage the team.

I met with the cheerleaders and told them how important they were to the team and the fans who attended our games. There had been very few pep assemblies in the past. I learned that he was not in favor of having them and even was vocal in discouraging them. I told the cheerleaders to plan on having a pep assembly during the school day of each home game and, if the away games had special significance, we'd have one then, also. I talked to the coach and told him what I'd planned. He said that they just got the players too fired up and didn't help them or the school. We had several successful pep assemblies during those first two years by using competitions to pick a grade-level winner at each assembly. He continued to be negative and talked against having them. Because we were winning most of our games, I let his negative attitude slide. I don't think that he ever bought into the concept that the basketball team was part of the whole school operation. I began to get the impression that he felt that it was just for the boys and the coaches.

The next year, the team went 6-12. The following year, the team won 6 and lost 13. In 1973, our record was 5-14. When I coupled those last three losing seasons with his increasing negativity about aiding in improving school spirit, I began to think that a new coach was needed. I knew a little somthing about basketball and I began to watch the offensive and defensive game plans a little closer. We had become very predictable. We did little to change game plans to match each separate opponent. Our rivals knew what to exepect from us. We ran the same plays game after game and year after year. In addiition, I'd begun to hear rumors of player dissension and of possible very good players not wanting to play for him.

At the end of the third straight losing season, I wrote a rather critical evaluation of him as our head basketball coach. I cited the reasons listed above for not recommending that his basketball coaching contract be renewed. In closed executive session of the school board, along with Mr. Cordier and myself, it was decided to not renew his contract at the next regular board meeting. As it was a personnel matter, the board was not obligated to cite reasons for the non-renewal.

As a courtesy, I told him of what the board had decided. It was difficult. He was a good man and a competent teacher. He had given long and devoted service to the school district. I sensed that he tried to control his anger. I told him my reasons for the recommendation. He responded by saying that I only did this because he didn't name my son as a starter in basketball or play him enough. I told him that that was the furthest thing from my mind. I sensed that he'd never believe that. We both became quiet. He got up to leave and I didn't stop him.

The furor began. The Akron Beacon Journal and the Kent-Ravenna Record Courier both carried big articles about his firing. He was well known in athletic circles and he received a lot of support and sympathy. Me, not so much. Following are some direct quotes from people who were interviewed by the papers' reporters:

The coach: "I will remain as a math and physical education teacher, but will resign as athletic director. I'm not going to try and fight it. If they don't want me, there is no use in staying. I'll divorce myself completely from athletics. But, at least, I got out when I could hold my head up high. I've enjoyed coaching at Mogadore and I'm not ashamed of anything I've done. This is something that everyone involved in this matter cannot say. The sun will come up tomorrow and I'll live. Mogadore lost probably their greatest coach in Ned Novell this same way."

Superintendent Jack Cordier: "This recommendation is based on the evaluation by Mr. Smith. The losses of the past several years had nothing to do with it."

Board member Jim Talbott: "I don't feel the coach had control of the team. And, I don't feel that he had an interest in getting qualified students into the basketball program. I think we can do better in this area. Age was not a factor. His performance has dropped."

Jim Chase, teacher and president of the Mogadore Education Association: "The MEA has stayed advised of the developments in the situation and realizes that the board of education makes the final decision. However, we hope that reasons are publicly given for not renewing any contract and that the board of education looks closely at the reasons given by the principal for the validity of those reasons. There is a possibility of the MEA demanding an explanation, but we are powerless to force the board to give us one. Our only alternative is legal action. Where else, after 20 years of service, can someone be eliminated so quickly. I don't think it can happen anywhere else."

Needless to say, many other comments were made by many other people over a period of years. I became a pariah in the minds of some people. When I attended our football game at Field High School the following fall, I was booed and cursed lustily when I walked up into the stands. Coach lived in the Field school district, so I was getting critisism from other than Mogadore citizens.

To replace the coach, we hired a young man who had graduated from Mogadore High School. He had been a great basketball player and had had some coaching experience. It didn't work out. Lack of discipline was why he lost control of the team. I began to second guess my recommendation for the firing . The young man lasted just one season. We conducted a more thorough search for a qualified coach. We hired a man with previous head-coaching experience. He was young, enthusiastic and presented a well thought-out plan for how he intended to turn our program around. The board, Mr. Cordier and I were impressed. Jerry Butcher was hired and began a great career at Mogadore. He encouraged all those who were interested to try out for the team and promised the cheerleaders complete cooperation in planning pep assemblies. School spirit and game attendance rose quickly. We began winning regulary and, even, in losing we looked good and played hard. Through shrewd coaching strategy, we beat teams that we shouldn't have beaten.

Donald E. Smith, Ph.D.

During the time frame discussed above, important things of a personal nature took place. My daughter, Kathy, graduated from Mogadore High School in 1971. She had survived being the principal's daughter. Mostly. She still remembers her embarrassment when she saw me in the hallway holding up a male student by the neck against the lockers for some breach of good conduct. She endured hearing comments about me from other students. She was accused by other students of receiving preferential treatment and grading because I was the principal. I take this opportunity to apologize publicly for inflicting deep psychological wounds on her tender psyche.

Also, in 1971, I was invited to take part in the National Association of Secondary School Principals' European Study Mission. The Mogadore School Board was gracious in allowing me to take part in this three-week program. I was granted the time off from my duties with full pay. We had briefings in Washington D.C. at the NASSP offices and at the Soviet Union and Hungarian embassies. During the trip, we visited schools in Denmark, The Soviet Union and Hungary. I had a brief, unscheduled lay-over in Sweden. I extended my stay for three additonal days in London before flying home. I learned a lot about schools in other countries during the trip and shared the information upon my return with school and civic groups. The downside was that I became ill during the last week of the trip with giardiasis, an amoebic parasite. I lost quite a bit of weight and only recovered when a doctor in Barberton prescribed quinine to kill the "bug." The little beasts encapsulated in my liver and I had to undergo liver scans for the next five years.

On a more serious note, on September 9, 1972, I received a phone call at the Mogadore Bowling Alley where my wife and I were taking part in a teachers' bowling league. It was from my step-mother who said that my dad had fallen off of a ladder at home while attempting to put tar around the chimney. She said that he had fallen onto a brick patio from the roof of the one-story bungalow. He had been covered in tar and the paramedics were on the way. By the time we arrived at his home, he had been taken to Akron City Hospital where he had been pronounced as being dead on arrival. He suffered a broken neck and fractured skull. The autopsy didn't reveal any medical reasons for his fall. It was declared to be an accident with no known cause for the fall.

My relationship with my dad had been an uneasy one as noted earlier in this story. What made it worse for me was that the day before he had called me to ask me to help him apply the tar. I said that I couldn't until the weekend. I was too busy with school activities. He didn't wait. That was dad. Impatient, eager to get things done. Logically, I shouldn't have blamed myself. But, I did. I still do.

Most of our faculty and many friends attended his funeral. Once, again, we made the long funeral procession to that little country graveyard in East Springfield Ohio where all of my relatives are buried. It's a peaceful, quiet place among the gently rolling hills of southeastern Ohio. But, underneath the parched sod lie too many memories and too many regrets. When we began the long trip back to Mogadore, I heard the sexton ring the bells in the steeple of the little white wooden church which stood like a Currier and Ives painting in stark contrast against the vivid blue of the bright fall sky.

Meanwhile, back at school, things were happening. Some good, some bad. I'll begin with a "Good" thing. At our staff meetings, we had begun to realize that we weren't doing much to help those students who had ability, but were doing failing work. We realized that the regular and normal classes were not providing the individual help and motivation that they needed.

After much discussion and head-scratching, we developed a plan for under-achieving seventh and eighth graders that we hoped would help them to reach their potentials. It would be a four-period class taught by Patricia Clayton. She was one of our newer teachers, but had impressed staff and students alike with her warm, caring approach to her job. She expressed interest in teaching the class when I explained the premise to her. We called it the "Opportunity Class."

The class would emphasize intensive personal help and encouragement from the teacher. It would stress attitude changes and improved work and study habits along with the basic subjects of English, mathematics, social studies and science. Special subjects such as art, music, physical education, industrial arts and home economics would be handled by the teachers in those areas.

The intent would be to promote feelings of success and a more positive self-image. The class will non-graded. If, at the end of the school year. Miss Clayton feels that the student has mastered the material required of a seventh or eighth grade student, the student will be promoted. My main point in recommending this type of class was that those students need a kind of "Mother-hen" person in their lives. Miss Clayton had that type of personality and caring attitude.

When I addressed the board about approving this class, I was quoted as saying, "This class will give those alienated students the opportunity to succeed if they give an honest effort. Maybe, having a year of successful school experience will give them a more positive outlook about school and, even, life itself." The board approved the program unanimously. Later, I wrote an article about the program in "The American Secondary Education Journal." Our idea seemed to resonate among school people around the country. We were asked to speak about it on the state and national levels.

More Problems

"You learn more and more that everything exists at once with its opposite, so the contradictions of life are never-ending and, somehow, the mediation between these opposites is the game of life."

Milton Glaser

Karen Rugerio, a new teacher, revitalized our drama department. She worked hard at recruiting new members for our drama club. She prepared them for presenting to the community a night of four one-act plays. They were presented to a large and enthusiastic audience in our little gymnasium which had a small stage at one end of the court.

I was pleased with the students' performance and with the size of the audience. The performance seemed to be received well. But, seeming doesn't make it so. A parent, who was, also, a teacher in the Akron area complained to Mr. Cordier and to the school board. She considered two of the plays, "The Widow" and "The Unknown Soldier" to be sadistic and violent. The other two, "The Magic Shop" and excerpts from Macbeth were described by her as being inappropriate for high school students.

I had, already, cleansed some foul language from the scripts and approved them as edited. But, the parent said that parents should have been notified of the content and that the four plays should have been given an "X" rating.

"The Unknown Soldier" won first place in the International Drama Festival and "The Widow" had a plot that was similar to "Arsenic and Old Lace," a highly regarded classic. "Macbeth" can stand on its own merits as a literary masterpiece.

The school board referred the complaint to a screening committee of faculty and school board members.

Nothing more came from the complaint other than it left Mrs. Rugerio wondering if all of her work had been worth the time and effort. I wondered about people who regard themselves as the guardians of community morality. The word "Hubris" came to mind.

It was about at this time when Mr. McBee, veteran social studies' teacher, asked to address the school board at one of our regular meetings. It took me by surprise. I had written some comments about his teaching style after I'd visited his Problems of Democracy class. He thought that I'd criticized him unfairly. I won't go into the details of my comments as they are classified information. But, suffice it to say, they were critical of how he was conducting this class. He chose to defend himself in the public forum of an open board meeting. I only responded by saying that I was not alone in questionning his out-dated teaching methods. I'd been hearing complaints from students and parents and my observation had validated those complaints.

Roscoe became very emotional and very critical of my daring to question one who had been teaching for many years. That was part of the problem. He had been teaching the same material in the same way for all of those many years. POD classes beg for student participation and free-style discussions, not "Read the chapter and answer the questions at the end of the chapter."

The board listened to his sermon-like delivery. He was a practicing Baptist preacher, after all. I listened quietly and invited the board members to read my written evaluation that was on file in my office. I, also, invited them to visit Mr. McBee's classes as often as they desired.

I only mention this here to illustrate how principals can create controversy by only doing their job. I thought that Mr. McBee's classes could be enlivened by doing some hands-on projects and encouraging more student involvement. I gave him some ideas as to how to do those things. He chose to defend himself in front of an audience instead of conferring with me in private. He was a long-time teacher who had many friends among the students, staff, former graduates and Mogadore residents in general. Needless to say, we weren't pals for the remainder of my time at MHS.

And, next, we have the "Great Book Controversary." This problem generated more newspaper coverage, public meetings, phone calls, letters and vitriol than any other situation that I ever encountered in my many years of working in the field of education.

When it's mentioned today, some 39 years later, it still creates strong feelings. It's too bad that the reading of a book served to divide a community and attracted such wide-spread attention. The act of reading should generate and evoke much of what is good and true in the human spirit. The assigned reading of "The Other Side of Midnight" for a senior class on contemporary literature evoked much of what is neither good nor true. It unleashed the furies.

The critics of the book called it "Dirty," "Obscene," "Trash," and "Filth." And, those were the nice terms.

The author of the book, Sidney Sheldon, was interviewed by phone by Record Courier reporter, Mary Gallagher. Here are some direct quotes from the interview:

"Senior students are old enough to read and discuss my book. Teachers are aware of their development."

"The book is realistic and students will say, I felt that way and was never able to put it into words."

"It is healthier to discuss sex than to snicker in dark corners. Many people are uptight about the subject and never discuss it with their children. But, I do feel that children should not be exposed to pornographic books or movies."

He said that four million copies of the book have been sold and a movie will be released soon. Sheldon was the producer and writer of "I Dream of Jeannie" and "The Patty Duke Show." No one ever drank or smoked on either show.

At the school board meeting on Monday, November 18, 1975, only one of the five board members, Laura Ingold, had bothered to read the book.

The other members listened to several parents voice complaints without having the background to make informed comments. But, that didn't deter them or other people in attendance. Following, are some examples of quotes from the large group in attendance:

Mrs. Richard Siers, parent: "Six out of the 40 students in Mr. Amedeo's two classes objected to the book. I don't think this book is good for anyone to read. We don't talk like this in our home. It is a filthy book. I read one paragraph and it turned my stomach. We shouldn't read it out loud tonight. Why not the Bible or the classics? My 17 year old son didn't like it. He was offended by 'Jaws.' He reads the Bible. It's a shame that the Good Book can't be in the schools. When asked if she'd read the book, she replied: "No, and I won't read it. I don't know what the book is about. It's bad enough for a boy to read it. Just let one of the girls get it."

I assured Mrs. Siers that classics were being read. "We're talking about one class here that is based on contemporary values. There are some moral values to be learned from reading the book." I added that I'd had parents visit my office to offer support for reading the book.

Bonnie Groves, parent: "These are still kids at age 17 and 18. We are adults. They are kids. We want them to continue to grow."

Joseph Amedeo, the teacher who assigned the book: "My seniors are not kids."

Mrs. Groves: "They don't act like adults in the community."

Mr. Amedeo: Your youngsters may leave Mogadore. They will learn these things. Instead of learning it elsewhere, wouldn't it be better if they learned it in a controlled atmosphere? Of the six students who objected to the book the strongest, four came to me today and apologized. They said it was one of the best books they ever read. It was just one of the books that I suggested for outside reading. I told them what was in the book. If the subject matter offended them, they could choose another book.

Board member Charles Carpenter: "I leafed through 40 or 50 pages. I didn't read it all. But, I don't think we're teaching college-level psychology. This is a high school English class. The book was brought to my house by a parent. I spent 22 years in the army and the book has some crude sections."

Superintendent Jack Cordier: "It's important to remember that this is a book on a list from which the students could choose, not one that they had to read. It tells a story that says that people make mistakes and have to pay for them. It was good that the book was discussed under the guidance of a teacher. No Summit County school has a specific reading policy. The choice of books is left in the hands of teachers and administrators."

Robert Glunt, Board Member: "I promise that the board will arrive at guidelines to stop the reading of such controversial books in the future."

Mr. Jack Clevenger, Board President: "I suggest that community people be asked to screen assigned books. Also, the teachers should be represented."

Mr. Carpenter: "I suggest that we organzize an Academic Booster Club to work in the school system. There is a lack of communication."

I spoke up: "I don't think that a small group of parents should impose their tastes on any other group. Teachers are trained to not only select materials for their classes but to handle discussions about the material in a balanced, non-biased manner. A chemist wouldn't want an English major to supervise or assist in his laboratory work unless that person had received sufficient training in the necessary science.

After the lengthy discussion, the board took no action on the parents' complaints, but decided to resume discussion in their next work session.

In the interim between the meeting described above and the next regular board meeting, more talk and more dissension was generated. Mrs. Watts, in a letter to the editor in the *Akron Beacon Journal*, said that she felt that the book was trash and that parents should keep a closer eye on what their students were assigned to read.

Students, Valerie Wilburne and Becky Briggs in "The Voice of the People" in the Beacon Journal stated: "Not only does this novel show us alternative moral values, it also deals with reality, everday living and the truth. We feel that we should be given more credit for being able to think like adults and to accept this book as an example of what is good and bad and what life has to offer. We've learned a lot from this novel. We openly discussed the characters and their lives. We, even, discussed our lives and benefitted from the comments of our fellow students and Mr. Amedeo. The novel has a good plot and theme. It's, also, a good education about life."

Sally Christman, in a "Letter to the Editor:" "Out of the whole community, only one person had taken the time to read the book, yet they all posed as authorities on the book. I agree with the principal, Don Smith, who said: "There are some moral values to be learned." I believed that that was the only true statement in the whole article about the school board meeting. If the people criticizing the book are examples of people trying to run the school, then, I feel sorry for the students who attend Mogadore and the other residents willing to keep an open mind."

In a Beacon Journal editorial, the following comments were made: The Mogadore School Board might be wise to establish a two-track system in literature classes such as "G" and "PG" like the movie system. Such a system could meet community standards, yet not deprive any student who had parental permission to read whatever the teacher offered. Community involvement might work, but, the guidelines must allow parents who so choose to place their faith in the teachers' ability to decide what is best for their children."

The school board failed to come up with a realistic, workable policy at its next work session. So, I developed an interim policy which required teachers to submit the books that were assigned to their classes to their departments for discussion and approval. If the departments couldn't reach a decision about a particular book, I would make the final decision. The department-approved reading lists would be distributed to me, the superintendent and the school board. The lists would be made available to parents and concerned citizens upon request. This policy was in effect for the balance of the school year with positive results. Later, it became the official board policy.

Controversy can bring about positive results if cooler heads are allowed to prevail. If all those with opposing views are permitted to voice their opinions, the mixture of differing viewpoints can be melded together into a satisfactory ending. Sometimes.

Joseph Amedeo was a good teacher and a good man. The book controversy wounded his pride and his ability to feel that Mogadore was a good fit for him. The next year, he moved on to teach successfully in another district. I appreciated his honesty, his understanding of today's youth and his ability to express that understanding.

Out of this controversy, we lost a good teacher. But, we gained a deeper understanding of how volatile the written word can become.

"Nothing that is worth knowing can be taught."

Oscar Wilde

Students who are members of the National Honor Society are supposed to be exemplary in both academic achievement and citizenship. One of our teachers called my attention to one member who had been rude and discourteous to her on several occasions. When that happens, the faculty is obligated to meet and discuss whether or not the violations are flagrant enough to warrant the student's removal from the society. We met in a special session of the society to discuss the situation. The rules of the society said that we could warn the student and give him the opportunity to improve his behavior or we could remove him permanently and include the findings in his permanent record. The debate over how to proceed was long and contentious. So much so, that we couldn't decide during the meeting.

The student in question was the daughter of a well-known and active Mogadore family. Making it even more difficult was the fact that her mother was an area educator. It was the kind of problem that would stir up another controversy. I would try very hard to have the case resolved quickly and fairly.

We scheduled another meeting and invited both the student and teacher to present their sides of the story. In the meantime, Mr. Cordier talked to me about the possible consequences of removing the student from the society. He and the girl's father were friends and the father had hinted about possible legal action if his daughter were removed. I was reminded that removal would be a black mark on her record and might eliminate her from college scholarships or, even, acceptance. I felt somewhat pressured and a little intimidated.

With these remarks in mind, I convened the next meeting of the faculty. We heard from both parties. They both presented cogent arguments. The teacher felt that the girl had been rude, impudent and downright insulting to her on several occasions. The girl felt that the teacher was singling her out unfairly for doing things that she hadn't done and had embarrassed her in front of the class. After a lengthy discussion, I called for a vote. The vote was whether or not to remove her from the society. The vote was very close. The result was that she would remain a member with the warning that future occurances of her poor behavior would result in dismissal. Many faculty members were upset by the decision and asked me why I just didn't remove her by executive order without the charade of holding meetings and having everyone vote. I explained that we followed the guidelines for dismissing a student from the society. Maybe, I shouldn't have discussed my meeting with Mr. Cordier prior to the vote and let the case stand on its own merits. "Maybes" were beginning to be a reoccuring theme.

Unless my memory is playing tricks with me, these problems and situations seem to have been bunched together very closely. They might be telescoped and condensed. I'm beginning to wonder if I were the cause of many of them. Or, was it because I chose to handle and resolve them when, before, they were overlooked or ignored?

I need to say once more that my memory is one of an 83 year-old. The exact years and months of many of these anecdotes are lost in the mists of time. I didn't keep personal notes at the time. What is important is that they happened and the circumstances are true to the best of my ability to recall. Those of you who lived through those times with me might have different memories and different viewpoints. But, this is my book and my memories. If you disagree with me and want to refute what I've written, write you own book. I hope that my recent evolvement into being a certified curmudgeon hasn't jaded my attitudes or thought processes. But, you know what? I don't care! This book is a kind of catharsis for me. So, play along. Enjoy the ride.

Back to the problems. One of our teachers came to me and said that some of her students had been following her to her home in Akron on several occasions. They'd parked in front of her house and stayed there for quite a while just looking at the house. She had felt threatened and intimidated. When she confronted them, they just told her that they were parked legally and had done nothing wrong. The students in question were receiving poor grades in most of their classes and had long behavior records. She had had occasion to keep them for detentions and had referred them to Mr. Murphy for disrupting her class.

She had, even, talked to an Akron police officer and had been told if they hadn't done harm to her or her house, he couldn't press charges. I called the boys into my office and told them that they were treading on dangerous grounds and that it would only lead to serious trouble for them. They listened quietly, were polite and said that they'd not intended any harm.

Two days later, the teacher came to my office in tears and said that she'd seen the same boys in the same car outside her house about 11pm and had heard the sound of glass shattering. She went outside and her car's headlights had been broken out and her side door window had been broken. The car was gone when she went outside. I asked her if she were certain that it was the same car and same boys. She assured me that they were. She said it looked like high-powered pellet guns had been used. I told her to call the Akron police to make a report.

That same day, I called the two boys back and told them that they were being suspended from school for an indefinite time until the police and

I had all of the facts. They didn't deny their involvement, but didn't confess either.

After the facts were all in, I recommended that the school board expel the two boys for the balance of the school year. The board upheld my recommendation. I advised the parents that they could request home instruction or use private tutors if they so chose. The boys and their families moved out of the Mogadore district before the school year ended.

"Rewards and punishments are the lowest forms of education."

Chuang Tzu

I guess that Mr. Tzu had never had his windows shot out.

In retrospect, it seems that my first few years at Mogadore revolved around handling problems and disputes. My mind seems to have stored those things at the expense of the many good things that happened. I guess that there is more drama surrounding those things that cause anguish and concern.

It was not all venom and spite. Some good things were happening, also. I had some ideas about improving and supplementing our curricular offerings. My assessment was that we were weak in some important areas. Our physical facilities precluded major improvements in certain areas such as science, industrial arts, music and home economics. But, we could fine- tune our subject offerings in many areas. We held lengthy discussions in our general staff meetings and in our departmental meetings as to how we could up-grade our subject offerings within the confines of budgetary limitations.

We presented our recommendations at a work session of the school board. Our main selling point was that none of the changes would require the expenditure of additional funds. I had been learning more about the collective psyche of our school board. The criterion by which things were judged seemed to be - "Go for it if it doesn't cost us money."

Of course, that was followed by the admonition - "Don't stir up any more controversies!"

We gave the school board the following recommendations for changes in existing courses and for new course offerings: We would add mini-courses of varying time lengths in English and American Studies for advanced juniors and seniors. Roscoe McBee, Chairman of the Social Studies Department told the board that the courses would be long enough to cover the subject and short enough to retain students' interest. I told the board that no new teachers would be needed and that the current staff would be able to operate in a more efficient manner. I added that the mini-courses would not cut subject matter, but would add to it. In the American Studies program, the traditional chronological approach to American history would be abandoned. Areas to be covered would include minority groups, civil rights and the responsibilities of American citizens. Mini-courses in English will provide seven additional offerings for students. We would add a behavioral science course that would combine psychology and sociology.

Other subjects to be offered include: advanced composition, music appreciation, French three and four, Spanish, notehand, developmental reading, journalism and credit offered for the newspaper and yearbook staffs.

Two periods will be added to the school day making a total of nine 42-minute periods daily. Teachers will teach more periods each day and will face a greater number of students daily.

I told the school board that the teachers' union had agreed to the increased work load in order to improve the school's curricular offerings. The agreement was not without its detractors. Some of whom have been vocal. It was an uneasy truce.

The crowning piece of the new program was the new humanities offering. Teacher Ross Morrow had spent the first semester of the school year visiting humanities programs in other school districts. Some of what he found would be incorporated into our program.

To support our reasons for offering the humanities program, I told the board the following: "I feel that we have a weakness in the cultural areas. The course will combine English, world history, art, music and, occasionally, other subject areas. The class will meet for two periods daily all year. A team of four subject teachers and a project coordinator will plan how time will be used. The team will share a common planning period prior to the double period class time.

This new course is designed to break away from the traditional pattern of teaching those areas as separate entitites with their usual emphasis upon textbook assignments and rote memorization of facts. We hope to provide meaningful experiences about other countries and their cultures. We shall emphasize similarities rather than differences among world cultures. We will examine man's continuing search for the meaning of life, his sense of identity and sense of direction. We will stress the interrelatedness of the various subjects and what mankind has experienced, felt, perceived and believed. The general theme is an attempt to answer the age-old questions of "Who am I?" "What am I?" and "Where am I going?"

In response to board members' questions about our goals for such a program, I answered: "We hope to show that literature, history, music and art are interconnected expressions of man's ideas, experiences and values. We hope to make the students not only more knowledgeable, but, also, more compassionate. We hope to develop students' powers of critical, analytical and reflective thinking. We plan to cultivate their ability to engage in independent inquiry.

The content of the course enables the students to meet college requirements and, if they don't plan on college, it is good preparation for living a productive life."

The school board seemed receptive to what was presented, but I did sense some skepticism as to how all these new offerings and changes would actually benefit the school.

At the school board meeting later that month, I presented an extensive report on what we needed to do to make Mogadore High School an even better, more relevant high school. The recommendations that I made were the result of an extensive self-study conducted by our staff and the recommendations of a visiting team of educators that were made during their three-day visit earlier in the school year. Those visits are required by The North-Central Association of Colleges and Schools. The visits generate a report that indicates whether or not the school being visited is meeting the association's stringent standards. If a school does meet those standards, it becomes an accredited school. Most colleges and universities do not accept students from a school that is not accredited by their regional associations.

Armed with data from our self-study and the visiting team's resports, I addressed the board by saying: "The board must decide whether its emphasis will be upon maintaining the status quo or upon reaching for excellence. Our school has problems that are inherent in operating a combined junior-senior high school. The range of ages and maturity levels is too great. The combination of grades and ages is not wise from educational, emotional or physical standpoints.

We try to operate complete academic and activity programs at all levels and the students and staff suffer. Only a new facility or drastic remodeling of our current facilities will solve the problem completely. We need a library/instructional materials center, a covered walkway between the two buildings, additional clerical help, data processing service for scheduling, report cards and attendance, a full-time assistant principal, additional custodial help and a larger budget for textbooks and other educational material.

I am not naive. I realize that our budget as it stands will not permit the expenditures needed to implement all of the needs listed above. The visiting team comes from many different area school districts. They enjoy many of the items that they recommend for us. Hopefully, we can prioritize those items and provide some of them in the future in a carefully phased manner.

But, we can make this a better school by approving the curricular changes that were presented earlier this month at the work session without doing any of the things which would require additional monies."

The meeting concluded with the board approving all of our curricular changes. I felt a sense of both relief and accomplishment. Now, it would be up to the staff and me to make it all work. I was excited. I hoped that the staff would be.

The humanities program was a work in progress. The team consisted of teachers who were accustomed to working alone and doing their own things. To work as a team for a common goal required a new mind set. Some bickering and arguments were a natural result of trying to meld several strong egos into one unified whole. Unfortunately, the team coordinator, Ross Morrow seemed to lose interest in the project. I was frustrated by the lack of leadership. I thought that the whole concept behind the humanities program was great. I wanted to see it work. During the second year of the program, Karen Rugerio arrived as a new teacher and as one who had had experience in team-teaching. She became the English teacher and the team coordinator. Unfortunately, not all of the team members played well together. They, apparently, hadn't learned in their respective sandboxes. After three years, the program died an untimely death. Culture would come slowly to the students of Mogadore. If at all. I shared some of the blame for the failure. I was unable to convince the team teachers of how important this program could be to the students and to the school. But, I guess that I was and am more of a humanist in my approach to life than they seemed to be. At heart and in practice, most people are still the rugged individualists of early American life. Team teaching, along with socialism, will struggle to gain a foothold in Mid-America. I can hear the mighty chorus in the background saying "Amen" to that.

I am proud of the fact that the school board approved the addition of a compulsary reading course for all tenth graders and a remedial reading course for students in the other grades who needed help in improving their reading skills. Also, we were able to offer speed-reading as an elective for any students who could fit it into their schedule. We hired a full-time reading specialist for these program. We became pioneers for these types of programs in our immediate area. Unfortunately, after I retired, the reading program was weakened and, eventually, dropped.

It was during this time period that I began investigating the possibility of beginning my doctoral work at The University of Akron. I scheduled an interview with the dean of the graduate school to gather more information. I was offered an internship to begin my course work. I would be expected to devote full-time to my doctoral work. In addition to taking the required courses, I would be expected to teach undergraduate courses in The College of Education. I would be paid $3,000 and my course fees would be waived. In order to do this, I would need to ask for a leave of absence from my job in Mogadore. Obviously, we couldn't live on the the $3,000 salary that Akron University offered.

I investigated my opportunities at The Ohio State University. I was offered a similar internship to what Akron University had offered. In addition, I was interviewed while on-campus at Ohio State for a principalship at the military dependents' school on the island of Guam. Guam is located in the Pacific Ocean south of Japan. I was led to believe that the job was mine if I desired it. A family discussion followed. We decided that I would stay at Mogadore and begin taking classes in night school at Akron University which would, eventually, lead to a Ph.D. in Education. At some point, I'd need to devote at least a semester in full-time work at the university. It was a start that wouldn't end until the year 2007.

Meanwhile, back in Mogadore, things were happening. They always do. I felt a rise in our school spirit. The sports' teams were not only winning, but receiving state-wide recognition in the year-end play-offs and tournaments. The new academic programs had given our students more choices and better preparation for college or for work in their chosen fields. An influx of new teachers who replaced those who retired or moved brought new life and enthusiasm.

Our enrollment had increased which caused me to devise a schedule with three different starting and ending times for the school day. We couldn't all fit into the rooms at the same times. My day began at 7a.m and ended at 5p.m. On days that we had games or other evening activities, I came back to school after eating dinner and returned home in time to go to bed.

Tom, my assistant principal, shared a lot of the duties of supervision. But, usually, we both attended evening and week-end events. We worked well together. I owe him much credit for any success that we might have achieved during the eighteen years that we worked together. He kept me grounded when I became too liberal, philosophical or patient. I kept him from becoming too conservative, pragmatic and impatient. I was pleased in 1984 when the school board hired him to replace me as principal.

In 1971, I was selected by the National Association of Secondary School Principals (NASSP) to take part in a three-week European Study Mission. We visited schools in Denmark, Sweden, The Soviet Union and Hungary. I remain grateful to our school board for permitting me to take part in this fascinating look into the educational practices in those countries. I still remember the students and teachers in Denmark who smoked during classes and enjoyed their beer during frequent breaks during the school days. I was amazed at how advanced the students were in the USSR. First and second graders spoke perfect English. Students in grade seven were taking algebra, geometry and, some, even calculus. High school students seemed as advanced as our college students, especially, in mathematics and science. The students in Sweden and Hungary seemed equally advanced when compared to our students of similar ages.

It should be noted that in many European countries, students had six-day school weeks and eight-hour school days. Also, their vacations were staggered at one or two weeks at a time throughout the calendar year. We, in comparison, still follow the old agrarian practice of taking off the summers to get the crops harvested. Few students in Mogadore harvest crops. Also, especially in the Soviet Union, not all students were approved to go on to a comprensive high school. The better students went to a pre-university secondary school. The middle-ability ones went to a technical school to prepare them for skilled jobs and the lesser-ability students were enrolled in vocational schools to train for menial jobs in labor and industry. In contrast, we try to educate all students in much the same way unless the parents can afford to send them to private schools where the elite of our younger generation are trained to be leaders in business and industry or the pure academic life.

In 1974, I was selected to be a delegate of the Institute For International Understanding under the auspices of the University of Pittsburgh. Once again, I was granted a sabbatical to take part in an educational program. I visited schools and health care facilities in England, France and The Soviet Union.

By taking part in these studies, I was able to return to Mogadore with some fresh ideas and outlooks. Some of what I learned colored my thinking as to what education should and could be. I discussed my findings with our staff and with the greater Akron area community through slide shows and other presentations. Some people felt that we shouldn't practice anything that was being taught or utilized in those decadent European countries. My feeling has always been that we should look around us, broaden our horizons and copy and use anything that would enable our students to become better, both as students and responsible citizens.

My memories of my time at Mogadore High School are beginning to look like the ever-changing swirls of color when one looks through a kaleidoscope. The bits of memories keep flashing in and out of my view. I'm having difficulty in pinning a flashing moment down long enough to flesh in the details. Ah! There's one! Gotcha!

In 1978, I took part in a principals' exchange program sponsored by NASSP. Richard Read from England arrived to stay in our home and work with me as I conducted the business of being a principal. He was the principal of a high school in Harrow-on-the-Hill, a suburb of London. The suburb was northwest of the sprawling city very near to Wembley Stadium.

Richard was a tall, thin sardonic Englishman of indeterminate age. He had a wry sense of humor and a precise, clipped British accent. I picked him up at Hopkins' Airport in Berea. His first comments were: "My, your car is quite large. Goodness, the roads are very bad."

He stayed at our home for three weeks during the winter. He complained of the cold and snow. England has relatively mild winters with hardly any snow or even freezing temperatures. We had to turn up the thermostat and provide extra blankets. He said that he missed the English food, but enjoyed our many fast food choices. My wife tried to make a lot of English-style meals - meat along with two or three different vegetables for dinnner, bacon, sausage and eggs for breakfast and different soups and stews for lunch. He was a big eater, but mangaged to stay thin. He complained about not finding satisfactory fish and chips.

Our children were grown and out of the house by then, but Jason, our grandson was enthralled by him and his tales of far-off England. Richard accompanied me to the meetings of the Summit County principals and the Portage County Athletic League. He attended our Athletic Committee meeting in the Rose Room and enjoyed the violin music. He said that the beer was too weak for his taste and that the coldness took away the flavor of the hops. He took an active part in the lively discussions. He felt that our curriculum was too soft and easy, our school weeks too short and our school year had that strange three-month void in the summer.

Our teachers found his stories and comments to be very interesting. Our weekly staff meetings took on a different hue and flavor when his pithy, pointed comments were added to the usual stew.

We began as strangers from very different educational and professional backgrounds and ended the three-weeks by becoming friends and confidantes. On our ride back to Hopkins' Airport, he said he looked forward to my visit with him in England during the next school year.

The next year, 1979, I made the trip to England to complete my part of the exchange program. I landed at Heathrow Airport, expecting Richard to meet me and drive me to his home some thirty miles away. No such luck. I had to take a train to King's Cross Station and take the "Tube" (subway) from central London some fifteen miles north to Harrow-on-the-Hill. Again, no Richard. I called him from one of those ubiquitous red phone booths and told him that I was there. He told me that the station was only about four blocks from his home. He gave me the walking directions. I was getting angry. I had driven a 100-mile round trip from Mogadore to Hopkins to pick him up and, now, he expected me to carry my large suitcase, carry-on and camera bag four long English blocks to his house. I complained on the phone. He said that he was busy and couldn't leave to pick me up. He said that I would enjoy the ambiance during the walk. I could see an historic English town along the way. I told him to stick his history up his scrawney English bum. He just laughed. Me, not so much.

So, I trudged along the brick-paved streets past tudor style homes and bright flowery gardens. I stopped frequently not only to take in the sights, but to rest my weary arms and back. I, finally, arrived at Richard's home. It was a two-story brick and stucco home on a quiet residential street. I knocked on the door with a large brass lion knocker. A tall, turbaned Indian man answered. I said, "Hello, is this Richard Read's home?" No response. I repeated my question. Still, no response. He gestured for me to come in. When I entered the hallway, a quiet, mousey little woman smiled at me from inside one of the open doors off of the hallway. She said very softly, "This is your bedroom."

I went into the small dark room that contained only a double-sized bed, a bureau and a night stand. I put down my luggage and went back out into the hallway. The Indian and the little woman stood quietly and looked at me. Just then, Richard appeared at the front door. He smiled at me and asked if I'd had a good trip. I thanked him for meeting me at the airport and driving me to his house. He just smiled and said that he'd been in a meeting at school.

He told me that I was to have his bedroom and that he'd take the guest room so that I'd have more room. He introduced me to the tall Indian who was a mute and the quiet lady. They both rented rooms from him so that he could supplement his principal's salary. Richard had been divorced and had to pay child support for his two children who lived with his former wife.

It was cold in the house. It was England. There was no central heating system. They relied on space heaters that were moved about the house as the needs arose. The little lady placed a heating pad under my bedspread each night before I went to bed.

The bathroom was very cold when I bathed each morning. The bath water was only tepid. But, the eggs, ham and potatoes were hot as was the coffee. I thought the English drank tea for breakfast, but they have coffee. It's either served black or black and white.

The lady turned out to be recovering from a mental illness and the government paid her rent. The Indian was an immigrant who was studying for his university degree. His government paid his tuition in a special program for the deaf and mute. Each time that I used the "Loo," the toilet, she mopped the bathroom floor and wiped down the toilet rim and the sink. One day, to test her, I went to the bathroom four times in one hour. She performed four times.

Richard's girl friend came over almost every evening and, often, stayed overnight with him. We were a motley crew - Richard, his girl friend, the seven-foot tall Indian, the recovering psychotic and me.

My purpose for being there was to take Richard's place in his school while he taught some classes at the local university. I occupied his office and, following his custom, served wine to senior students each day at lunch time from his private liquor cabinet. I thought of bringing this custom back to Mogadore. But, I didn't.

The students were mostly black from former British colonial possessions. They wore red and white uniforms and spoke with crisp English accents. In addition to being a temporary quasi principal, I spoke at the local elementary and middle schools and at the local university to education classes. The students at all of the facilities were very interested in my life, my job and all things American.

I enjoyed my four weeks there which included a side-trip to Scotland to visit schools in the Edinburgh area. Scotland would have been even more interesting if I had been able to understand the language and enjoy the obligatory haggis. A tour of Bell's Distillery which produced fine scotch was a highlight. I tasted 20 year old scotch that went down my throat like melted butter.

I had to take the tube back to London and the bus to Heathrow without the assistance of Richard. After all that I'd done for him in Mogadore, he treated me that way. But, we stayed in touch down through the years, exchanging letters and holiday cards. Several years later, my wife and I escorted a tour group to England, Scotland, Wales and Ireland. Four of us visited Richard and his new wife in their home along Thames, just south of London. He didn't meet our train there, either.

I came back to Mogadore and regaled anyone who would listen to the stories from my trip, most of which were true.

"Teaching, may I say, Is the noblest profession of all in a democracy."

Kurt Vonnegut

School dances should be entertaining and fun for all who attend. That wasn't the case at Mogadore High School in the early 1970's. The ones that our own clubs and organizations sponsored were well-attended and caused few problems. We didn't allow students from other schools to attend unless they were the date of one of our students. We didn't permit any non-students to attend. They were well-chaparoned and the bands were screened before they were given a contract.

This was not the case with dances sponsored by our Athletic Booster Club. They used the proceeds from the dances to support our athletic programs. The dances were well attended. Students from other schools and young adults were permitted to attend. The Boosters hired the bands, provided their own hired security and were approved by Superintendent Cordier and our Community Education Director, David Storey. On the night in question, the attendance was estimated at 1200. At the 11p.m. closing time, a big fight broke out. Three non-Mogadore residents were arrested for disorderly conduct and possession of intoxicating liquor. I had attended out of curiosity and a desire to be of help. The fight was bad enough, but the hard feelings that arose carried over into our school-sponsored dances.

A few weeks later, at our Sweetheart Dance, students from Ellet and Mogadore appeared at the dance armed with tire chains, steel pipes, large wrenches, a tire iron, some knives and a night stick. It turned out that students from both schools had argued and threatened each other at the previous Booster's Dance. The band had heard of the possible trouble that might occur at the dance and they came armed with weapons, also.

I, along with Mr. Murphy, and the two local policemen that we had hired, ended up wrestling and rolling on the floor with the students who had weapons before we could get them out of the gymnasium. Before peace was restored, one student was beaten unconscious, one had a broken nose and one had a severe blow to the head. The police station was called and more officers arrived to try to secure the area. Nine Ellet students were charged with disturbing the peace along with two students from Mogadore. Of course, the dance was cancelled.

The result of all of this was that the police department along with school officials set up a program for students in grades six through twelve being given identification cards which were to be carried at all times. All dances in the future would be closed to all except Mogadore students.

Those occurances served as a wake-up call to the people of Mogadore. Our quiet little village could erupt at any time given the right mixture of volatile ingredients. Some of our students were not exemplary citizens. That came as a big suprise to many local citizens. It seems that there is always trouble in paradise even when it goes by the name of Mogadore.

> *"The most valuable of all education is the ability to*
> *make yourself do the things that you have to do, when*
> *it has to be done, whether you like it or not."*

Aldous Huxley

In addition to hosting Richard Read as part of the NASSP principals' exchange program, I had the good fortune to be asked to host a Japanese English teacher and a school administrator from India, both of whom stayed with me and my family in Mogadore. I, my family, the students, the staff and the village all profited from having them live for a short time among us. They shared their stories of life in their countries and of how their schools were operated.

The following quotation is from a letter that I received from Mr. Singh, the Indian administrator after he had returned to his home:

"My dear Donald, I shall remember the sweet and interesting conversations that I had with you at your home. I am really much influenced by your hospitality and kind behavior.

I am very thankful to you for your kind offer to allow me to visit your school and other interesting places in the area. I am thankful to Mrs. Smith for her hospitality. To your bonny daughter and your lively son, I express my affection and love.

Yours sincerely, Vidyapodi Singh"

The three visits from educators from other countries were of great value to all with whom they came into contact. They, also, deepened my desire to visit as many countries as my limited finances would permit. It's difficult to fear and dislike those whom we come to know as individual people, not just as stereotypes that we might read about.

In 1974, my son, Michael, graduated from Mogadore High School. In retrospect, I'm certain that he suffered far more than he has ever admitted from my being his principal for six years. I know that he heard a lot of comments about me, some of which were true and some of which were blatant lies and exaggerations.

He never really complained to me about my being his principal except in a joking manner. But, I'm certain that the hurts were deep and his behavior and attitude were altered towards me, school and life in general. He became known as "PK," the principal's kid.

To add to my family's consternation about my being their principal, my grandson Jason came to live with us and attended MHS during his high school years. After overcoming his initial shyness, he joined the marching band as a drummer and made many new friends. He was and is a talented artist who, later, illustrated my first book, "When the Muses Came to Call."

Our daughter, Kathy, has a degree in elementary education and a certificate as a reading specialist. She was a library aide in The Barberton Public Library until lack of funding caused a reduction in staff. She was a victim of the "Last in, first out policy." She is, now, the Christian Education Director at Oak Hill U.P. Church. Michael, our son, retired from being a technical director at CBS television stations and is, now, working at On24 television in San Francisco. He was part of the technical crew on the Irish rock group U2's world tour several years ago.

In 1978 and, again, in 1980, I was invited by the United States Department of Justice to serve as a consultant to review and rate alternative educational programs for juvenile delinquents. The programs were submitted by school districts from around the country to try to win government funding for their programs. I and eleven other individuals read the programs and rated them according to their perceived effectiveness.

I stayed in Washington, D.C. for a week during each of the two years. I was flown first-class to Washington and lodged in a three-room suite in a hotel along the Potomac near to the National Theater. I was given $50.00 daily to buy meals and paid $100.00 daily. I spent about $15.00 daily to eat and saved the remainder. The suite had a kitchenette and I could eat breakfast and dinner en suite. My desk each year was next to Mr. Barrron, the owner and editor of Barron's Financial Newsletter. I had some free time which permitted me to explore Washington as a tourist. I spent a lot of my free time in the Smithsonian.

After a lot of lively discussion, we selected five programs to receive grant monies. While there, I was able to ride the subway to Rock Creek to visit my old roommate from my first trip to visit schools in The Soviet Union. I asked his wife if he still snored.

During this time period, I became more involved in North-Central Association work. I was asked to chair several visiting teams that spent up to a week at a time determining if the high schools that we visited met the stringent standards of the association. I selected teams of 15 to 20 members composed of area educators in secondary schools and the local universities. I enjoyed the work and received many compliments from the schools that we visited for being well-organized, impartial and completely fair.

As a result of my leading those teams, I was selected by Stanley Fox, the director of Ohio's North Central Committee to be the chief assistant to Dr. Charles Wood of Akron University who chaired the Northeastern Ohio District. In that capacity, I served as a consultant to the schools being visited and to the visiting teams. I appreciated that our school board permitted me to do these duties in addition to my the being high school principal.

COMPETENCY TESTING

"Everybody is a genius, but, if you judge a fish by its ability to climb a tree, it will live its life believing that it is stupid."

Albert Einstein

It's difficult to know if a student is prepared to meet the world and its challenges when he is ready to graduate. I'm certain that, in my years as a principal, I certified many students as being qualified to graduate who weren't prepared to do just that. Basic to meeting the world, should be knowledge of how to read and to understand what is being read. A graduate should be able to speak clearly and intelligently enough for people to understand what he is saying. He should be able to put his thoughts and ideas into writing that is understood by those for whom the writing is intended. He should have been exposed to some of the writings of the world's great thinkers and doers and be able to explain some of those writings.

Because we live in an ever-increasing world of technology, basic knowledge of mathematics is paramount to understanding the vagaries of the explosion of scientific advancement. Even every-day living requires some mathematical ability. Paying our bills, balancing our checkbooks, deciphering the complexities of loans, mortgages and interest rates test those abilities.

I knew that at Mogadore, as was true at Buchtel High School in Akron, we had graduated students who didn't have those basic skills.

So, I challenged our staff at Mogadore High School to come up with competency tests in both English and mathematics that students would be required to pass before we would certify them for graduation.

At that time, such tests were not required by the state, the county or our local school district. I ran the idea by our school board and superintendent at a board work session. Their attitude was generally supportive, but they would wait for approval until we presented them with the actual tests.

The English and mathematics departments worked hard on them for the balance of that school year. Near the end of the year, we presented the final drafts to the school board. I suggested that each member take the tests. Some did, but some quietly side-stepped them. The ones who took the tests said that they were demanding, but fair. We discussed the individual test items and with the help of the English and mathematics' teachers, we fine-tuned them by eliminating a few items and substituting new and better ones. The board accepted the final drafts and approved them for use beginning the next school year. The local papers ran feature stories about them. We felt that we were pioneers in this field of testing.

We all realized that the first few years of implementation would be difficult. Some seniors who had passed all of the required subjects and earned the compulsory number of credits might not graduate if they failed one or both of the competency tests. We built into the policy that students could take the test at the end of the tenth, eleventh or twelfth grades. If, at the end of grade twelve, he or she still hadn't passed the test, it could be given again up to two weeks before the date of graduation. After that, the student could take take the test again in the summer, but would not take part in the spring graduation program. After passing the summer test, he could pick up his diploma in the office. All of us hoped that it wouldn't come down to that. But, it did.

We had to notify a few students that they wouldn't walk across the stage with their peers during the next several years. Ultimately, they all received diplomas. I feel, in retrospect, that the tests had positive results. The fear of not graduating was a powerful motivation. The parents, fearing embarrassment, applied a little more presssure for their unmotivated offspring to work and study harder.

We wrote about our testing program in professional journals and spoke about it at educators' meetings. It generated quite a bit of curiosity and some copy-cat followers.

Later, the State of Ohio devised its own competency testing program which replaced our home-grown version. Some educators, parents and students liked the home-cooking better.

Some of the things that I tried didn't work as I had planned. The weekly lesson plans that I asked the teachers to submit had unexpected consequences. At first, everyone turned them in as requested. Eventually, it became a game. Denny and Fred began to turn in the same ones each week. I accepted them without comment. Some other teachers submitted plans that, very obviously, had no relationship to what they were teaching or planned to teach. I realized that the group intelligence about the plans' usefulness was that they were not necessary.

I had no qualms about admitting that my request for the plans was not working and, in honesty, was not necessary. But, I continued to request them and send green notes to those who didn't. The teachers needed something to unify them and provide a common goal. Their goal was to submit the plans, but to do so in a way that showed their resisitance to authority without going far enough to warrant my anger or retribution. The game lasted for years. I got a kick out of the creativity that the teachers showed in subverting the reasons for my request. So, the lesson plans flowed in weekly and my green notes followed in predictable fashion.

We had a good staff. By giving department chairpersons an additional preparation period to do departmental work, we were able to do many good things with our curriculum. The department chairpersons played an important role in whatever success that we had. I persuaded the school board to give them a small stipend each year in payment for the additional responsibility. We added a second full-time counselor in order to make certain that all students who needed extra help and advice would get the assistance that they needed.

Our athletic programs in the Portage County League prospered. Norm Lingle, our new football coach, brought energy and enthusiasm to the program. Our basketball teams, under Jerry Butcher and, later, Tom McClary, were respected and, even, feared. The baseball, track, golf and volleyball teams prospered and won several league and tournament titles.

We were proud of our academic programs and the success that our graduates were having in college and in the work force. We received accolades from visiting North Central teams and the Summit County supervisors about our programs and students.

There are many more stories, anecdotes and personalities that I could write about. The cast of "Characters" is long. The pull and tug of emotions and feelings as I reminisce is very strong. I feel guilty about omitting stories of each one with whom I lived and worked for those eighteen years I was at Mogadore High School. Each one deserves to be mentioned either with praise or censure. But, I need to limit those observations to those that came to mind quickly. My intention is not to chronicle everthing and everyone. This is not an historical document. It is just some very personal recollections that emanate from an aging and faulty memory.

In 1984, Mr. Cordier, our superintendent, Mr. Adams, the elementary principal and I decided that we would retire at the same time. We felt that we'd accomplished many of our goals and would move on to see what retirement would bring. And, so it came to pass.

While doing research for this book, I looked at many of the MHS yearbooks. I was surprised at how many of the board members, faculty and support staff members have died. Here are some of the ones that I know about:

Ruth Corbin, my secretary; Myra Bowlin, clerk of the board; Harold Shaffer, board member; Bill Frieden, board member; Charles Carpenter, board member; Jack Heldreth, English teacher; Joe Gerin, math teacher; Charlie Spangler, math teacher; Denny Brawley, social studies teacher; Jim Outland, science teacher; Roscoe McBee, history teacher; Grace Fleming, P.E teacher; Bill Evans, drafting teacher and coach; Phyllis Read, counselor: Mrs. Stuber, cook; Mr. Riggs, custodian; Paul Held, custodian; Harlan Fry, board member; ; Doris Kot, business education teacher and Ross Morrow, English teacher.

As is the case with most lists, there might be several more to add to this list. One would hope not. These were all good people. The all helped to make the Mogadore School District a good place to send your children and a good place to work.

Today, the men of the MHS faculty who were members when I was principal meet every other month for breakfast. We look at each other in wonder and amazement, not quite believing that we are still vertical (most of the time) and still of reasonably sound mind. Some have gained weight. Some have lost weight. Many have lost hair. Many ask frequently, "What did you say?" Our peculiarities are still evident for all to see and hear. And, that brings us happiness.

"It's only worth knowing about the things that make one's life worth living, and whether there are, in fact, things that make it worth living."

Adam Phillips

RETIREMENT FROM THE
PUBLIC SCHOOLS -1984

I continued teaching evening and summer classes at Akron University for several years after I retired from the public schools. I added supervising student teachers to my schedule. I was assigned student teachers over a wide, too wide, four-county area. I had assignments in Summit, Portage, Wayne and Medina counties. I had enjoyed my career as a part-time university instructor in spite of the relatively low pay. Akron University paid less than Kent State did and I, along with many others, resented that fact.

I resented, also, the fact that in summer sessions, I was assigned three or four classes to teach while the full-time faculty taught one or two classes for far more money. My classes would be spread all over the campus making it almost impossible to get from one class to the other in the allotted time. The same was true with the supervision of the student teachers. I had to drive great distances between the schools where they were assigned.

I was given a tiny office with no windows and only a desk and one chair. I shared it with one other part-time instructor. The only perk was that I could eat in the faculty dining room with the full-time staff.

I was given no syllabus or course of study to guide me as to what and how to teach the assigned classes. I taught Principles of Secondary School Administration, Freshman English, Creative Writing and Appreciation of Poetry.

But, the final insult was when I was informed that there would be no parking passes for part-time instructors. We would need to scrounge around the area for a place to park. It was then that I decided to accept an offer to be a sales' representative for Ohio School Pictures which was based in Berea.

I had used that company to do our school photography at Mogadore. Bob, the owner, had told me that, when I retired, I could go to work for him. He knew that I knew many school administrators around the state and that I'd be able to secure a lot of new contracts for the company. I called him and we agreed upon the terms of employment. I would receive a per diem salary, a commission based upon picture-packets sold, the year-around use of a company car and a company credit card to use for gasoline and to entertain potential and current clients. After a period of time, I'd become vested in the company's profit-sharing plan. I would work out of my home and go to Berea for meetings not more than once each week and, sometimes, not that often. It sounded like a plan.

I worked for Ohio School Pictures for ten years. During that time, I had over 100 schools under contract. I enjoyed the travel, the freedom and the people whom I met on my sales' calls. But, after the ten years, I grew tired of the daily work and the, often, long hours.

I had begun to do a little work as a standardized patient at NEOUCOM, the medical school in Rootstown on weekends and in the evening. I enjoyed working with medical students and doctors, so I submitted my resignation to Bob at Ohio School pictures.

My choir director at Oak Hill U.P. church in the Ellet section of Akron was the director of the standardized patient program at NEOUCOM, now, NEOMED. She knew that I had retired from teaching and from Ohio School Pictures. She said that I'd be a good candidate for being a standardized patient. She explained the program to me in this way: The job is, basically, an acting job. I would be given a script for a doctor/patient scenario. I would play the part of the patient in a variety of situations. The student doctors would play the role of practicing physicians. Most roles were scripted heavily, meaning that I would need to say the same things and act the same way with each student doctor with whom I role-played. Hence, the term "Standardized."

In some scenarios, I would be angry about something. In some, I would seek medical information. In some, I would be the recipient of bad news concerning my health. A few scenarios called for acting as though I would have Alzheimer's or other mental/emotional problems. That was called type-casting. The situations were many and varied. In a few scenarios, I would be able to ad-lib and say whatever I wished. Mostly, I'd work with medical students, but, sometimes, it would be with practicing doctors who were having difficulty relating to their patients and were sent to the medical school for additional sensitivity training.

It sounded fascinating and the pay was good. It ranged from $10.00 to $20.00 per hour depending upon the case. One could also submit his body for non-invasive head-to-toe physicals for $18.00 an exam. If you felt more daring and less inhibited, you could serve as a model for prostrate, rectal or gynecological exams for $30-40 an exam. I signed up only for the acting roles.

After each scenario, I would give the student an oral feed-back as to how I felt as the patient. I would, also, write a written evaluation. In most cases, the encounters would be video-taped and used for teaching tools in the students' classrooms.

It was another way for me to use my experience as an educator and evaluator. I began to work at NEOUCOM, Case-Western Reserve Medical School, The Cleveland Clinic, Cleveland Metro Hospital and Sagamore Hills Osteopathic Training Facility in 1985 shortly after I retired from public school education. It was part-time work that occured, usually, during the medical schools' testing periods. I have continued doing this work up to the present time.

Obviously, I was busy. For a while, I worked at both Ohio School Pictures and the medical schools at the same time. When I had a gig at the medical schools, I didn't make sales' calls to sell the pictures.

To make it more interesting, I ran for for the Mogadore School Board in 1986 and was elected to a four-year term. I served as its president for the last two years of my term. It gave me an entirely different perspective about the operation of a school district. We had to worry about generating enough money to, not only, maintain the status quo, but to continue to improve the quality of the schools. As a principal, I would request money. As a board member, I had to try to save money.

Two difficult things happened during my term in office. The other board members had come to believe that our local superintendent was not doing a good job. They felt that he wasn't giving the job the attention and time that was needed to do the job correctly. He lived quite a distance away and, often, arrived quite late each morning. His operating philosophy didn't match the viewpoints of the other four members. They had each been in office several years before my term began. The idea of firing him had been germinating in their minds for quite a long time. During our work sessions, we discussed his performance at length. I wanted to have a meeting with him to state orally and in writing the exact reasons for the board's dissatisfaction and give him a period of time to try to improve in those areas. The other members wanted to non-renew his contract when it expired at the end of the current year. I objected, but the majority prevailed. I have alway felt that he was not given due process or a fair chance to change if he so desired. I apologized to him. He went on to secure a better paying job in a larger district where he remained until his retirement.

The other difficult event occured when an elementary student was struck by one of our school buses as he attempted to cross the busy street which ran in front of his house. It turned into a highly publicized case that created a lot of controversy for the school district. In most cases, children were exited from our school buses on the same side of the street on which their homes were located. This is true, especially, on streets with a high volume of traffic. In this case, the road was our town's main street, Cleveland Avenue or route 532.

As I understood the facts, the family had wanted the child to exit the bus on the opposite side of Cleveland Avenue in front of their home, not the regular bus stop on their side which was about a block away. In any event, the nanny came out in front of the house to escort the boy but he didn't wait for her and he darted across the busy street and was struck. He suffered brain damage which affected his cognitive ability.

His mother, who was a school board member with me, appeared on my door-step one evening and announced her resignation. She cited a conflict of interest. As board president, I encouraged the board to accept it without prejudice.

I was naive and didn't realize until later that the family intended to sue the school district for negligence up to the amount of our insurance policy. There were some extenuating circumstances surrounding the case, but boy did need and, still needs, continuing assistance with his physical and mental problems. There were some people who complained about how the situation was handled, but the boy needed financial help to assure that he could lead as normal a life as possible and the school district was insured heavily for this very kind of situation. Today, the young man has a steady job which he has held for several years. He is able to function quite normally. I guess that you could say that it was one of those situations where a tragic occurance was partially eased by being able to work the system.

In retrospect, I wonder often why people run for places on the school boards. Some, I know, do it with a sincere desire to be of service to the school district. They have no specific agenda. Some do it to try to change the way that the school system operates. Some do it to get a teacher or administrator fired. Some just like to be in a position of authority and power. Some like to be in the know about things. They like to be in the loop. Why did I run? I'd like to think that it was for purely altruistic reasons. It, certainly, wasn't for the pittance that we received for being a member.

One term on the school board was enough for me. I chose not to run for a second term. I have no masochistic tendencies.

1998 - Mogadore High School Redux

*"The real object of education is have a man in the
condition of continually asking questions."*

Mandell Creighton

In November of 1997, I received a phone call from the president of the Mogadore Board of Education. He wanted to talk to me about a serious problem. We met over coffee in a local establishment. He said that the current high school principal had made some serious mistakes and the board had decided to ask him to leave before they were forced to make his indiscretions known. He decided to leave as of the first of the year.

The board president asked if I would be interested in serving as both high school principal and acting superintendent. The superintendent's position was open and the board was in the search mode for a new one. He outlined the terms of the contract which would run from January to July in 1998. I would receive a daily salary which matched what the departing principal had been receiving and a car allowance for school-related business. As I had retired already and was receiving benefits and health coverage, retirement and the cost of the health plan would not be deducted from my salary. I could not add anthing to my retirement package by working those additional months. After talking it over with my wife, I decided to accept the terms of employment. I hoped to save all of my salary and invest it in stocks and bonds. It would be the first time that I could afford to do that. But, after being retired from school administration work for 14 years, I had some doubts about my ability to readjust to the rigors of the principalship.

I learned later that those retirement items would be deducted from my salary, but would be returned with interest at the end of my contract in June. This was just another example of foolish bureaucratic policies.

I didn't know at the time, but I was inheriting that proverbial bucket of worms. The previous principal and, in fact, the previous two principals had left a huge mess. I played catch-up for the first month. Teacher evaluations had not been done. North Central reports had not been filed. Grants had not been renewed. Teacher morale was low. Student behavior was, often, out of hand. There was constant tension and open arguments between the staff in the senior high building and the staff in the junior high building. The school had been operating as two separate schools instead of the harmonious one school when I left in 1984.

I received, almost daily, letters from individual and businesses about money being owed to them from the former principals. I recieved court documents from various legal entities about violations and proceedings involving my predecessors.

After getting the important things back in order, I went about trying to reassure students and teachers that it was a new day. I visited every English class to talk to students. In that way, I would reach all of them. The seniors, especially, were concerned about their records and grades being handled properly. I asssured them that any errors would be corrected prior to graduation time.

A woman had been hired to do nothing but keep track of and supervise detentions that teachers and administrators had assigned. Apparently, the teachers had abandoned their individual responsibilities for handling their own disciplinary problems. The woman had an office and was employed full-time to do what teachers and administrators once did. It was a huge operation. It was a waste of tax-payer's money and made the disciplinary process very impersonal and far removed from the teacher-student relationship that should be paramount in the process.

In addition to assuming the duties of being both principal and superintendent, I had no assistant principal to pick up the slack. I found the jobs to be both time-consuming and tiring. I was almost 70 years old and was beginning to suffer from sciatica in my right leg. The pain became almost debilitating. I had difficulty walking and standing for even short periods of time. Then, I came down with what is known as walking pneumonia. I was put on drugs to fight the infection. I came close to being hospitalized.

Some of my former teachers were still there, but the majority were new-comers. With a few exceptions, I received a lot of support and encouragement from the staff. I had told the school board that the person hired to manage the growing detention program was unnecessary and that the position should be eliminated. When she heard of my recommendation, she became an instant enemy. It was an uncomfortable situation because her office was next to mine.

My old secretary, Ruth, had passed away. But, my new secretary, Kathy Miller, was efficient and supportive. That was a good thing because I needed all the support that I could get.

A bad thing was that the junior and senior high school teachers were at odds constantly over almost every topic that came up. They argued about curriculum, money allocations, comments made and supposedly made. It was annoying and petty. The culmination came one day just after lunch period. I heard loud yelling in the area between the two buildings which was just outside my office windows.

I looked out and one female teacher from the junior high building and a female high school teacher were yelling insults at each other. I went outside immediately to quiet them down. Students from both buildings were hanging out of the classroom windows whooping and hollering with excitement. They were yelling "Fight," "Fight." I told the two women to get back into their classrooms and act like grown-ups. The two women tried to give me their respective sides of the disagreement, but I told them to be quiet and go to their rooms. If they didn't, I promised them that disciplinary action would be taken against each of them. The students were still watching from the windows and I called to them to go back to their seats as the entertainment was over.

The dispute had been over a remark that one teacher had supposedly made about the other teacher's ability to teach properly. I found this out when I invited them to stay after school hours to meet with me in my office. I told them that I would be the judge of their teaching ability, not them. They left my office after they shook hands grudgingly. I heard each of them mutter something softly as they left my office together. But, I ignored it.

The balance of the year went by slowly. I did not feel well. My sciatica got worse and the pneumonia made me tired and lethargic for several weeks.

But, I muddled through with a lot of help from most of the teaching and support staff. Instead of the previous separate staff meetings for the two buildings, I had combined staff meetings and emphasized the importance of being one unified school, not two opposing entitities. Most of the teachers bought into the idea that we were one school which happened to be in two buildings, not two separate schools.

Most of the discipline problems centered around a few students who were from outside our school district who were there due to the open enrollment policy. The policy might have brought in some needed money, but it brought, also, some unneeded problems. Most of the open enrollment students seemed to be there because of the problems they'd had in their home schools. They came to Mogadore with a chip on their shoulders and an aggressive mind-set to prove how tough they were. I had to break up and/or prevent several fights. I ended up asking our school board to revoke the open enrollment status of a few of those students.

But, by graduation time, things had settled down to just a minimal roar. I managed to limp around enough to enable me to keep an eye on things. Soon after my contractual period was over, I had to have spinal fusion surgery for the increasingly severe sciatica. Three of my lumbar vertebrae were fused together using a piece of bone from my pelvis.

Was it worth it to make a few more dollars? This note that I received just before the graduation service made it very worthwhile:

Donald E. Smith, Ph.D.

"Dear Mr. Smith,

The reason that I am writing this letter is to thank you for filling in as principal this school year. You helped to make my senior year a very pleasant and enjoyable time. Past principals have been lazy, power-hungry and/or bad decision-makers. Our principal last year tried to entirely change our school and its schedule, but he was quick to leave when he found a higher paying job. The following guy was also a quitter. He only lasted half of a year. Then, Mr. Smith came back. It was very encouraging to see someone who actually cared about Mogadore and cared about our school's future to come out of retirement and lead us in the right direction. Your kindness and concern for high school students is seen in your eyes and through the things that you do. You are able to mantain order and receive respect without being tyrannical. You treat the students with respect and that is why we respect you so much. All of the kids love you -- and its not just because you gave us a longer lunch period. We know how much you care about us and we appreciate your efforts more than you will ever know. Thanks again!"

Sincerely,

Josh Cameron, Senior Class President.

That note and a picture from Nate Lyons with this on the back: "To Mr. Smith, Finally! A great principal" made the time, effort and, yes, even the pain, more than worth while.

Those two notes and the one that I saved from Linda Shaw from Simon Perkins Junior High School back in the mid-1950's and the one from Prince Washington from Buchtel High School in the mid-1960's have been saved for a reason. They are not about me. They are about the strong bond that can be created between students and educators as they intermingle their lives for those brief moments in time. Down through the years, past trials and triumphs, through careers, marriages, divorces, and deaths, those connections, those meetings of mind and spirit remain strong and form part of who we are as humans.

It helps, also, to receive kind words from your colleagues and fellow-workers. One note that I've kept since 1984 is from my long-time assistant principal at Mogadore High School, Tom Murphy. It reads: "Don, Thanks for all of the kind words. Though, most of all, for the years of guidance you gave me. Without your patience, I could not have survived. Tom"

That meant a lot to me. We faced a lot of adversity together. But, we shared a lot good times and success, also. He always had my back. He was loyal to me even when we disagreed on how to handle students and how to motivate teachers. He would voice his opinion clearly and openly. If we disagreed, he would just say, "You're the boss!" The survival that you mentioned in your note worked both ways. I will always be grateful for your ability to work with me and not just for me.

"Yes," I can say with certainty as I look back over what I can remember from 84 years of living, "It was worth it." It was worth every minute of it. It was worth being considered to be not among the elite movers and doers. It was worth living below, at, and just above the poverty level. It was worth spending more time with your children than I did with my own. It was worth staying up late at night trying to figure out how to motivate students who were disinterested, remote and, even, antagonistic. It was worth the verbal abuse from parents who blamed me and other educators for their children's failures.

I, still, feel some resentment over the fact that most school board members seemed to think that Mogadore teachers and administrators shouldn't be paid as much those who worked in larger districts. If anything, we deserved as much or more than our big-city peers. We were exposed to more scrutiny because of the closer contact with parents and other residents. The administrators had less help and spent more time performing their duties. But, of course, I didn't have to stay. But, I did.

But, there are shining moments that remain embedded in my memory and nourish me in moments of sadness and regret. I remember the look of surprise and excitement when a student suddenly grasps an idea or difficult concept. I remember the silent "Thank you" when I paid a compliment to a student who had seldom heard a compliment from anyone. Yes, I remember the tears on the faces of macho athletes who had just won a state championship. I remember the handshake and the eye contact from parents who thanked me for assisting them with a troubled child.

But, those notes and others that I haven't cited, are not about me. They are about how educators throughout the entire world are part of your extended family. As in all families, we have squabbles, disagreements and jealousies. But, also, as in all families, there is an underlying love that needs to acknowledged openly and warmly. Teachers need to tell students and parents how well they are doing and, if need be, how they might do better. Students and their parents need to tell teachers how much they appreciate what they do for them and for all of their students. It should be a two-way street based upon love and mutual respect.

Before I wax too emotionally about receiving notes and verbal compliments about my work as an educator, I need to admit that not everyone liked or respected me. Over the years, I received several nasty notes and letters. Some of them could be labeled as being of the Poison-Pen variety. I admit to tossing them after I'd read them. Evidence of the crime and all of that, you know.

Some people said that I was too liberal. Some said that I was too conservative. Some said that I always defended the teachers. Some said that I didn't support the teachers. Some said that I made too much money. Some said I shouldn't teach at Akron University in the evenings. Some said that my trips overseas made me a socialist or, even, worse, a communist. Some said that I was too mean and used the paddle too often. Some said that I wasn't stern enough and should paddle more.

At least, those who took the time to write or call took an active interest in the school and its employees. I tried not to let criticism deter me from doing what I thought was right and proper. But, insults and unjust criticisms always hurt. I think that I can say that, over the years, I heard more compliments than criticisms. Of course, I didn't hear all of the comments. And, that's a good thing.

As I drive by the impressive new junior-senior high school, I have regrets that I wasn't able to work in the shiny new building with its modern classrooms and labs. An, oh, the big gym! What a change that is. But, nice as it is, it's just a building. It's the people who work in it that make it a school. Before I segue into more philosophical things, I'd like to mention some great teachers from my years at MHS whom I didn't mention earlier. They deserve recognition for being outstanding educators and adults who served as great role models for their students: Vicki Wilkinson, English and French teacher who ranks among the best teachers with whom I've worked - Jim Martin, music teacher and band instructor who, not only was a fine teacher, but a first-class musician himself - Jerry Reller, industrial arts teacher who brought fresh ideas and enthusiasm to an area that was dying of terminal ennui - Jerry Schaible, social studies teacher who made history and maps favorite subjects of many of our students - John Hrib, who, along with Phyllis Read, combined to give our students very personal guidance and counseling - Norm Lingle, physical education teacher, football coach and athletic director, who brought organization, spirit and expertise to our athletic programs - Grace Fleming, physical education teacher and girls' athletic director who championed the rights of female athletes to have equal athletic opportunities with the male students - Tom McClary who continued the excellent basketball program and doubled as a fine teacher

I know that other teachers are worthy of recognition, but the line is drawn here in the sand.

Special recognition goes to Jack Cordier who was my superintendent during all of the first eighteen years that I worked in Mogadore. I owe him thanks for allowing me the freedom to be the principal that I tried to be. Some of my ideas and plans were new and different. It would have been easy for him to tell me to slow down and stick with the status quo. But, he didn't and shared the blame with me for my failures. He had the welfare of the students as his main motivation in all things that he did. Jack was and is a good man. We were lucky to have him as our boss for many years.

SOME THINGS THAT
I LEARNED

"Education would be so much more effective if its purpose were to ensure that by the time they leave school every boy and girl should know how much they don't know, and be imbued with a lifelong desire to know it."

Sir William Haley

One thing that I learned is that, the teacher, while teaching, learns more than his students. The learning is from the students, not the subject material. After finally realizing how important my students were in my development and maturation, I began to acknowledge that I was a receiver of the benefits of education, not just an imparter of facts. For that and for countless other blessings that I have received from being an educator, I am truly thankful.

I am sad that I am nearing the end of my ability and strength to be part of this noble profession. I am seguing out of the active mode and into the passive mode of memories and reveries.

I am slowly phasing out of working with medical students. I enjoy helping to make them more sensitive to the needs of their patients. I began to tutor on-line with Tutor.com, a large national company that supplements the assistance that their regular classroom teachers provide for them. I tutored students in essay writing and history. I found the work to be tedious and lacking in the personal encounters that are so necessary in a learning environment. I have taken a hiatus from doing that. I might resume some day. Some day.

I am volunteering with The Agency on Aging as a long-term care ombudsman. I serve as an advocate for the residents of the nursing home to which I'm assigned. I look for violations of the codes of the Ohio State Department of Health and for signs of poor treatment of the residents. I try to establish a personal relationship with the residents so that they will feel comfortable in discussing their problems and concerns. Some of them never get visitors. I try to fill in that void. I'd like to continue doing this. Who knows, I might be able to use what I've learned if my wife or I were placed in a nursing home. That word "If" becomes more possible with each passing day.

But, for now, I'd like to empty my brain and my heart of those things that I think are important in education - important to both the student and the teacher - important in any place, in any type of learning situation - in any place - at any time.

I feel that the goal of education should be to create students who are capable of doing new things, not simply repeating what other generations have done. We should create students who are creative, inventive, able to discover, and who can be critical and not accept everything that they are offered.

Public education has become the whipping boy of the media and of many of our citizens. Home schooling and charter schools are on the rise. Widely published statistics show that the United States has slipped in the world rankings of students' mastery in many subject areas. But, we are measured against countries who, often, separate their students into groups based upon past achievement and innate ability. They only offer higher level courses to the academically gifted. We, on the other hand, try to educate all of our young people in much the same way. The democratic ideal, you know. As a consequence, especially in math and science, we are compared against only the top students from other countries in those highly scrutinized areas. But, do we want our students to be grinds and drudges who spend most of their time in studying and worrying about getting into a pretigious college? I have seen examples of those kinds of students in many other countries which I've visited. They look old and worn out long before they reach maturity. Our schools offer much more than academics. In many other countries, those extra-curriculars are handled by the communities in which they live. Don't be confused by statistics. They are, often, misleading. In our country, the schools have become the way by which we judge the livability of where we live. If the schools are good, life is good. The quality of a school district is often measured by how many parents decide where to live and raise their children. Providing and maintaining quality schools is a tremendous responsibility. It takes all of us to do it.

Public education does not exist solely for the students and their parents. It is necessary to maintain and preserve the social order. Many people object to paying school taxes, especially, if they no longer have children in school. They forget that people just like them helped to pay for their education. Would you want to live in a country surrounded only by stupid, uneducated people? I hear some of you saying, "But, I already do!"

We live in a country that has a strong tradition of schools being controlled by the local communities with minimal control and influence from the state and national governments. But, generally, decisions our made by school boards at the local level. This is in comparison to much of the rest of the world where there are national educational systems. There are good arguments for both forms of control. But, unless things change dramatically, we, at the local level, control much of our own destinies. That means that we can approve or turn down requests for monies to operate our local schools. It's a mixed blessing. School money issues are one of the few taxes over which citizens have control. But, times and situations will change. It's inevitable. We might be looking at more state and federal control in the future.

As I write this, I am looking at a newspaper article which gives the results of the vote on an additional tax levy which would be used by The Mogadore Local School District for operating expenses. It lost by an unhealthy margin. It has lost three times in a row. As a senior citizen living on a fixed income, I can sympathize with those who voted against it. But, as a retired educator, I am able to take a broader view even as I worry about my ability to pay the additional annual amount in perpetuity. We need to support our schools. I won't belabor the point as to why should. We know that already. Threats about cutting services won't change our minds. Sob stories about the poor underpaid teachers and administrators won't do it. The only thing that will work is taking a long, introspective look at what quality education means to our community and to our country. We need to soften our hearts and open our minds to the fact that, even though it might make our budgets a little bit tighter, we need our schools as much as the schools need us. Do I hear an "Amen?"

As I near the end of writing this book, I can't help but to reminisce a little bit more. I'd like to share with you a few more of my ideas and thoughts about what I feel about teaching, about being a principal and what it took to be an educator.

Back in the mid-70's when I was mid-way through my tenure at Mogadore High School, Helen Carringer from the Akron Beacon Journal, interviewed me about my thoughts about being a high school principal. Following are some of my comments that are taken from her article:

"The principal's role is a difficult and, often, ambiguous one. In staffing reports required by the state, he is lumped under 'Instruction," but in the minds of teachers and the public, he is considered to be 'Administration.' He must be able to consolidate the, often, disparate goals of teachers and parents into something compatible with his own goals. He is the man in the middle between those administrators above him and the teacher-union power below.

I feel that a principal should have a broad liberal arts' background, not just training in how to be a teacher and principal. At the expense of being labeled as being too liberal, I feel that recent supreme court decisions, which might be seen as being liberal, will have a good effect of how we operate our schools.

I created a 'Survival Kit' for principals which I presented at the state high school principals' convention in Columbus. I'd like to share the important points with you:

LIVE in today's world. Don't rely only on old verities. Today's accepted practices were yesterday's fads and fancies.

DON'T be paranoid. Not everyone is out to get you. But, be aware, some are.

Donald E. Smith, Ph.D.

RESERVE anger for the important things. Don't sweat the small stuff.

BE INDEPENDENT - Be friendly and cooperative, but keep your social and school lives separate.

BE ACCESSIBLE - Open your office door frequently and let in some fresh air and ideas.

BE AMBULATORY - Be visible. Go out in the hall and get to know the students. Check the restrooms. Lead a cheer in pep assemblies. Eat in the cafeteria, but not too often.

GIVE responsibility. Don't try to do it all yourself. Share the acclaim and the blame.

ALLOW your students and teachers to save face. Don't back them into corners with no escape route.

SOLICIT - ideas from teachers, students and the community

INSIST - that the superintendent and the school board listen to your ideas, recommendations and complaints.

KEEP a sense of humor. Don't take yourself and your position too seriously. No one else does.

DON'T hide behind policy. Use as few rules as possible. People are far more important than rules.

DISCIPLINE is a last resort. The only guideline that should be needed is: "Be kind to each other." "Should" is the operative word."

Soon after Miss Carringer's interview with me was published, I received the following anonymous note in the mail: "Dear Mr. Know-it-All,

Why don't you practice what you preach? I'm tired of paying your salary for sitting behind closed doors. You didn't tell the truth!"

Usually, I don't pay much attention to people who refuse to state their names, but I did this one. It hurt. It caused me to spend some time in introspection. Was I really guilty of what the note implied? Did other people see me in this same way? After much soul-searching, I decided that I would only sit when my door was open. Apparently, sitting when my door was closed was the problem.

"I wondered why the baseball was getting bigger. Then, it hit me!"

In "A Man For All Seasons" Sir Thomas More asked Richard: "Why not be a teacher? You'd be a fine one.. Perhaps, a great one." Richard replied: "And, if I was who would know it?" Sir Thomas: "You, your pupils, your friends, God. Not a bad public, that."

The best teachers are those who keep learning from the world around them and from their students. They have their own drive to know more about more and more things and are able to transmit that drive and that knowledge to their students. That's how great teachers resonate through time. It's how they become immortal.

John Cage, composer, and Sister Corita Kent, artist, combined their ideas into "Ten Rules for Students, Teachers, and Life." Following, are the ten rules and one hint:

1. Find something or someone that you trust and try trusting it for a while
2. General duties of a student - pull everything out of your teacher; pull everything out of fellow students.
3. Central duties of a teacher - pull everything out of your students
4. Consider everything an experiment
5. Be self-disciplined - find someone wise or smart and follow them. To be disciplined, is to follow in a good way. To be self-disciplined, is to follow in a better way.
6. Nothing is a mistake. There's no win and no fail. There's only make.
7. The only rule is work. If you work, it will lead to something.
8. Don't try to create and analyze at the same time. They're different processes.

9. Be happy when you can manage it. Enjoy yourself. It's lighter than you think.
10. Break all of the rules. Even our own rules. Leave plenty of room for the X quantities.

The Hint: Always be around. Come or go to everything. Always go to classes. Read anything you can get your hands on. Look at movies carefully, often. Save everything. It might come in handy later.

Some of those rules might seem simplistic, even a little silly. But, when one thinks about them carefully, the genius of the authors' creative minds shines through. Both were known for their minimalist style in music and art. It worked for them. Why not us?

"Our schools are failing, especially, the public schools." We hear some variation of that statement almost every time that the discussion turns to American schools.

Our Secretary of Education has said it. Even our president has said it. CNN has said it. So, it must be true, mustn't it? We've spent billions of dollars on No Child Left Behind and the Race To The Top. Now it's the Common Core. So far, none of it has provided measurable improvements. We've tried high-stake standardized testing, test prep and teacher accountability programs for several years with the main goal of bringing up student test scores and it hasn't worked.

Value-added measures, school vouchers, charter schools - none have given us positive results. We do know that wealthy districts produce the best test scores. Kids who live in poverty don't do nearly as well. The majority of all public school students in one third of our states come from low-income families.

The most powerful factor in determing student achievement is their parents' economic status. Students who live in poverty have enough trouble just surviving, much less achieving success in school.

Why don't we turn to realistic school reform tactics? Let's try to spend more money on things that might actually help kids to learn? Things such as extra tutoring, child care, basic health programs and other services for low-income level schools.

Let's think about giving poverty area schools the same funding as schools in wealthy neighborhoods. Let's give high-poverty schools *more* funds than rich districts because combating poverty is expensive.

We should consider helping impoverished students' parents - raise the minimum wages, provide funding for daycare and legislate a real jobs' bill to get people back to work. If the powers that be shy away from fighting poverty as they probably will, we need to change our aniquated school system itself. Yes, it's antiquated. Our public schools still operate as if they were preparing students to work in factories. Those jobs have been shipped overseas where costs are lower and they, probably, won't be coming back. We need to educate our students for the jobs of the future - in science and technology, especially.

Instead of "Standardizing" everything and everybody, we should be "Individualizing." Teachers are told to individualize their lessons, but standardize their tests. Does that make sense?

Students should be allowed to have more of a say in their own educations as they get older and grow in maturity. Instead of assigning obligatory books to read as is done in the Common Core, let them pick some of their reading based on personal interest. Teach them to be media savvy and computer literate. Don't give them any answers. Help them to find the answers. Sitting all in a row and filling in the bubbles on a standardized test is not what education should be. The open mind should replace the multiple-choice mind.

Only well-informed, warm-hearted people can teach others the things that they will always remember and love. Computers and television can't do that. A computer teaches a child what a computer can become. An educated human being teaches a child what a child can become.

Schools need not only reflect the collective attitudes and tastes of the communities which they serve, but they should, also, take the lead in changing those same attitudes and tastes when wisdom and common sense indicate that change is needed. Sometimes, people need to be urged, cajoled, even pushed in order to change biases and prejudicial thinking.

Students should be exposed to all kinds of stimuli: things to read, to see, to hear, to feel and, yes, even smell. Control of those stimuli should be lessened each year of a child's education. Ideally, when a student reaches his senior year of high school, he should be able to select his own stimuli and respond intelligently to all of them. He should be able to make value judgements and decisions based upon his past experiences and rational reasoning. That is what education is all about.

Students must learn to be discriminating. Topics relating to real life such as marriage, divorce, sex, abortion, politics, religion and other "Touchy" subjects should be able to be discussed freely and openly with the guidance of a trained teacher. I believe in the open discussion of all topics that relate to the lives that young people will face upon their graduation.

At Mogadore High School, we had guest speakers who discussed such topics with students both in the classrooms and school-wide assemblies. We invited John Glenn, Senator Ocasek, a black congressional leader, pro-abortion organizers, atheists, a former Grand Dragon of the KKK and the Pastor of Bourbon Street among others. Older students are able to sift through such information using their innate intelligence and good sense in order to keep what has value and reject what is worthless.

Both aspects of life, the virtuous and the profane, need open discussion in a neutral atmosphere so that their values and messages can stand on their own merits and face the test of public scrutiny. We are fortunate to live in a country where we can do these things.

In order to make some sense, some meaning, out of all of the many pullings and tuggings that we endure as we spin through space on the orb that we call earth, we need to to be exposed to all of the knowledge that is available to us and that we are able to absorb.

We need more than just factual knowledge. We need the understanding that is rooted deeply in the wisdom of the ages. We need to understand the exhileration that Debussy, Piccasso, Michelangelo and Tchaikovsky must have felt when they created things of beauty and knew intuitively that they were, in fact, beautiful.

We need the knowledge and compassion that permits us to empathize with the survivors of the horrors of concentration camps and with the loved ones of the victims of brutal and senseless killings.

To survive the realities of everday life, we must be able to place apparently random happenings into the proper historical perspective or in their place in the future that brilliant theoriticians project for us.

An educational system should be able to provide us with those abilities. The question for you, for us, is "Are your schools doing those things?" If not, why not?

In our country, there are as many types of schools as there are communities, administrators and teachers. The basic question in the United States where we still have mostly locally-controlled schools is: "What kind of school do *you* want?"

Do you want only safe, sanitized material to be presented? Do you want a curricula that is free from controversial material? Or, do you want free discussion in a controlled atmosphere for students who have the maturity and the need for it?

The realities of life are not textbook abstractions. The realities make up the fabric of how we live and act on this stage that we call life. We cannot hide or shield our eyes from the reality that is all around us.

Schools, through the interaction between students and teachers can help young people to not only survive life's many perils, but can help to make reality more understandable and more bearable.

We don't need to just react to what life throws at us. We can be proactive and help to create our own lives. We can learn, if exposed to beauty, to appreciate beauty. We can learn to abhor and reject ugliness, prejudice and narrow-mindedness. We don't need to just endure. We can learn those things that will enable us to control and change our lives.

Next, and most importantly, we need both dreamers and thinkers. We need students who are immersed in what humanity has learned about being human. We need the stories, the poetry, and the music that has been handed down through the ages. Only then, can we decide what is needed to fulfill the destiny of mankind in our current age and in the ages to come.

The two basic groups, the thinkers and the doers, the artists and the scientists, must work together to form the kind of world that all of us need so badly.

This should be the working philosphy of our schools. Is it the philosophy of *your* school?

"How To Be An Explorer of the World

1. Always be looking - notice the ground beneath your feet

2. Consider everthing alive and animate

3. Everthing is interesting - look closer"

Unknown

A FINAL THOUGHT

'The greatest sign of success for a teacher is to be able to say,
"The children are now working as if I didn't exist."

Maria Montessori

Building self esteem in students should be one of a teacher's primary goals. The mastery of subject matter and the insistence upon "Good" behavior are secondary to nurturing confidence and sense of personal worth.

Students learn soon that a wide variety of actions, behaviors and attitudes will get them attention, praise and rewards (good grades).

They build their self confidence around those situations and tend to repeat them.

Teachers need to place their students in positions that will enable them to experience those things that engender that sense of worth and self-confidence. Students build that esteem around those things that promise a good return and learn to avoid the things that deflate those positive feelings.

This is true of all of us, not just students. We build bubbles around ourselves to hold in those things that make us feel good and hold out the things that make us feel bad and destroy our sense of worth.

Self-esteem and the confidence that it produces are what gets us all out of bed in the morning to face an, often, unforgiving world.

It's what makes students want to go to a school that offers more rewards than it does punishments.

And, those rewards can take many forms. Sometimes, a simple "Good Job!" will do.

"The truth is, most of us discover where we are headed after we arrive."

Bill Watterson

In this book, I have tried to show you how one person came to be a teacher, an educator, if you will. It was not a unique journey. Similar journeys have been taken by countless others. Working second jobs, foregoing vacations and new cars were part of the process. We bought a house in Mogadore in 1958 for $15,000 and we've lived there ever since. That's not a unique situation for many educators. I, also, tried to highlight some of the rewarding things and some of the tragic things that all teachers experience during their careers. When one works with people on a daily basis, he will experience the entire gamut of the human condition. Human frailty and human nobility will be on full display.

As teachers, we work with whomever is placed in our care. We don't pick and choose. As parents, you send us the best that you have. If we're lucky, your best and our best will combine to produce young people who will be prepared and ready to not only face the world, but to change the world. And, that change will be for the common good.

I worked both with and for many wonderful students, colleagues and parents over the many years that I spent in my various roles in the field of education. In retrospect, I couldn't have chosen a more rewarding career. It caused headaches, heartaches and bellyaches, but, at the end of each day, my sense of accomplishment overcame those aches. I felt, as most teachers do, that I had made that elusive thing called "A difference." I hope that my students, my fellow educators and all those with whom I had contact, felt the same way.

I plan to keep busy with my work on the village Planning and Zoning Committee, the personnel committee at Oak Hill Church, my work with medical students at NEOMED and my volunteer job with The Agency on Aging. But, these jobs do not and will not define me and absorb me as did my jobs in public education. They are just a postcript to my life in the greatest profession in the world. Teaching!

Thank you, grandma Jenny, dad, coach Joe, Mrs. Wee, the grad assistant, Joy and Goodyear Tire and Rubber Company for steering me away from a less rewarding job. Thank you for saying that I'd make a good teacher. I hope that I've earned that title.

Now, with a tip of the hat to author, Joan Didion, I will begin "Slouching towards my own private Bethlehem."

Addendum

The following information is not meant to be self-serving and boastful. It's included here to show how I was able to arrive at this stage of my life and what I was able to accomplish with limited abilities and limited resources. The same story could be told of countless other educators.

JOBS THAT I HELD TO FINANCE MY EDUCATION AND TO SUPPLEMENT MY TEACHER'S INCOME

lawn services - self employed - 1946-1949

hardware store clerk - 1947

drug store clerk - 1948

public library - page - 1947-1949

The A&P Tea Company - produce clerk & night stock clerk - 1949-1951

The Goodyear T&R Company - production worker - 1950-1956

The City of Akron -recreation department - 1954-1956

The J.C. Penney Company - clothing sales - summers, holidays -1956-1959

Garner Brothers Drive-In - nights while at Simon Perkins - 1956-1957

The Retail Credit Corporation - insurance investigator - four summers

The Waldorf Ice Cream Company - ice cream truck driver and office manager - six summers

Various local travel agencies - outside sales - overseas' tour group organizer and escort - 1981-1993

Donald E. Smith, Ph.D.

Ohio School Pictures - district sales' manager - 1984-1994

NEOMED, Cleveland Clinic, Case-Western Reserve, Cleveland Metro Hospital, Sagamore Hill's Osteopathic Training Center, BioInnovations - standardized patient and medical student evaluator - 1991 to current

Census Enumerator - 2010

EDUCATION-RELATED JOBS AND VOLUNTEER EXPERIENCES

Akron Public Schools - teacher, counselor, assistant principal - 1954-1966

Mogadore Local Schools - high school principal, acting superintendent, school board member and president - 1966- 1984, 1986-1990, 1998

The University of Akron - evening college counselor, instructor in the English and education departments, supervisor of student teachers - 1960-1990

The Ohio North-Central Accreditation Association - regional coordinator for Northeastern Ohio, chaired many evaluation teams - speaker at yearly Association meetings in Chicago, Illinois - 1976-1984

United States Department of Justice - consultant to a federal program to devise alternate educational programs to prevent juvenile delinquency - worked in Washington D. C. for two weeks in 1978 and 1980

I visited schools in the Soviet Union, Denmark, Sweden and Hungary - 1971

I was an exchange principal in Harrow-on-the-Hill, England - 1979

Global Volunteers - I taught English on the island of Java in Indonesia. - 1991

Global Volunteers - I taught English in Tanzania, East Africa - 1992

Global Volunteers - I taught English in the Russian Republic in the city of Tver - 1994

Global Volunteers - I visited schools, universities and health facilities on the island nation of Cuba - 2002

Global Volunteers - I tutored students in Metcalf, Mississippi - 2004

EDUCATION-RELATED PUBLICATIONS AND SPEECHES

"An Opportunity Class" - American Secondary Education Journal - 1970

"Surviving Student Behavior Problems" - as above - 1975

"School Evaluation - Why Everyone Benefits" - Journal of American Education - 1976

"The Benefits of a Small Suburban High School" - American Secondary Education Journal - 1976

"The Reluctant Student" - as above - 1976

"An Innovative English Program" - as above - 1977

"What I've Learned- a retrospective after three decades in education" - as above - 1984

"The Humane High School - Is It a Contradiction in Terms?" - as above - 1984

"Evaluating the Secondary School in a Painless Way" - a keynote speech at the annual North Central meeting in Chicago in 1975

"How To Prepare Your School For Evaluation" - featured speaker at the annual OASSP meeting in Columbus - 1981

"A New Way to Teach English - Mogadore High School's Innovative Program" - speech delivered at the annual OASSP meeting in Columbus - 1982

EDUCATIONAL AWARDS AND HONORARIES

Martha Holden Jennings Foundation Award - for administrative leadership and excellence - 1980

O. H. Somer's Award - for school and community leadership - 1985

Peace and Justice Award - from the Presbyterian Church U.S. A. for volunteer teaching in Indonesia, Tanzania and Russia - 1992

Phi Delta Kappa, Kappa Delta Pi - education honoraries

CIVIC AND COMMUNITY ACTIVITIES

United Way fund-raising captain - The Akron Public Schools

The University of Akron Development Fund canvasser

The Oak Hill Presbyterian Church

> Board of trusees - member and president
> Teacher - adult and post-high school classes
> Long Range Planning Committee
> Pastor Nominating Committe
> Staff Relations' Committee - current
> Chancel choir - member and former soloist -current

Summer Festival Parade, Mogadore - Grand Marshal 2003 & 2007

Village of Mogadore Charter Review Commission - 2010

Village of Mogadore Planning and Zoning Commission - 2010 to present

TRAVEL

In addition to traveling throughout the United States, I've visited 52 countries since 1971, many of them several times each. I went as an observer of school systems, tour escort, volunteer teacher, vacationer, photographer and world-class voyeur. Oh, yes, also, as a reluctant shopper for souvenirs at the coaxing of my wife.

Having a world-view changed my outlook on education and life in general. We are all part of the whole and of each other. Politics and religion aside, we are inter-connected by virtue of all being human and children of whatever God is your God. We need to embrace that concept and make it the universal credo.

The gift of travel is one of the greatest gifts that one can bestow on children and grandchildren. It takes them out of the petty and inconsequential and opens their eyes to larger, more important values and ideals. It should be an important component of a well-rounded education.

GETTING PERSONAL

Born - February 5, 1931 in Carrollton, Ohio

Married - June 18, 1950 to Mary Joyce (Joy) Carter

Children - Kathy - age 61, Michael - age 58

Grandchildren - Jason, Aaron, Ryan, Caitlin, Cooper

Greatgrandchildren - Zachary, Morrigan, Madison, Hannah, Amara, Jaden

BOOKS PUBLISHED PREVIOUSLY

"Travel and the Human Condition" - 2008

Donald E. Smith, Ph.D.

"When The Muses Came To Call" - 2009

"Ducks, Yaks Camels and the Vast Mongolian Sky, Oh, My!" - 2009

"Cuba - One Mojito At A Time" - 2010

"The Hopeful Agnostic" - 2012

They are available at Amazon, Barnes & Noble, the Akron-Summit Library System and from AuthorHouse, the publisher.

The end, la fin, eind, das ende, akhir, an deireadh, fine, koheu, mwisho, el fin

The assignment for tomorrow is to identify the country for each of the "The end terms" that are listed above. 30